THE
POET'S TONGUE

THE
POET'S TONGUE

An Anthology
chosen
by
W. H. AUDEN
and
JOHN GARRETT

LONDON
G. BELL & SONS LTD
1949

First published 1935

Reprinted 1935, 1936, 1937, 1938, 1940, 1941, 1943, 1945, 1946, 1948, 1949

Printed in Great Britain by
NEILL & CO. LTD., EDINBURGH

INTRODUCTION

Of the many definitions of poetry, the simplest is still the best: 'memorable speech.' That is to say, it must move our emotions, or excite our intellect, for only that which is moving or exciting is memorable, and the stimulus is the audible spoken word and cadence, to which in all its power of suggestion and incantation we must surrender, as we do when talking to an intimate friend. We must, in fact, make exactly the opposite kind of mental effort to that we make in grasping other verbal uses, for in the case of the latter the aura of suggestion round every word through which, like the atom radiating lines of force through the whole of space and time, it becomes ultimately a sign for the sum of all possible meanings, must be rigorously suppressed and its meaning confined to a single dictionary one. For this reason the exposition of a scientific theory is easier to read than to hear. No poetry, on the other hand, which when mastered is not better heard than read is good poetry.

All speech has rhythm, which is the result of the combination of the alternating periods of effort and rest necessary to all living things, and the laying of emphasis on what we consider important; and in all poetry there is a tension between the rhythm due to the poet's personal values, and those due to the experiences of generations crystallised into habits of language such as the English tendency to alternate weak and accented syllables, and conventional verse forms like the hexameter, the heroic pentameter, or the French Alexandrine. Similes, metaphors of image or idea, and auditory metaphors such as rhyme, assonance, and alliteration help further to clarify and strengthen the pattern and internal relations of the experience described.

Poetry, in fact, bears the same kind of relation to Prose, using prose simply in the sense of all those uses of words that are not poetry, that algebra bears to arithmetic. The poet writes of personal or fictitious experiences, but these are not important in themselves until the reader has realised them in his own consciousness.

> Soldier from the war returning,
> Spoiler of the taken town.

It is quite unimportant, though it is the kind of question not infrequently asked, who the soldier is, what regiment he belongs to, what war he had been fighting in, etc. The soldier is you or me, or the man next door. Only when it throws light on our own experience, when these lines occur to us as we see, say, the unhappy face of a stockbroker in the suburban train, does poetry convince us of its significance. The test of a poet is the frequency and diversity of the occasions on which we remember his poetry.

Memorable speech then. About what? Birth, death, the Beatific Vision, the abysses of hatred and fear, the awards and miseries of desire, the unjust walking the earth and the just scratching miserably for food like hens, triumphs, earthquakes, deserts of boredom and featureless anxiety, the Golden Age promised or irrevocably past, the gratifications and terrors of childhood, the impact of nature on the adolescent, the despairs and wisdoms of the mature, the sacrificial victim, the descent into Hell, the devouring and the benign mother? Yes, all of these, but not these only. Everything that we remember no matter how trivial: the mark on the wall, the joke at luncheon, word games, these, like the dance of a stoat or the raven's gamble, are equally the subject of poetry.

We shall do poetry a great disservice if we confine it only to the major experiences of life:

> The soldier's pole is fallen,
> Boys and girls are level now with men,
> And there is nothing left remarkable
> Beneath the visiting moon.
>
> They had a royal wedding.
> All his courtiers wished him well.
> The horses pranced and the dancers danced.
> O Mister it was swell.
>
> And masculine is found to be
> Hadria the Adriatic Sea,

have all their rightful place, and full appreciation of one depends on full appreciation of the others.

A great many people dislike the idea of poetry as they dislike over-earnest people, because they imagine it is always worrying about the eternal verities.

Those, in Mr Spender's words, who try to put poetry on a pedestal only succeed in putting it on the shelf. Poetry is no better and no worse than human nature; it is profound and shallow, sophisticated and naïve, dull and witty, bawdy and chaste in turn.

In spite of the spread of education and the accessibility of printed matter, there is a gap between what is commonly called 'highbrow' and 'lowbrow' taste, wider perhaps than it has ever been.

The industrial revolution broke up the agricultural communities, with their local conservative cultures, and divided the growing population into two classes: those whether employers or employees who worked and had little leisure, and a small class of shareholders who did no work, had leisure but no responsibilities or roots, and

vii

were therefore preoccupied with themselves. Literature has tended therefore to divide into two streams, one providing the first with a compensation and escape, the other the second with a religion and a drug. The Art for Art's sake of the London drawing-rooms of the '90's, and towns like Burnley and Rochdale, are complementary.

Nor has the situation been much improved by the increased leisure and educational opportunities which the population to-day as a whole possess. Were leisure all, the unemployed would have created a second Athens.

Artistic creations may be produced by individuals, and because their work is only appreciated by a few it does not necessarily follow that it is not good; but a universal art can only be the product of a community united in sympathy, sense of worth, and aspiration; and it is improbable that the artist can do his best except in such a society.

Something of this lies behind the suspicion of and attack upon the intellectual which is becoming more and more vocal. It is hardly possible to open a number of *Punch* without seeing him spectacled, round-shouldered, rabbit-toothed, a foil to a landscape of beautifully unconscious cows, or a whipping-boy for a drawing-room of dashing young sahibs and elegant daughters of the chase. Cross the channel and this dislike, in more countries than one, has taken a practical form, to which the occasional ducking of an Oxford æsthete seems a nursery tiff.

If we are still of the opinion that poetry is worth writing and reading, we must be able to answer such objections satisfactorily at least to ourselves.

The 'average' man says: 'When I get home I want to spend my time with my wife or in the nursery; I want to get out on to the links or go for a spin in the car, not to read poetry. Why should I? I'm quite happy without it.' We must be able to point out to him that whenever, for example, he makes a good joke he is creating poetry, that one of the motives behind poetry is curiosity, the wish to know what we feel and think, and how, as E. M. Forster says, can I know what I think till I see what I say, and that curiosity is the only human passion that can be indulged in for twenty-four hours a day without satiety.

The psychologist maintains that poetry is a neurotic symptom, an attempt to compensate by phantasy for a failure to meet reality. We must tell him that phantasy is only the beginning of writing; that, on the contrary, like psychology, poetry is a struggle to reconcile the unwilling subject and object; in fact, that since psychological truth depends so largely on context, poetry, the parabolic approach, is the only adequate medium for psychology.

The propagandist, whether moral or political, complains that the writer should use his powers over words to persuade people to a particular course of action, instead of fiddling while Rome burns. But Poetry is not concerned with telling people what to do, but with extending our knowledge of good and evil, perhaps making the necessity for action more urgent and its nature more clear, but only leading us to the point where it is possible for us to make a rational and moral choice.

In compiling an anthology such considerations must be borne in mind. First, one must overcome the prejudice that poetry is uplift and show that poetry can appeal to every level of consciousness. We do not want to read 'great' poetry all the time, and a good anthology should contain poems for every mood. Secondly, one must disabuse people of the idea that poetry is primarily an escape from reality. We all need escape at times, just as we need food and sleep, and some escape poetry there must always be. One must not let people think either that poetry never enjoys itself, or that it ignores the grimmer aspects of existence. Lastly, one must show those who come to poetry for a message, for calendar thoughts, that they have come to the wrong door, that poetry may illuminate but it will not dictate.

As regards arrangement we have, after some thought, adopted an alphabetical, anonymous order. It seems best to us, if the idea of poetry as something dead and suitable for a tourist-ridden museum—a cultural tradition to be preserved and imitated rather than a spontaneous living product—is to be avoided, that the first approach should be with an open mind, free from the bias of great names and literary influences, the first impression that of a human activity, independent of period and unconfined in subject.

W. H. AUDEN.
JOHN GARRETT.

INDEX OF FIRST LINES AND AUTHORS

PART I

xii

Index
to Part I

xiii

Index
to PART I

xiv

Index
to PART I

Index
to PART I

XVI

Index
to PART I

INDEX OF FIRST LINES AND AUTHORS

PART II

Index
to Part II

xix

Index
to PART II

xx

Index
to PART II

xxi

xxii

Index
to PART II

Index
to PART II

APPENDIX

Index
to PART II

INDEX OF AUTHORS

[*N.B.*—The numbers refer to the number of the poem, except the Roman numbers, which indicate the Part.]

INDEX OF SUBJECTS

[*N.B.*—The numbers refer to the number of the poem,
except the Roman numbers, which indicate the Part.]

ACKNOWLEDGMENTS TO FIRST PART

For permission to include the copyright poems whose numbers are given in the following list, we wish to thank the Authors thereof (or their Executors or Literary Representatives), and the Publishers.

Mr Hilaire Belloc	for Nos. 20 & 54	from *Sonnets and Verses* and *Cautionary Tales for Children* (Duckworth & Co., Ltd.).
Mr Edmund Blunden	„ No. 95	„ *Collected Poems*, 1914–1930 (Cobden-Sanderson,Ltd.).
The Representatives of "Lewis Carroll"	„ Nos. 43 & 119	„ *Through the Looking Glass* (Macmillan & Co., Ltd.).
Messrs Cobden-Sanderson, Ltd.	„ No. 100	„ John Clare's *Poems*.
Mr Charles Dalmon	„ No. 68	„ *The Manx Song Book, with Music* (Chappell).
Mr Walter de la Mare	„ No. 130	„ *Peacock Pie* (Constable & Co., Ltd.).
Mr Robin Flower	„ No. 78	„ *Poems and Translations* (Constable & Co., Ltd.).
Mr Colin Francis	„ No. 77	„ *Come Hither* (Constable & Co., Ltd.).
Mr Robert Frost	„ No. 114	„ *New Hampshire* (Henry Holt & Co., New York).
Mrs Frieda Lawrence	„ No. 10	„ *Birds, Beasts and Flowers*, by D. H. Lawrence (Martin Secker, Ltd.).
Executors of the late Vachel Lindsay	„ No. 21	„ The Author's *Collected Poems* (Macmillan & Co., Ltd.).
Sir Henry Newbolt	„ No. 35	„ Mary Coleridge's *Poems* (Elkin Mathews & Marrot, Ltd.).
Messrs Martin Secker, Ltd.	„ Nos. 75 & 103	„ Emily Dickinson's *Poems*.
Miss Edith Sitwell	„ No. 126	„ *Troy Park* (Duckworth & Co., Ltd.).
Messrs Frederick Warne & Co., Ltd.	„ Nos. 112, 125, & 129	„ *Nonsense Songs* and *Stories*, by Edward Lear.
Mr W. B. Yeats	„ Nos. 14 & 32	„ *Collected Poems* (Macmillan & Co., Ltd.).

For particular versions of the following old poems and plays we are indebted to the work of former editors in translating, adapting, editing, discovering or recording, and we extend our thanks, accordingly, to the firms and individuals mentioned, for permission to include these versions. If, through inadvertence, there are omissions from this list, we beg to offer the editors and publishers concerned our sincere apologies.

Messrs Chatto & Windus	for No. 97	from Alice Meynell's *Flowers of the Mind.*
Messrs Chatto & Windus and Mr Norman Douglas	„ Nos. 34, 42, 73, 81, & 115	„ *London Street Games.*
The Clarendon Press	„ Nos. 55, 86, & 92	modernised from *Fourteenth Century Verse and Prose*, edited by Kenneth Sisam.
„ „ „	„ Nos. 132 & 133	from *The English Folk Play*, edited by E. K. Chambers.
„ „ „	„ No. 128	„ *The Mummer's Play*, edited by R. J. E. Tiddy.
„ „ „	„ No. 84	„ *English Madrigal Verse*, by E. H. Fellowes.
Messrs J. B. Cramer & Co., Ltd.	„ No. 63	„ *English County Songs*, by Lucy Broadwood and J. A. Fuller-Maitland.
Mr Walter de la Mare	„ Nos. 29, 60, 104, 105, 106, 113	„ *Come Hither* (Constable & Co., Ltd.).
Mr Walter de la Mare and Mrs Lyon	„ No. 59	„ Do. do.
Mr Walter de la Mare and Mr Ralph Hodgson	„ No. 107	„ Do. do.
Messrs J. M. Dent & Sons, Ltd.	„ No. 46	„ *Anglo-Saxon Poetry*, edited by A. K. Gordon.
Miss Maud Karpeles (Lit. Executor of Cecil Sharp)	„ Nos. 48 & 74	„ *Folk Songs of English Origin collected in the Southern Appalachians* (Novello).
„ „ „	„ Nos. 66 & 110	„ *English Folk Songs for Schools* (Curwen Press).
„ „ „	„ No. 108	„ *Folk Song Carols* (Novello.)
„ „ „	„ Nos. 25 & 41	„ *Nursery Songs from the Appalachian Mountains* (Novello).
Messrs Longmans Green & Co., Ltd., and Mr Norman Ault.	„ Nos. 7, 27, 31, 82, 83, & 123	„ *Elizabethan Lyrics.*

Messrs Methuen & Co., Ltd.	for Nos. 11, 13, 17, 47, 53, 56, 72, 85, 102, 118, 120	from *The Sailor's Garland*, edited by John Masefield.
The Nonesuch Press	,, No. 40	,, *The Week-End Book.*
The Oxford University Press	,, Nos. 39, 62	,, *The Scottish Psalter.*
,, ,, ,,	,, Nos. 38, 80	,, *The Oxford Book of Carols.*
,, ,, ,,	,, Nos. 16, 58	,, *American Tramp and Underworld Slang*, edited by Godfrey Irwin.
Messrs Sidgwick & Jackson, Ltd.	,, No. 49	,, *Song Books of the Elizabethan Age*, edited by A. H. Bullen.

W. H. A.
J. G.

ACKNOWLEDGMENTS TO SECOND PART

For permission to include the copyright poems whose numbers are given in the following list, we wish to thank the Authors thereof (or their Executors or Literary Representatives), and the Publishers.

Mr Hilaire Belloc	for No. 82	from *Sonnets and Verses* (Duckworth & Co., Ltd.).
Mr Edmund Blunden	,, Nos. 43 & 115	,, *Collected Poems, 1914–1930, and Half-Way House* (Cobden-Sanderson, Ltd.).
The Executors of the late Robert Bridges	,, Nos. 101 & 116	,, *Poetical Works of Robert Bridges* (Clarendon Press, Oxford).
The Representatives of the late "Lewis Carroll"	,, No. 7	,, *Through the Looking Glass* (Macmillan & Co., Ltd.).
Mr T. S. Eliot	,, Nos. 1, 60, & 111	,, *The Journey of the Magi, Animula,* and *The Rock* (Faber & Faber, Ltd.).
Mr Colin Ellis	,, No. 142	,, *Mournful Numbers* (Macmillan & Co., Ltd.).
Lady Gilbert	,, No. 148	,, *Savoy Operas* by W. S. Gilbert (Macmillan & Co., Ltd.).

The Executors of the late A. D. Godley	for No. 138	from	*Fifty Poems* (Oxford University Press).
Capt. Harry Graham	„ Nos. 86, 141, & 144	„	*More Ruthless Rhymes* (Edward Arnold & Co.).
Mr G. Rostrevor Hamilton	„ No. 94	„	*Epigrams* (William Heinemann, Ltd.).
The Executors of the late Thomas Hardy	„ Nos. 56, 147, 150, & 153	„	*The Dynasts* and *Collected Poems* (Macmillan & Co., Ltd.).
Mr Maurice Hare	„ No. 3		
The Executors of the late Gerard Manley Hopkins	„ Nos. 37, 47, & 85	„	*Poems* (Oxford University Press).
Prof. A. E. Housman	„ Nos. 33, 57, 143, & 145	„	*Last Poems* (The Richards Press, Ltd.).
The Executor of the late "Charles Inge," Mrs Gardiner	„ No. 126		
Mr E. V. Knox	„ No. 46	„	*Poems of Impudence* (Ernest Benn, Ltd.).
Mrs Frieda Lawrence	„ No. 87	„	*Pansies* (Martin Secker, Ltd.).
Mr C. Day Lewis	„ No. 102	„	*A Time to Dance and Other Poems* (Hogarth Press).
Mr John Masefield	„ No. 26	„	*Collected Poems* (William Heineman, Ltd.).
The Executors of the late Barry Pain	„ No. 92	„	*Playthings and Parodies* (Cassell & Co., Ltd.).
Mrs Wilfred Owen	„ Nos. 30, 71, 104, & 132	„	*Poems of Wilfred Owen* (Chatto & Windus).
The Executors of the late Sir Walter Raleigh	„ No. 49	„	*Poems* (Constable & Co., Ltd.).
Messrs Martin Secker, Ltd.	„ Nos. 5 & 125	„	Emily Dickinson's *Poems*.
Mr Stephen Spender	„ Nos. 24 & 117	„	*Poems* (Faber & Faber, Ltd.).
Sir John Squire	„ No. 20	„	*Tricks of the Trade* (William Heinemann, Ltd.).
Mr R. E. Warner	„ No. 66	„	*The Listener* (British Broadcasting Corporation).
Mr W. B. Yeats	„ Nos. 40, 61, & 74	„	*Collected Poems* (Macmillan & Co., Ltd.).

For particular versions of the following old poems we are indebted to the work of former editors in translating, adapting, editing, discovering or recording, and we extend our thanks, accordingly, to the firms and individuals mentioned, for permission to include these versions. If, through inadvertence, there are omissions from this list, we beg to offer the editors and publishers concerned our sincere apologies.

The Clarendon Press, Oxford	for No. 59	from	*The Oxford Book of Ballads*, edited by Sir A. Quiller-Couch.
„ „ „	„ No. 27	„	*The Apocryphal New Testament*, edited by M. R. James.
„ „ „	„ Nos. 64, 77, 99, 100, 109, 119, & 135	„	*English Madrigal Verse*, edited by E. H. Fellowes.
Messrs J. M. Dent & Sons, Ltd.	„ No. 136	„	*Anglo-Saxon Poetry*, edited by A. K. Gordon.
Mr John Murray	„ Nos. 19 & 97	„	*Byron's Poems*, edited by E. M. Coleridge.
The Oxford University Press	„ No. 29	„	*The English Hymnal.*
„ „	„ No. 41	„	*Soldier's Song and Slang*, edited by J. Brophy and E. H. Partridge.
The Porpoise Press	„ Nos. 31 & 45	„	*The Poems of William Dunbar*, edited by William Mackenzie.
Miss Clara L. Skeat	„ No. 122	„	*Piers Plowman*, edited by Prof. Skeat (Medieval Library) (Chatto & Windus).

W. H. A.
J. G.

THE
POET'S TONGUE

PART I

A CARRION crow sat on an oak,
  Fol de riddle, lol de riddle, hi ding do,
Watching a tailor shape his cloak;
  Sing heigh ho, the carrion crow,
  Fol de riddle, lol de riddle, hi ding do.

Wife, bring me my old bent bow,
  Fol de riddle, lol de riddle, hi ding do,
That I may shoot yon carrion crow;
  Sing heigh ho, the carrion crow,
  Fol de riddle, lol de riddle, hi ding do.

The tailor he shot and missed his mark,
  Fol de riddle, lol de riddle, hi ding do,
And shot his own sow quite through the heart;
  Sing heigh ho, the carrion crow,
  Fol de riddle, lol de riddle, hi ding do.

Wife, bring brandy in a spoon,
  Fol de riddle, lol de riddle, hi ding do,
For our old sow is in a swoon;
  Sing heigh ho, the carrion crow,
  Fol de riddle, lol de riddle, hi ding do.

2.

A FARMER's dog leapt over the stile,
  His name was little Bingo;

There was B. with an I., and I. with an N.,
   N. with a G., G. with an O.;
      There was B.I.N.G.O.,
And his name was little Bingo.

The farmer loved a cup of ale,
   And called it very good stingo;
There was S. with a T., and T. with an I.,
   N. with a G., G. with an O.;
      There was S.T.I.N.G.O.,
And its name was jolly Stingo.

The farmer loved a pretty lass,
   And gave her a wedding Ring-O;
There was R. with an I., and I. with an N.,
   N. with a G., G. with an O.;
      There was R.I.N.G.O.,
      She curtsied and took the Ring-O.

3.

A WIDOW bird sate mourning for her love
   Upon a wintry bough;
The frozen wind crept on above,
   The freezing stream below.

There was no leaf upon the forest bare,
   No flower upon the ground,
And little motion in the air
   Except the mill-wheel's sound.

4. THE STRANGE VISITOR

A WIFE was sitting at her reel ae night;
And aye she sat, and aye she reeled, and aye she
wished for company.

In came a pair o' braid braid soles, and sat down at
the fireside;
And aye she sat, and aye she reeled, and aye she
wished for company.

In came a pair o' sma' legs, and sat down on the
braid braid soles;
And aye she sat, and aye she reeled, and aye she
wished for company.

In came a pair o' muckle muckle knees, and sat down
on the sma' sma' legs;
And aye she sat, and aye she reeled, and aye she
wished for company.

In came a pair o' sma' sma' thees, and sat down on
the muckle muckle knees;
And aye she sat, and aye she reeled, and aye she
wished for company.

In came a pair o' muckle muckle hips, and sat down
on the sma' sma' thees;
And aye she sat, and aye she reeled, and aye she
wished for company.

In came a sma' sma' waist, and sat down on the
muckle muckle hips;
And aye she sat, and aye she reeled, and aye she
wished for company.

In came a pair o' braid braid shouthers, and sat
down on the sma' sma' waist;
And aye she sat, and aye she reeled, and aye she
wished for company.

In came a pair o' sma' sma' arms, and sat down on
the braid braid shouthers;
And aye she sat, and aye she reeled, and aye she
wished for company.

In came a pair o' muckle muckle hands, and sat
down on the sma' sma' arms;
And aye she sat, and aye she reeled, and aye she
wished for company.

In came a sma' sma' neck, and sat down on the braid
braid shouthers;
And aye she sat, and aye she reeled, and aye she
wished for company.

In came a great big head, and sat down on the sma'
sma' neck;
And aye she sat, and aye she reeled, and aye she
wished for company.

"What way hae ye sic braid braid feet?" quo' the
wife.
"Muckle ganging, muckle ganging.".
"What way hae ye sic sma' sma' legs?"
"*Aih-h-h*!—late—and *wee-e-e* moul."
"What way hae ye sic muckle muckle knees?"
"Muckle praying, muckle praying."

4

"What way hae ye sic sma' sma' thees?"
"*Aih-h-h*!—late—and *wee-e-e* moul."
"What way hae ye sic big big hips?"
"Muckle sitting, muckle sitting."
"What way hae ye sic a sma' sma' waist?"
"*Aih-h-h*!—late—and *wee-e-e* moul."
"What way hae ye sic braid braid shouthers?"
"Wi' carrying broom, wi' carrying broom."
"What way hae ye sic sma' sma' arms?"
"*Aih-h-h*!—late—and *wee-e-e* moul."
"What way hae ye sic muckle muckle hands?"
"Threshing wi' an iron flail, threshing wi' an iron
    flail."
"What way hae ye sic a sma' sma' neck?"
"*Aih-h-h*!—late—and *wee-e-e* moul."
"What way hae ye sic a muckle muckle head?"
"Muckle wit, muckle wit."
"What do you come for?"
"For YOU!"

5.

ALL people that on earth do dwell,
Sing to the Lord with cheerful voice.
Him serve with mirth, his praise forth tell;
Come ye before him and rejoice.

Know that the Lord is God indeed;
Without our aid he did us make:
We are his flock, he doth us feed,
And for his sheep he doth us take.

O enter then his gates with praise,
Approach with joy his courts unto;
Praise, laud, and bless his name always,
For it is seemly so to do.

For why? the Lord our God is good,
His mercy is for ever sure;
His truth at all times firmly stood,
And shall from age to age endure.

6.

AND did those feet in ancient time
 Walk upon England's mountains green?
And was the holy Lamb of God
 On England's pleasant pastures seen?

And did the Countenance Divine
 Shine forth upon our clouded hills?
And was Jerusalem builded here
 Among these dark Satanic Mills?

Bring me my bow of burning gold!
 Bring me my arrows of desire!
Bring me my spear! O clouds, unfold!
 Bring me my chariot of fire!

I will not cease from mental fight,
 Nor shall my sword sleep in my hand,
Till we have built Jerusalem
 In England's green and pleasant land.

6

7.

ART thou gone in haste?
    I'll not forsake thee!
Runn'st thou ne'er so fast,
    I'll o'ertake thee!
O'er the dales or the downs,
    Through the green meadows,
From the fields, through the towns,
    To the dim shadows!

All along the plain,
    To the low fountains;
Up and down again,
    From the high mountains:
Echo, then, shall again
    Tell her I follow,
And the floods to the woods
    Carry my holla.
                Holla!
Ce! la! ho! ho! hu!

8.

As I was going by Charing Cross,
I saw a black man upon a black horse;
They told me it was King Charles the First;
Oh dear, my heart was ready to burst!

9. JOHN DORY

As it fell on a holy-day,
  And upon a' holy-tide-a.
John Dory brought him an ambling nag,
  To Paris for to ride-a.

And when John Dory to Paris was come,
  A little before the gate-a,
John Dory was fitted, the porter was witted,
  To let him in thereat-a.

The first man that John Dory did meet,
  Was good King John of France-a;
John Dory could well of his courtesie,
  But fell down in a trance-a.

"A pardon, a pardon, my liege and my king
  For my merie men and for me-a;
And all the churles in merie England,
  Ile bring them all bound to thee-a."

And Nicholl was then a Cornish man,
  A little beside Bohide-a,
And he mande forth a good blacke barke,
  With fifty good oares on a side-a.

"Run up, my boy, unto the maine top,
  And looke what thou canst spie-a":
"Who ho! who ho! a goodly ship I do see,
  I trow it be John Dory-a."

8

They hoist their sailes, both top and top,
    The meisseine and all was tride-a;
And every man stood to his lot,
    Whatever should betide-a.

The roring cannons then were plide,
    And dub-a-dub went the drumme-a;
The braying trumpets lowd they cride,
    To courage both all and some-a.

The grapling-hooks were brought at length,
    The browne bill and the sword-a;
John Dory at length, for all his strength,
    Was clapt fast under board-a.

10. BAT

At evening, sitting on this terrace,
When the sun from the west, beyond Pisa, beyond
    the mountains of Carrara
Departs, and the world is taken by surprise. . . .

When the tired flower of Florence is in gloom
    beneath the glowing
Brown hills surrounding. . . .

When under the arches of the Ponte Vecchio
A green light enters against stream, flush from the
    west,
Against the current of obscure Arno. . . .

9

Look up, and you see things flying
Between the day and the night;
Swallows with spools of dark thread sewing the
    shadows together.

A circle swoop, and a quick parabola under the
    bridge arches
Where light pushes through;
A sudden turning upon itself of a thing in the air.
A dip to the water.

And you think:
"The swallows are flying so late!"

Swallows?

Dark air-life looping
Yet missing the pure loop. . . .
A twitch, a twitter, an elastic shudder in flight
And serrated wings against the sky,
Like a glove, a black glove thrown up at the light,
And falling back.

Never swallows!
Bats!
The swallows are gone.

At a wavering instant the swallows give way to bats
By the Ponte Vecchio. . . .
Changing guard.

Bats, and an uneasy creeping in one's scalp
As the bats swoop overhead!
Flying madly.

Pipistrello!
Black piper on an infinitesimal pipe.
Little lumps that fly in air and have voices in-
    definite, wildly vindictive;

Wings like bits of umbrella.

Bats!

Creatures that hang themselves up like an old rag,
    to sleep;
And disgustingly upside down.
Hanging upside down like rows of disgusting old rags
And grinning in their sleep.
Bats!

In China the bat is symbol of happiness.

Not for me!

II.

AWAY, haul away, boys, haul away together,
    Away, haul away, boys, haul away O;
Away, haul away, boys, haul away together,
    Away, haul away, boys, haul away O.

Louis was the King of France afore the Revoluti-on,
    Away, haul away, boys, haul away O;
Louis was the King of France afore the Revoluti-on,
    Away, haul away, boys, haul away O.

11

But Louis got his head cut off, which spoiled his
 con-stitu-ti-on,
 Away, haul away, boys, haul away O;
But Louis got his head cut off, which spoiled his
 con-sti-tu-tion,
 Away, haul away, boys, haul away O.

12.

Beautiful Soup, so rich and green,
 Waiting in a hot tureen!
Who for such dainties would not stoop?
Soup of the evening, beautiful Soup!
Soup of the evening, beautiful Soup!
 Beau-ootiful Soo-oop!
 Beau-ootiful Soo-oop!
Soo-oop of the e-e-evening,
 Beautiful, beautiful Soup!

Beautiful Soup! Who cares for fish,
Game, or any other dish?
Who would not give all else for two p
ennyworth only of beautiful Soup?
Pennyworth only of beautiful Soup?
 Beau-ootiful Soo-oop!
 Beau-ootiful Soo-oop!
Soo-oop of the e-e-evening,
 Beautiful, beauti-FUL SOUP!

Boney was a warrior,
Away-i-oh;
Boney was a warrior,
John François.

Boney fought the Proosh-i-ans,
Away-i-oh;
Boney fought the Proosh-i-ans,
John François.

Boney fought the Roosh-i-ans,
Away-i-oh;
Boney fought the Roosh-i-ans,
John François.

Drive her, captain, drive her,
Away-i-oh;
Drive her, captain, drive her,
John François.

Give her the top-gallant sails,
Away-i-oh;
Give her the top-gallant sails,
John François.

It's a weary way to Baltimore,
Away-i-oh;
It's a weary way to Baltimore,
John François.

14. THE HAWK

'CALL down the hawk from the air;
Let him be hooded or caged
Till the yellow eye has grown mild,
For larder and spit are bare,
The old cook enraged,
The scullion gone wild.'

'I will not be clapped in a hood,
Nor a cage, nor alight upon wrist,
Now I have learnt to be proud
Hovering over the wood
In the broken mist
Or tumbling cloud.'

'What tumbling cloud did you cleave,
Yellow-eyed hawk of the mind,
Last evening? that I, who had sat
Dumbfounded before a knave,
Should give to my friend
A pretence of wit.'

15. THE DEATH OF NELSON

COME all gallant seamen that unite a meeting
Attend to these lines that I'm going to relate
And, when that you hear, it will move you with pity
To hear how Lord Nelson he met with his fate.
For he was a bold and undaunted commander
As ever did sail on the ocean wide
And he made both the French and the Spaniards
    surrender
By always pouring into them a broadside.

Chorus

Mourn England mourn; mourn and complain
For the loss of Lord Nelson, who died on the main.

From aloft to aloft, where he was commanding
All by a French gun he received a ball
And by the contents, he got mortally wounded
And that was the occasion of Lord Nelson's fall.
Like an undaunted hero, exposed to the fire
As he gave the command, on the quarter deck stood
And to hear of his actions, you would much admire,
To see the decks all covered with human blood.

One hundred engagements he had been into
And never in his time was he known to be beat;
For he had lost an arm, likewise his right eye, sir
No powers on earth could ever him defeat.
His age at his death, it was forty and seven
And as long as I live, his great praises I'll sing;
For the whole navigation was given unto him
Because he was loyal and true to his king.

Then up steps the doctor in a very great hurry
And unto Lord Nelson these words he did say
Indeed then my Lord I am very sorry
To see you lying and bleeding this way.
No matter no matter whatever about me
My time it has come, I'm almost at the worst,
And there's my gallant seamen who'se fighting so
    boldly
Go and discharge your duty to them first.

Then with a loud voice he called out to his captain
Pray let me know how this battle does go
I think that our guns continue to rattle
Though death approaches I very well know.
The antagonist's ship has gone to the bottom
Eighteen we've captured, and brought them on
    board
And here are two of them quite blown out of the
    ocean
So that is the news I've brought you, my Lord.

Come all gallant seamen that unite a meeting
Always let Lord Nelson's memory go round
For it is your duty when you unite a meeting
Because he was loyal and true to the crown.
So now to conclude and to finish these verses,
My time it is come, I am quite at the worst.
May the heavens go with you and ten thousand
    blessings
May rest in the Fleet with you, Lord Collingwood.

16. CASEY JONES

Come all you rounders if you want to hear
The story of a brave engineer;
Casey Jones was the hogger's name,
On a big eight-wheeler, boys, he won his fame.
Caller called Casey at half-past four,
He kissed his wife at the station door,
Mounted to the cabin with orders in his hand,
And took his farewell trip to the promised land.

> Casey Jones, he mounted to the cabin,
> Casey Jones, with his orders in his hand!
> Casey Jones, he mounted to the cabin,
> Took his farewell trip into the promised land.

Put in your water and shovel in your coal,
Put your head out the window, watch the drivers
roll,
I'll run her till she leaves the rail,
'Cause we're eight hours late with the Western
Mail!
He looked at his watch and his watch was slow,
Looked at the water and the water was low,
Turned to his fireboy and said,
"We'll get to 'Frisco, but we'll all be dead!"

(Refrain)

Casey pulled up Reno Hill,
Tooted for the crossing with an awful shrill,
Snakes all knew by the engine's moans
That the hogger at the throttle was Casey Jones.

He pulled up short two miles from the place,
Number Four stared him right in the face,
Turned to his fireboy, said "You'd better jump,
'Cause there's two locomotives that's going to
    bump!"

                                  (*Refrain*)

Casey said, just before he died,
"There's two more roads I'd like to ride."
Fireboy said, "What can they be?"
"The Rio Grande and the Old S.P."
Mrs Jones sat on her bed a-sighing,
Got a pink that Casey was dying,
Said, "Go to bed, children; hush your crying,
'Cause you'll get another papa on the Salt Lake
    line."

    Casey Jones!   Got another papa!
    Casey Jones, on the Salt Lake Line!
    Casey Jones!   Got another papa!
    Got another papa on the Salt Lake Line!

17.   THE DEATH OF ADMIRAL BENBOW

    Come all you sailors bold,
      Lend an ear,
    Come all you sailors bold,
      Lend an ear:
    'Tis of our Admiral's fame,
    Brave Benbow called by name,
    How he fought on the main
      You shall hear.

Brave Benbow he set sail
  For to fight,
Brave Benbow he set sail
  For to fight:
Brave Benbow he set sail,
With a fine and pleasant gale,
But his captains they turned tail
  In a fight.

Says Kirkby unto Wade,
  "I will run,"
Says Kirkby unto Wade,
  "I will run:
I value not disgrace,
Nor the losing of my place,
My foes I will not face
  With a gun."

'Twas the *Ruby* and *Noah's Ark*,
  Fought the French,
'Twas the *Ruby* and *Noah's Ark*,
  Fought the French:
And there was ten in all,
Poor souls they fought them all,
They recked them not at all
  Nor their noise.

It was our Admiral's lot,
  With a chain-shot,
It was our Admiral's lot,
  With a chain-shot:

Our Admiral lost his legs,
And to his men he begs
"Fight on, my boys," he says,
   "'Tis my lot."

While the surgeon dressed his wounds,
   Thus he said,
While the surgeon dressed his wounds,
   Thus he said:
"Let my cradle now in haste
On the quarter-deck be placed,
That the Frenchmen I may face,
   Till I'm dead."

And there bold Benbow lay,
   Crying out,
And there bold Benbow lay,
   Crying out:
"O let us tack once more,
We'll drive them to the shore,
As our fathers did before
   Long ago."

18.   FOR THE VICTORY AT AGINCOURT

DEO gratias Anglia redde pro victoria!
Owre kynge went forth to Normandy,
With grace and myzt[1] of chivalry;
The God for him wrouzt marvelously,
Wherefore Englonde may calle, and cry
         Deo gratias:
   Deo gratias Anglia redde pro victoria.

[1] z=gh

20

He sette a sege, the sothe for to say,
To Harflue toune with ryal aray:
That toune he wan and made a fray,
That Fraunce shall rywe [1] tyl domes day.
Deo gratias, etc.

Then went owre kynge with alle his oste
Thorowe Fraunce for all the Frenshe boste;
He spared [for] drede of leste ne most,
Tyl he come to Agincourt coste.
Deo gratias, etc.

Than for sothe that knyzt comely
In Agincourt feld he fauzt manly,
Thorow grace of God most myzty
He had both the felde and the victory:
Deo gratias, etc.

Ther dukys and erlys, lorde and barone,
Were take and slayne and that wel sone,
And some were ledde in to Lundone
With joye and merthe and grete renone.
Deo gratias, etc.

Now gracious God he save owre kynge,
His peple and all his wel wyllynge,
Gef him gode lyfe and gode endynge,
That we with merth mowe savely synge
Deo gratias:
Deo gratias Anglia redde pro victoria.

[1] rue

21

Deep in the shady sadness of a vale
Far sunken from the healthy breath of morn,
Far from the fiery noon, and eve's one star,
Sat grey-hair'd Saturn, quiet as a stone,
Still as the silence round about his lair;
Forest on forest hung about his head
Like cloud on cloud.   No stir of air was there,
Not so much life as on a summer's day
Robs not one light seed from the feather'd grass,
But where the dead leaf fell, there did it rest.
A stream went voiceless by, still deaden'd more
By reason of his fallen divinity
Spreading a shade: the Naiad 'mid her reeds
Press'd her cold finger closer to her lips. . . .

20. TARANTELLA

Do you remember an Inn,
Miranda?
Do you remember an Inn?
And the tedding and the spreading
Of the straw for a bedding,
And the fleas that tease in the High Pyrenees,
And the wine that tasted of the tar?
And the cheers and the jeers of the young
    muleteers
(Under the vine of the dark verandah)?
Do you remember an Inn, Miranda,
Do you remember an Inn?

And the cheers and the jeers of the young
    muleteers
Who hadn't got a penny,
And who weren't paying any,
And the hammer at the doors and the Din?
And the Hip! Hop! Hap!
Of the clap
Of the hands to the twirl and the swirl
Of the girl gone chancing,
Glancing,
Dancing,
Backing and advancing,
Snapping of the clapper to the spin
Out and in——
And the Ting, Tong, Tang of the Guitar!
Do you remember an Inn,
Miranda?
Do you remember an Inn?

      Never more;
      Miranda,
      Never more.
      Only the high peaks hoar:
      And Aragon a torrent at the door.
      No sound
      In the walls of the Halls where falls
      The tread
      Of the feet of the dead to the ground
      No sound:
      But the boom
      Of the far Waterfall like Doom.

21. THE CONGO

I. *Their Basic Savagery*

Fat black bucks in a wine-barrel room,
Barrel-house kings, with feet unstable,

A deep rolling bass. Sagged and reeled and pounded on the
table,
Pounded on the table,
Beat an empty barrel with the handle of a
broom,
Hard as they were able,
Boom, boom, Boom,
With a silk umbrella and the handle of a
broom,
Boomlay, boomlay, boomlay, Boom.
Then I had religion, Then I had a vision.
I could not turn from their revel in derision.

More deliberate.
Solemnly chanted. Then I saw the Congo, creeping through
the black,
Cutting through the forest with a
golden track.
Then along that riverbank
A thousand miles
Tattooed cannibals danced in files;
Then I heard the boom of the blood-lust
song

A rapidly piling
climax of speed and
racket. And a thigh-bone beating on a tin-pan gong.
And "Blood" screamed the whistles and
the fifes of the warriors,
"Blood" screamed the skull-faced lean
witch-doctors,
"Whirl ye the deadly voo-doo rattle,

24

Harry the uplands,
Steal all the cattle,
Rattle-rattle, rattle-rattle,
Bing.
Boomlay, boomlay, boomlay, BOOM,"
A roaring, epic, rag-time tune

With a philo-sophic pause.

From the mouth of the Congo
To the Mountains of the Moon.
Death is an Elephant,
Torch-eyed and horrible,

Shrilly and with a heavily accented metre.

Foam-flanked and terrible.
BOOM, steal the pygmies,
BOOM, kill the Arabs,
BOOM, kill the white men,
Hoo, Hoo, Hoo.
Listen to the yell of Leopold's ghost

Like the wind in the chimney.

Burning in Hell for his hand-maimed host.
Hear how the demons chuckle and yell
Cutting his hands off, down in Hell.
Listen to the creepy proclamation,
Blown through the lairs of the forest-nation,
Blown past the white-ants' hill of clay,
Blown past the marsh where the butter-
    flies play:—
"Be careful what you do,
Or Mumbo-Jumbo, God of the Congo,

All the O sounds very golden.

And all of the other

Heavy accents very heavy.

Gods of the Congo,
Mumbo-Jumbo will hoo-doo you,

Light accents very light. Last line whispered.

Mumbo-Jumbo will hoo-doo you,
Mumbo-Jumbo will hoo-doo you."

II. *Their Irrepressible High Spirits*

Rather shrill and high.

Wild crap-shooters with a whoop and a call
Danced the juba in their gambling-hall
And laughed fit to kill, and shook the town,
And guyed the policemen and laughed them
down
With a boomlay, boomlay, boomlay, Boom.

Read exactly as in first section.

THEN I SAW THE CONGO, CREEPING THROUGH
THE BLACK,
CUTTING THROUGH THE FOREST WITH A
GOLDEN TRACK.

Lay emphasis on the delicate ideas. Keep as light-footed as possible.

A negro fairyland swung into view,
A minstrel river
Where dreams come true.
The ebony palace soared on high
Through the blossoming trees to the even-
ing sky.
The inlaid porches and casements shone
With gold and ivory and elephant-bone.
And the black crowd laughed till their sides
were sore
At the baboon butler in the agate door,
And the well-known tunes of the parrot
band
That trilled on the bushes of that magic land.

With pomposity.

A troupe of skull-faced witch-men came
Through the agate doorway in suits of
flame,
Yea, long-tailed coats with a gold-leaf crust
And hats that were covered with diamond-
dust.

And the crowd in the court gave a whoop
    and a call
And danced the juba from wall to wall.
But the witch-men suddenly stilled the
    throng

With a great deliberation and ghostliness.

With a stern cold glare, and a stern old
    song :—
"Mumbo-Jumbo will hoo-doo you." . . .
Just then from the doorway, as fat as
    shotes,

With overwhelming assurance, good cheer, and pomp.

Came the cake-walk princes in their long
    red coats,
Canes with a brilliant lacquer shine,
And tall silk hats that were red as wine.
And they pranced with their butterfly
    partners there,

With growing speed and sharply marked dance-rhythm.

Coal-black maidens with pearls in their
    hair,
Knee-skirts trimmed with the jassamine
    sweet,
And bells on their ankles and little black-
    feet.
And the couples railed at the chant and
    the frown
Of the witch-men lean, and laughed them
    down.
(O rare was the revel, and well worth while
That made those glowering witch-men
    smile.)

The cake-walk royalty then began
To walk for a cake that was tall as a man

To the tune of "Boomlay, boomlay, Boom,"

With a touch of negro dialect, and as rapidly as possible toward the end.

While the witch-men laughed, with a sinister
　　air,
And sang with the scalawags prancing
　　　there:—
"Walk with care, walk with care,
Or Mumbo-Jumbo, God of the Congo,
And all of the other
Gods of the Congo,
Mumbo-Jumbo will hoo-doo you.
Beware, beware, walk with care,
Boomlay, boomlay, boomlay, boom.
Boomlay, boomlay, boomlay, boom,
Boomlay, boomlay, boomlay, boom,
Boomlay, boomlay, boomlay,
Boom."

Slow philosophic calm.

Oh rare was the revel, and well worth while
That made those glowering witch-men smile.

III. *The Hope of their Religion*

Heavy bass. With a literal imitation of camp-meeting racket, and trance.

A good old negro in the slums of the town
Preached at a sister for her velvet gown.
Howled at a brother for his low-down ways,
His prowling, guzzling, sneak-thief days.
Beat on the Bible till he wore it out
Starting the jubilee revival shout.
And some had visions, as they stood on
　　　chairs,
And sang of Jacob, and the golden stairs,
And they all repented, a thousand strong
From their stupor and savagery and sin and
　　　wrong

28

And slammed with their hymn books till
    they shook the room
With "glory, glory, glory,"
And "Boom, boom, BOOM."

THEN I SAW THE CONGO, CREEPING THROUGH
    THE BLACK
CUTTING THROUGH THE JUNGLE WITH A
    GOLDEN TRACK.

Exactly as in the first section. Begin with terror and power, end with joy.

And the gray sky opened like a new-rent
    veil
And showed the Apostles with their coats of
    mail.
In bright white steel they were seated
    round
And their fire-eyes watched where the Congo
    wound.
And the twelve Apostles, from their thrones
    on high
Thrilled all the forest with their heavenly
    cry:—

"Mumbo-Jumbo will die in the jungle;
Never again will he hoo-doo you,
Never again will he hoo-doo you."

Sung to the tune of "Hark, ten thousand harps and voices."

Then along that river, a thousand miles
The vine-snared trees fell down in files.
Pioneer angels cleared the way
For a Congo paradise, for babes at play,
For sacred capitals, for temples clean.
Gone were the skull-faced witch-men lean.

With growing deliberation and joy.

There, where the wild ghost-gods had wailed
A million boats of the angels sailed

In a rather high key —as delicately as possible.

29

With oars of silver, and prows of blue
And silken pennants that the sun shone
    through.
'Twas a land transfigured, 'twas a new
    creation.
Oh, a singing wind swept the negro nation
And on through the backwoods clearing
    flew:—

To the tune of "Hark, ten thousand harps and voices."

"Mumbo-Jumbo is dead in the jungle.
Never again will he hoo-doo you.
Never again will he hoo-doo you."

Redeemed were the forests, the beasts and
    the men,
And only the vulture dared again
By the far, lone mountains of the moon
To cry, in the silence, the Congo tune:—

Dying down into a penetrating, terrified whisper.

"Mumbo-Jumbo will hoo-doo you,
Mumbo-Jumbo will hoo-doo you.
Mumbo . . . Jumbo . . . will . . . hoo-doo
    . . . you."

22. HUGH OF LINCOLN

Four and twenty bonny boys
    Were playing at the ba,
And by it came him sweet Sir Hugh,
    And he played oer them a'.

He kicked the ba with his right foot,
　　And catchd it wi his knee,
And throuch-and-thro the Jew's window
　　He gard the bonny ba flee.

He's doen him to the Jew's castell,
　　And walkd it round about;
And there he saw the Jew's daughter,
　　At the window looking out.

"Throw down the ba, ye Jew's daughter,
　　Throw down the ba to me!"
"Never a bit," says the Jew's daughter,
　　"'Till up to me come ye."

"How will I come up?　How can I come up?
　　How can I come to thee?
For as ye did to my auld father,
　　The same ye'll do to me."

She's gane till her father's garden,
　　And pu'd an apple red and green;
'Twas a' to wyle him sweet Sir Hugh,
　　And to entice him in.

She's led him in through ae dark door,
　　And sae has she thro nine;
She's laid him on a dressing-table,
　　And stickit him like a swine.

And first came out the thick, thick blood,
　　And syne came out the thin,
And syne came out the bonny heart's blood;
　　There was nae mair within.

She's rowd him in a cake o lead,
  Bade him lie still and sleep;
She's thrown him in Our Lady's draw-well,
  Was fifty fathom deep.

When bells were rung, and mass was sung,
  And a' the bairns came hame,
When every lady gat hame her son,
  The Lady Maisry gat nane.

She's taen her mantle her about,
  Her coffer by the hand,
And she's gane out to seek her son,
  And wanderd oer the land.

She's doen her to the Jew's castell,
  Where a' were fast asleep:
"Gin ye be there, my sweet Sir Hugh,
  I pray you to me speak."

She's doen her to the Jew's garden,
  Thought he had been gathering fruit:
"Gin ye be there, my sweet Sir Hugh,
  I pray you to me speak."

She neard Our Lady's deep draw-well,
  Was fifty fathom deep:
"Whareer ye be, my sweet Sir Hugh,
  I pray you to me speak."

"Gae hame, gae hame, my mither dear,
  Prepare my winding sheet,
And at the back o merry Lincoln
  The morn I will you meet."

Now Lady Maisry is gane hame,
　　Made him a winding sheet,
And at the back o merry Lincoln
　　The dead corpse did her meet.

And a' the bells o merry Lincoln
　　Without men's hands were rung,
And a' the books o merry Lincoln
　　Were read without man's tongue,
And neer was such a burial
　　Sin Adam's days begun.

23. SONG FOR ST. CECILIA'S DAY

FROM harmony, from heavenly harmony
　　This universal frame began.
When nature underneath a heap
　　Of jarring atoms lay,
　　And could not heave her head,
The tuneful voice was heard from high,
　　Arise, ye more than dead.
Then cold, and hot, and moist, and dry,
In order to their stations leap,
　　And Music's power obey.
From harmony, from heavenly harmony
　　This universal frame began:
　　From harmony to harmony
Through all the compass of the notes it ran,
The diapason closing full in Man.

What passion cannot Music raise and quell?
　　When Jubal struck the corded shell,

His listening brethren stood around,
    And, wondering, on their faces fell
    To worship that celestial sound.
Less than a God they thought there could not dwell
    Within the hollow of that shell,
    That spoke so sweetly and so well.
What passion cannot Music raise and quell?

    The trumpet's loud clangor
        Excites us to arms,
    With shrill notes of anger,
        And mortal alarms.
    The double double double beat
        Of the thundering drum
Cries "Hark! the foes come;
Charge, Charge, 'tis too late to retreat!"

    The soft complaining flute
    In dying notes discovers
    The woes of hopeless lovers,
Whose dirge is whisper'd by the warbling lute.

    Sharp violins proclaim
Their jealous pangs, and desperation,
Fury, frantic indignation,
Depth of pains, and height of passion,
    For the fair disdainful dame.

    But oh! what art can teach,
    What human voice can reach
The sacred organ's praise?
    Notes inspiring holy love,
Notes that wing their heavenly ways
    To mend the choirs above.

Orpheus could lead the savage race;
And trees unrooted left their place,
   Sequacious of the lyre:
But bright Cecilia rais'd the wonder higher:
When to her organ vocal breath was given,
An angel heard, and straight appear'd,
   Mistaking Earth for heaven!

Grand Chorus:

As from the power of sacred lays
   The spheres began to move,
And sung the great Creator's praise
   To all the bless'd above;
So when the last and dreadful hour
This crumbling pageant shall devour,
The trumpet shall be heard on high,
The dead shall live, the living die,
And Music shall untune the sky.

24.

GAY go up, and gay go down,
To ring the bells of London town.

Bull's eyes and targets,
Say the bells of St. Marg'ret's.

Brickbats and tiles,
Say the bells of St. Giles'.

Halfpence and farthings,
Say the bells of St. Martin's.

Oranges and lemons,
Say the bells of St. Clement's.

Pancakes and fritters,
Say the bells of St. Peter's.

Two sticks and an apple,
Say the bells at Whitechapel.

Old Father Baldpate,
Say the slow bells at Aldgate.

You owe me ten shillings,
Say the bells at St. Helen's.

Pokers and tongs,
Say the bells at St. John's.

Kettles and pans,
Say the bells at St. Ann's.

When will you pay me?
Say the bells at Old Bailey.

When I grow rich,
Say the bells at Shoreditch.

Pray when will that be?
Say the bells at Stepney.

I am sure I don't know,
Says the great bell at Bow.

Here comes a candle to light you to bed,
And here comes a chopper to chop off
   your head.

25. THE OLD GREY GOOSE

Go and tell Aunt Nancy,
Go and tell Aunt Nancy,
Go and tell Aunt Nancy
The old grey goose is dead.

The one that she'd been saving
For to make her feather-bed.

She died last Friday
With a pain all in her head.

Old gander is weeping
Because his wife is dead.

The goslings are mourning
Because their mother's dead.

26.

Gup, Scot,
Ye blot:
Laudate
Caudate,
Set in better
Thy pentameter.
This Dundas,
This Scottishe as,
He rymes and railes
That Englishmen have tailes.

. . . .

Skelton laureat
After this rate
Defendeth with his pen
All Englysh men
Agayn Dundas,
That Scottishe asse.
Shake thy tayle, Scot, lyke a cur,
For thou beggest at every mannes dur:
Tut, Scot, I sey,
Go shake thy dog, hey!

. . . . . .

Dundas, dronken and drowsy,
Skabed, scurvy, and lowsy,
Of unhappy generacion
And most ungracious nacion.
Dundas,
That dronke asse,
That ratis and rankis,
That prates and prankes
On Huntley bankes,
Take this our thankes;
Dunde, Dunbar,
Walke, Scot,
Walke, sot,
Rayle not to far.

27.

Ha ha! ha ha! This world doth pass
  Most merrily I'll be sworn,
For many an honest Indian ass
  Goes for a unicorn.
        Fara diddle dyno,
        This is idle fyno.

Tie hie! tie hie! O sweet delight!
  He tickles this age that can
Call Tullia's ape a marmasyte
  And Leda's goose a swan.
        Fara diddle dyno,
        This is idle fyno.

So so! so so! Fine English days!
  For false play is no reproach,
For he that doth the coachman praise
  May safely use the coach.
        Fara diddle dyno,
        This is idle fyno.

28.

Here lies the preacher, judge and poet, Peter,
Who broke the laws of God, and man, and metre.

29. A NEW YEAR CAROL

Here we bring new water
  from the well so clear,
For to worship God with,
  this happy New Year.

Sing levy dew, sing levy dew,
    the water and the wine;
The seven bright gold wires
    and the bugles that do shine.

Sing reign of Fair Maid,
    with gold upon her toe,—
Open you the West Door,
    and turn the Old Year go.

Sing reign of Fair Maid
    with gold upon her chin,—
Open you the East Door,
    and let the New Year in.

Sing levy dew, sing levy dew,
    the water and the wine;
The seven bright gold wires
    and the bugles they do shine.

30.

HERE we come a piping
First in spring, and then in May;
The queen she sits upon the sand,
Fair as a lily, white as a wand:
King John has sent you letters three,
And begs you'll read them unto me.—
We can't read one without them all,
So pray, Miss Bridget, deliver the ball!

31.

Hey nonny no!
Men are fools that wish to die!
Is't not fine to dance and sing
When the bells of death do ring?
Is't not fine to swim in wine,
And turn upon the toe
And sing hey nonny no,
When the winds do blow,
And the seas do flow?
Hey nonny no!

32.

'I am of Ireland,
And the Holy Land of Ireland,
And time runs on,' cried she.
'Come out of charity,
Come dance with me in Ireland.'

One man, one man alone
In that outlandish gear,
One solitary man
Of all that rambled there
Had turned his stately head.
'That is a long way off,
And time runs on,' he said,
'And the night grows rough.'

'I am of Ireland,
And the Holy Land of Ireland,
And time runs on,' cried she.
'Come out of charity
And dance with me in Ireland.'

'The fiddlers are all thumbs,
Or the fiddle-strings accursed,
The drums and the kettledrums
And the trumpets all are burst,
And the trombone,' cried he,
'The trumpet and trombone,'
And cocked a malicious eye,
'But time runs on, runs on.'

'I am of Ireland,
And the Holy Land of Ireland,
And time runs on,' cried she.
'Come out of charity
And dance with me in Ireland.'

33.

I DO not love thee, Doctor Fell;
The reason why I cannot tell.
But this I'm sure I know full well,
I do not love thee, Doctor Fell.

34.

I HAD a black man, he was double-jointed,
I kissed him, and made him disappointed,
All right, Hilda, I'll tell your mother
Kissing the black man round the corner.
How many kisses did he give you?
One, two, three, etc.

35.

I HAD a boat, and the boat had wings;
And I did dream that we went a flying
Over the heads of queens and kings,
Over the souls of dead and dying,
Up among the stars and the great white rings,
And where the Moon on her back is lying.

36.

I HAD a little nut-tree, nothing would it bear
But a silver nutmeg and a golden pear;
The King of Spain's daughter came to visit me,
And all was because of my little nut-tree.
I skipp'd over water, I danced over sea,
And all the birds in the air couldn't catch me.

37.

I SAW a peacock with a fiery tail
I saw a blazing comet drop down hail

I saw a cloud wrapped with ivy round
I saw an oak creep upon the ground
I saw a pismire swallow up a whale
I saw the sea brimful of ale
I saw a Venice glass full fifteen feet deep
I saw a well full of men's tears that weep
I saw red eyes all of a flaming fire
I saw a house bigger than the moon and higher
I saw the sun at twelve o'clock at night
I saw the man that saw this wondrous sight.

38.

I SAW three ships come sailing in,
On Christmas Day, on Christmas Day,
I saw three ships come sailing in,
On Christmas Day in the morning.

And what was in those ships all three,
On Christmas Day, on Christmas Day?
And what was in those ships all three,
On Christmas Day in the morning?

Our Saviour Christ and His Lady,
On Christmas Day, on Christmas Day,
Our Saviour Christ and His Lady,
On Christmas Day in the morning.

Pray, whither sailed those ships all three,
On Christmas Day, on Christmas Day?
Pray, whither sailed those ships all three,
On Christmas Day in the morning?

O they sailed into Bethlehem,
  On Christmas Day, on Christmas Day,
O they sailed into Bethlehem,
  On Christmas Day in the morning.

And all the bells on earth shall ring,
  On Christmas Day, on Christmas Day,
And all the bells on earth shall ring,
  On Christmas Day in the morning.

And all the angels in Heaven shall sing,
  On Christmas Day, on Christmas Day,
And all the angels in Heaven shall sing,
  On Christmas Day in the morning.

And all the souls on earth shall sing,
  On Christmas Day, on Christmas Day,
And all the souls on earth shall sing,
  On Christmas Day in the morning.

Then let us all rejoice amain,
  On Christmas Day, on Christmas Day,
Then let us all rejoice amain,
  On Christmas Day in the morning.

39.

I TO the hills will lift mine eyes,
  From whence doth come mine aid.
My safety cometh from the Lord,
  Who heaven and earth hath made.

Thy foot he'll not let slide, nor will
    He slumber that thee keeps.
Behold, he that keeps Israel,
    He slumbers not, nor sleeps.

The Lord thee keeps, the Lord thy shade
    On thy right hand doth stay:
The moon by night thee shall not smite,
    Nor yet the sun by day.
The Lord shall keep thy soul; he shall
    Preserve thee from all ill.
Henceforth thy going out and in
    God keep for ever will.

40.

I wish I were a
Elephantiaphus
And could pick off the coconuts with my nose.
But, oh! I am not,
(Alas! I cannot be)
An Elephanti-
Elephantiaphus.
But I'm a cockroach
And I'm a water-bug,
I can crawl around and hide behind the sink.

I wish I were a
Rhinosceréeacus
And could wear an ivory toothpick in my nose.

But, oh! I am not,
(Alas! I cannot be)
A Rhinoscōri-
Rhinosceréeacus.
But I'm a beetle
And I'm a pumpkin-bug,
I can buzz and bang my head against the wall.

I wish I were a
Hippopōpotamus
And could swim the Tigris and the broad Gangés.
But, oh! I am not,
(Alas! I cannot be)
A hippopōpo-
Hippopōpotamus.
But I'm a grasshopper
And I'm a katydid,
I can play the fiddle with my left hind-leg.

I wish I were a
Levilevīathan
And had seven hundred knuckles in my spine.
But, oh! I am not,
(Alas! I cannot be)
A Levi-ikey-
A Levi-ikey-mo.
But I'm a firefly
And I'm a lightning-bug,
I can light cheroots and gaspers with my tail.

(*And so ad infinitum.*)

47

In Nottamun Town not a soul would look up,
Not a soul would look up, not a soul would look
    down,
Not a soul would look up, not a soul would look
    down
To tell me the way to Nottamun Town.

I rode a big horse that was called a grey mare,
Grey mane and tail, grey stripes down his back,
Grey mane and tail, grey stripes down his back,
There weren't a hair on him but what was called
    black.

She stood so still, she threw me to the dirt,
She tore my hide and bruised my shirt;
From stirrup to stirrup I mounted again
And on my ten toes I rode over the plain.

Met the King and the Queen and a company of
    men
A-walking behind and a-riding before.
A stark naked drummer came walking along
With his hands in his bosom a-beating his drum.

Sat down on a hot and cold frozen stone,
Ten thousand stood round me yet I was alone.
Took my heart in my hand to keep my head warm.
Ten thousand got drowned that never were born.

42.

I-N spells in—
I was in my kitchen
Doing a bit of stitching,
Old Father Nimble
Came and took my thimble,

I got up a great big stone,
Hit him on the belly bone—
O-U-T spells out.

43.

[The asterisks indicate Alice's interruptions.]

In winter, when the fields are white,
I sing this song for your delight——
  * * *
In spring, when woods are getting green,
I'll try and tell you what I mean——
  * * *
In summer, when the days are long,
Perhaps you'll understand the song:

In autumn, when the leaves are brown,
Take pen and ink, and write it down.
  * * *
I sent a message to the fish:
I told them "This is what I wish."

The little fishes of the sea
They sent an answer back to me.

The little fishes' answer was
"We cannot do it, Sir, because——"
      *   *   *

I sent to them again to say
"It will be better to obey."

The fishes answered with a grin
"Why what a temper you are in!"

I told them once, I told them twice:
They would not listen to advice.

I took a kettle large and new,
Fit for the deed I had to do.

My heart went hop, my heart went thump;
I filled the kettle at the pump.

Then some one came to me and said
"The little fishes are in bed."

I said to him, I said it plain,
"Then you must wake them up again."

I said it very loud and clear;
I went and shouted in his ear.
      *   *   *

But he was very stiff and proud;
He said "You needn't shout so loud!"

And he was very proud and stiff;
He said "I'd go and wake them, if——"

I took a corkscrew from the shelf:
I went to wake them up myself.

And when I found the door was locked,
I pulled and pushed and kicked and knocked.

And when I found the door was shut
I tried to turn the handle, but——

There was a long pause.
"Is that all?" Alice timidly asked.
"That's all," said Humpty Dumpty.
"Good-bye."

44. KUBLA KHAN

In Xanadu did Kubla Khan
   A stately pleasure-dome decree:
Where Alph, the sacred river, ran
Through caverns measureless to man
    Down to a sunless sea.
So twice five miles of fertile ground
With walls and towers were girdled round:
And there were gardens bright with sinuous rills
Where blossom'd many an incense-bearing tree;
And here were forests ancient as the hills,
Enfolding sunny spots of greenery.

But Oh, that deep romantic chasm which slanted
Down the green hill athwart a cedarn cover!
A savage place! as holy and enchanted
As e'er beneath a waning moon was haunted
By woman wailing for her demon-lover!

And from this chasm, with ceaseless turmoil seething,
As if this earth in fast thick pants were breathing,
A mighty fountain momently was forced;
Amid whose swift half-intermitted burst
Huge fragments vaulted like rebounding hail,
Or chaffy grain beneath the thresher's flail:
And 'mid these dancing rocks at once and ever
It flung up momently the sacred river.
Five miles meandering with a mazy motion
Through wood and dale the sacred river ran,
Then reach'd the caverns measureless to man,
And sank in tumult to a lifeless ocean:
And 'mid this tumult Kubla heard from far
Ancestral voices prophesying war!

   The shadow of the dome of pleasure
      Floated midway on the waves;
   Where was heard the mingled measure
      From the fountain and the caves.
It was a miracle of rare device,
A sunny pleasure-dome with caves of ice!

   A damsel with a dulcimer
      In a vision once I saw:
   It was an Abyssinian maid,
      And on her dulcimer she play'd,
   Singing of Mount Abora.
   Could I revive within me,
      Her symphony and song,
To such a deep delight 'twould win me,
That with music loud and long,
I would build that dome in air,
That sunny dome! those caves of ice!

And all who heard should see them there,
And all should cry, Beware! Beware!
His flashing eyes, his floating hair!
Weave a circle round him thrice,
And close your eyes with holy dread,
For he on honey-dew hath fed,
And drunk the milk of Paradise.

45. THE LAY OF ST. CUTHBERT

It's in Bolton Hall, and the clock strikes One,
And the roast meat's brown and the boil'd meat's
done,
And the barbecu'd sucking-pig's crisp'd to a turn,
And the pancakes are fried, and beginning to burn;
The fat stubble-goose   Swims in gravy and
juice,
With the mustard and apple-sauce ready for use;
Fish, flesh, and fowl, and all of the best,
Want nothing but eating—they're all ready drest,
But where is the Host, and where is the Guest?

Pantler and serving-man, henchman and page,
Stand sniffing the duck-stuffing (onion and sage),
And the scullions and cooks,   With fidgety
looks,
Are grumbling and mutt'ring, and scowling as black
As cooks always do when the dinner's put back;
For though the board's deckt, and the napery, fair
As the unsunn'd snow-flake, is spread out with care,

And the Daïs is furnish'd with stool and with chair,
And plate of *orfèvrerie* costly and rare,
Apostle-spoons, salt-cellar, all are there,
        And Mess John in his place,   With his rubicund
            face,
And his hands ready folded, prepared to say Grace,
Yet where is the Host?—and his convives—where?

The Scroope sits lonely in Bolton Hall,
And he watches the dial that hangs by the wall,
He watches the large hand, he watches the small,
        And he fidgets and looks   As cross as the cooks,
And he utters—a word which we'll soften to
    'Zooks!'
And he cries, 'What on earth has become of them
    all?—
        What can delay   De Vaux and De Saye?
What makes Sir Gilbert de Umfraville stay?
What's gone with Poyntz, and Sir Reginald Braye?
Why are Ralph Ufford and Marny away?
And De Nokes, and De Styles, and Lord Marmaduke
    Grey?
        And De Roe?   And De Doe?—
Poynings, and Vavasour—where be they?
Fitz-Walter, Fitz-Osbert, Fitz-Hugh, and Fitz-John,
And the Mandevilles, *père et filz* (father and son)?
Their cards said, "Dinner precisely at One!"
        There's nothing I hate, in   The World, like
            waiting!
It's a monstrous great bore, when a Gentleman
    feels
A good appetite, thus to be kept from his meals!'

54

It's in Bolton Hall, and the clock strikes Two!
And the scullions and cooks are themselves in 'a
   stew,'
And the kitchen-maids stand, and don't know what
   to do,
For the rich plum-puddings are bursting their bags,
And the mutton and turnips are boiling to rags,
   And the fish is all spoil'd, And the butter's all
      oil'd,
And the soup's got cold in the silver tureen,
And there's nothing, in short, that is fit to be seen!
While Sir Guy Le Scroope continues to fume,
And to fret by himself in the tapestried room,
   And still fidgets, and looks More cross than the
      cooks,
And repeats that bad word, which we've soften'd to
   'Zooks!'

Two o'clock's come, and Two o'clock's gone,
And the large and the small hands move steadily on,
   Still nobody's there, No De Roes, or De Clare,
To taste of the Scroope's most delicate fare,
Or to quaff off a health unto Bolton's Heir,
That nice little boy who sits there in his chair,
Some four years old, and a few months to spare,
With his laughing blue eyes, and his long curly hair,
Now sucking his thumb, and now munching his
   pear.

Again, Sir Guy the silence broke,
'It's hard upon Three!—it's just on the stroke!
Come, serve up the dinner!—A joke is a joke!'—

Little he deems that Stephen de Hoaques,
Who 'his fun,' as the Yankees say, everywhere
   'pokes,'
And is always a great deal too fond of his jokes,
Has written a circular note to De Nokes,
And De Styles, and De Roe, and the rest of the folks,
    One and all,   Great and small,
Who were asked to the Hall
To dine there and sup, and wind up with a ball,
And had told all the party a great bouncing lie, he
Cook'd up, that 'the *fête* was postponed *sine die*,
The dear little curly-wigg'd heir of Le Scroope
Being taken alarmingly ill with the croup!'

    When the clock struck Three,   And the Page on
      his knee
Said 'An't please you, Sir Guy Le Scroope, *On a
    servi!*'
And the Knight found the banquet-hall empty and
    clear,
    With nobody near   To partake of his cheer,
He stamp'd, and he storm'd—then his language!—
    Oh dear!
'Twas awful to see, and 'twas awful to hear!
And he cried to the button-deck'd Page at his knee,
Who had told him so civilly '*On a servi*,'
'Ten thousand fiends seize them, wherever they be!
—The Devil take *them!* and the Devil take *thee!*
And the DEVIL MAY EAT UP THE DINNER FOR ME!!'

    In a terrible fume   He bounced out of the room,
He bounced out of the house—and page, footman,
    and groom,

Bounced after their master; for scarce had they
    heard
Of this left-handed Grace the last finishing word,
Ere the horn at the gate of the Barbican tower
Was blown with a loud twenty-trumpeter power,
    And in rush'd a troop Of strange guests!—
    such a group
As had ne'er before darken'd the door of the
    Scroope!

This looks like De Saye—yet—it is not De Saye—
And this is—no, 'tis not—Sir Reginald Braye—
This has somewhat the favour of Marmaduke
    Grey—
But stay!—*Where on earth did he get those long nails?*
Why, they're *claws!*—then Good Gracious!—they've
    all of them *tails!*
That can't be De Vaux—why, his nose is a bill,
Or, I would say a beak!—and he can't keep it
    still!—
Is that Poynings?—Oh Gemini!—look at his feet!!
Why, they're absolute *hoofs!*—is it gout or his corns
That have crumpled them up so?—by Jingo, he's
    horns!
Run! run!—There's Fitz-Walter, Fitz-Hugh, and
    Fitz-John,
And the Mandevilles, *père et filz* (father and son),
And Fitz-Osbert, and Ufford—*they've all got them on!*
    Then their great saucer eyes— It's the Father
    of lies
And his Imps—run! run! run!—they're all fiends in
    disguise,

Who've partly assumed, with more sombre com-
plexions,
The forms of Sir Guy Le Scroope's friends and con-
nexions,
And He—at the top there—that grim-looking elf—
Run! run!—that's the 'muckle-horned Clootie'
himself!

And now what a din   Without and within!
For the court-yard is full of them.—How they begin
To mop, and to mowe, and make faces, and grin!
Cock their tails up together,   Like cows in hot
weather,
And butt at each other, all eating and drinking,
The viands and wine disappearing like winking.
And then such a lot   As together had got!
Master Cabbage, the steward, who'd made a
machine
To calculate with, and count noses,—I ween
The cleverest thing of the kind ever seen,—
Declared, when he'd made,   By the said
machine's aid,
Up, what's now called, the 'tottle' of those he
survey'd,
There were just—how he proved it I cannot divine,—
Nine thousand, nine hundred, and ninety, and nine,
Exclusive of Him,   Who, giant in limb,
And black as the crow they denominate *Jim*,
With a tail like a bull, and a head like a bear,
Stands forth at the window,—and what holds he there,
Which he hugs with such care,   And pokes out
in the air,

And grasps as its limbs from each other he'd tear?
    Oh! grief and despair! I vow and declare
It's Le Scroope's poor, dear, sweet, little, curly-
    wigg'd Heir!
Whom the nurse had forgot, and left there in his
    chair,
Alternately sucking his thumb and his pear!

    What words can express   The dismay and
    distress
Of Sir Guy, when he found what a terrible mess
His cursing and banning had now got him into?
That words, which to use are a shame and a sin too,
Had thus on their speaker recoil'd, and his malison
Placed in the hands of the Devil's own 'pal' his son!—
    He sobb'd and he sigh'd,   And he scream'd, and
    he cried,
And behaved like a man that is mad, or in liquor,—he
Tore his peak'd beard, and he dash'd off his 'Vicary,'
    Stamped on the jasey   As though he were crazy,
And staggering about just as if he were 'hazy,'
Exclaimed, 'Fifty pounds!' (a large sum in those
    times)
'To the person, whoever he may be, that climbs
To that window above there, *en ogive*, and painted,
And bring down my curly-wi'——' here Sir Guy
    fainted!

    With many a moan,   And many a groan,
What with tweaks of the nose, and some *eau de
    Cologne*,
He revived,—Reason once more remounted her
    throne,

Or rather the instinct of Nature,—'twere treason
To Her, in the Scroope's case, perhaps, to say
    Reason,—
But what saw he then?—Oh! my goodness! a sight
Enough to have banished his reason outright!—
    In that broad banquet hall   The fiends one and
      all,
Regardless of shriek, and of squeak, and of squall,
From one to another were tossing that small
Pretty, curly-wigg'd boy, as if playing at ball:
Yet none of his friends or his vassals might dare
To fly to the rescue, or rush up the stair,
And bring down in safety his curly-wigg'd Heir!

    Well a day! Well a day! All he can say
Is but just so much trouble and time thrown away;
Not a man can be tempted to join the *mêlée*,
E'en those words cabalistic, 'I promise to pay
Fifty pounds on demand,' have, for once, lost their
    sway,
    And there the Knight stands, Wringing his
    hands
In his agony—when on a sudden, one ray
Of hope darts through his midriff!—His Saint!—Oh,
    it's funny,
    And almost absurd, That it never occurr'd!—
'Ay! the Scroope's Patron Saint!—he's the man for
    my money!
Saint—who is it?—really I'm sadly to blame,—
On my word I'm afraid,—I confess it with shame,—
That I've almost forgot the good Gentleman's
    name,—

Cut—let me see—Cutbeard?—no!—CUTHBERT!—
    egad
St. Cuthbert of Bolton!—I'm right—he's the lad!
Oh, holy St. Cuthbert, if forbears of mine—
Of myself I say little,—have knelt at your shrine,
And have lashed their bare backs, and—no matter—
    with twine,
    Oh! list to the vow Which I make to you now,
Only snatch my poor little boy out of the row
Which that Imp's kicking up with his fiendish bow-
    wow,
And his head like a bear, and his tail like a cow!
Bring him back here in safety!—perform but this
    task,
And I'll give!—Oh!—I'll give you whatever you
ask!—
    There is not a shrine In the County shall shine
With a brilliancy half so resplendent as thine,
Or have so many candles, or look half so fine!—
Haste, holy St. Cuthbert, then,—hasten in pity!'—
    —Conceive his surprise
    When a strange voice replies,
'It's a bargain!—but, mind, sir, THE BEST SPER-
    MACETI!'—
Say, whose that voice?—whose that form by his side,
That old, old, grey man, with his beard long and wide,
    In his coarse Palmer's weeds,
    And his cockle and beads?—
And, how did he come?—did he walk?—did he ride?
Oh! none could determine,—oh! none could
    decide,—
The fact is, I don't believe any one tried,

For while ev'ry one stared, with a dignified stride,
     And without a word more, He march'd on
          before,
Up a flight of stone steps, and so through the front
          door,
To the banqueting-hall, that was on the first floor,
While the fiendish assembly were making a rare
Little shuttlecock there of the curly-wigg'd Heir.—
—I wish, gentle Reader, that you could have seen
The pause that ensued when he stepp'd in between,
With his resolute air, and his dignified mien,
And said, in a tone most decided, though mild,
'Come!—I'll trouble you just to hand over that
          child!'

     The Demoniac crowd In an instant seem'd
          cowed;
Not one of the crew volunteer'd a reply,
All shrunk from the glance of that keen-flashing eye,
Save one horrid Humgruffin, who seem'd by his talk,
And the airs he assumed, to be Cock of the walk,
He quailed not before it, but saucily met it,
And as saucily said, 'Don't you wish you may get it?'

My goodness!—the look that the old Palmer gave!
And his frown!—'twas quite dreadful to witness—
          'Why, slave!
     You rascal!' quoth he, 'This language to ME!!
—At once, Mr. Nicholas! down on your knee,
And hand me that curly-wigg'd boy!—I command
          it—
Come!—none of your nonsense!—you know I won't
          stand it.'

Old Nicholas trembled,—he shook in his shoes,
And seem'd half inclined, but afraid, to refuse.
 'Well, Cuthbert,' said he, 'If so it must be,
—For you've had your own way from the first time
  I knew ye;—
Take your curly-wigg'd brat, and much good may
  he do ye!
But I'll have in exchange'—here his eye flash'd with
  rage—
'That chap with the buttons—he *gave me* the Page!'

'Come, come,' the Saint answer'd, 'you very well
  know
The young man's no more his than your own to
  bestow—
Touch one button of his if you dare, Nick—no! no!
Cut your stick, sir—come, mizzle! be off with you!—
  go!'—
 The Devil grew hot— 'If I do I'll be shot!

An you come to that, Cuthbert, I'll tell you what's
  what;
He has *asked* us to *dine here*, and go we will not!
 Why you Skinflint,—at least You may leave us
  the feast!
Here we've come all that way from our brimstone
  abode,
Ten million good leagues, sir, as ever you strode,
And the deuce of a luncheon we've had on the road—
—"Go!"—"Mizzle!" indeed—Mr. Saint, who are
  you,
I should like to know?—"Go!"—I'll be hanged if
  I do!

He invited us all—we've a right here—it's known
That a Baron may do what he likes with his own—
Here, Asmodeus—a slice of that beef;—now the
    mustard!—
What have *you* got?—oh, apple-pie—try it with
    custard!'

    The Saint made a pause As uncertain, because
He knew Nick is pretty well 'up' in the laws,
And they *might* be on *his* side—and then, he'd such
    claws!
On the whole, it was better, he thought, to retire
With the curly-wigg'd boy he'd pick'd out of the fire,
And give up the victuals—to retrace his path,
And to compromise—(spite of the Member for Bath).
    So to old Nick's appeal, As he turn'd on his heel,
He replied, 'Well, I'll leave you the mutton and veal,
And the soup *à la Reine*, and the sauce *Bechamel*;
As the Scroope *did* invite you to dinner, I feel
I can't well turn you out—'twould be hardly
    genteel—
But be moderate, pray,—and remember thus much,
Since you're treated as Gentlemen, show yourselves
    such,
    And don't make it late, But mind and go
        straight
Home to bed when you've finish'd—and don't steal
    the plate!
Nor wrench off the knocker, or bell from the gate.
Walk away, like respectable Devils, in peace,
And don't "lark" with the watch, or annoy the
    police!'

Having thus said his say,   That Palmer grey
Took up little Le Scroope, and walk'd coolly away,
While the Demons all set up a 'Hip! hip! hurray!'
Then fell, tooth and claw, on the victuals, as they
Had been guests at Guildhall upon Lord Mayor's
        day,
All scrambling and scuffling for what was before 'em,
No care for precedence or common decorum.
        Few ate more hearty   Than Madame Astarte,
And Hecate,—considered the Belles of the party.
Between them was seated Leviathan, eager
To 'do the polite,' and take wine with Belphegor;
Here was *Morbleu* (a French devil), supping soup-
        meagre,
And there, munching leeks, Davy Jones of Tredegar
(A Welsh one), who'd left the domains of Ap Morgan
To 'follow the sea,'—and next him Demogorgon,—
Then Pan with his pipes, and Fauns grinding the
        organ
To Mammon and Belial, and half a score dancers,
Who'd joined, with Medusa to get up 'the Lancers';
—Here's Lucifer lying blind drunk with Scotch
        ale,
While Beëlzebub's tying huge knots in his tail.
There's Setebos, storming because Mephistopheles
        Gave him the lie,   Said he'd 'blacken his eye,'
And dash'd in his face a whole cup of hot coffee-
        lees;—
        Ramping and roaring,   Hiccoughing, snoring,
Never was seen such a riot before in
A gentleman's house, or such profligate revelling
At any *soirée*—where they don't let the Devil in.

Hark!—as sure as fate The clock's striking
      Eight!
(An hour which our ancestors called 'getting late,')
When Nick, who by this time was rather elate,
Rose up and addressed them.

                           ' 'Tis full time,' he said,
'For all elderly Devils to be in their bed;
For my own part I mean to be jogging, because
I don't find myself now quite so young as I was;
But, Gentlemen, ere I depart from my post,
I must call on you all for one bumper—the toast
Which I have to propose is,—OUR EXCELLENT
      HOST!
—Many thanks for his kind hospitality—may
     We also be able To see at *our* table
Himself, and enjoy, in a family way,
His good company *downstairs* at no distant day!
     You'd, I'm sure, think me rude If I did not
      include
In the toast my young friend there, the curly-wigg'd
      Heir!
He's in very good hands, for you're all well aware
That St. Cuthbert has taken him under his
      care;
     Though I must not say "bless,"—
     —Why you'll easily guess,—
May our curly-wigg'd Friend's shadow never be
      less!'
Nick took off his heel-taps—bow'd—smiled—with an
      air
Most graciously grim,—and vacated the chair.—

66

Of course the *élite*   Rose at once on their feet,
And followed their leader, and beat a retreat;
When a sky-larking Imp took the President's seat,
And, requesting that each would replenish his cup,
Said, 'Where we have dined, my boys, there let us
      sup!'—
—It was three in the morning before they broke
      up!!!

  .   .   .   .   .   .

    I scarcely need say   Sir Guy didn't delay
To fulfil his vow made to St. Cuthbert, or pay
For the candles he'd promised, or make light as day
The shrine he assured him he'd render so gay.
In fact, when the votaries came there to pray,
All said there was nought to compare with it—nay,
    For fear that the Abbey   Might think he was
      shabby,
Four Brethren thenceforward, two cleric, two lay,
He ordained should take charge of a new-founded
      chantry,
With six marcs apiece, and some claims on the
      pantry;
    In short, the whole County   Declared, through
      his bounty
The Abbey of Bolton exhibited fresh scenes
From any displayed since Sir William de Meschines,
And Cecily Roumeli came to this nation
With William the Norman, and laid its foundation.

    For the rest, it is said,   And I know I have read
In some Chronicle—whose, has gone out of my
      head—

That, what with these candles, and other expenses,
Which no man would go to if quite in his senses,
      He reduced, and brought low   His property so
That, at last, he'd not much of it left to bestow;
And that, many years after that terrible feast,
Sir Guy, in the Abbey, was living a Priest;
And   there,   in   one   thousand   and—something,
      deceased.
      (It's supposed by this trick   He bamboozled
      Old Nick,
And slipped through his fingers remarkably 'slick.')
While, as to young Curly-wig,—dear little Soul,
Would you know more of him, you must look at 'The
      Roll,'
      Which   records   the   dispute,   And   the   sub-
      sequent suit,
Commenced in 'Thirteen sev'nty-five,'—which took
      root
In Le Grosvenor's assuming the arms Le Scroope
      swore
That none but *his* ancestors, ever before,
In foray, joust, battle, or tournament wore,
To wit, '*On a Prussian-blue Field*, a *Bend Or*';
While the Grosvenor averred that *his* ancestor bore
The same, and Scroope lied like a—somebody tore
Off the simile,—so I can tell you no more,
Till some A double S shall the fragment restore.

MORAL

      This Legend sound maxims exemplifies—*e.g.*
1mo   Should anything tease you,   Annoy, or
      displease you,

68

Remember what Lilly says, '*Animum rege!*'
And as for that shocking bad habit of swearing,
—In all good society voted past bearing,—
Eschew it! and leave it to dustmen and mobs,
Nor commit yourself much beyond 'Zooks!' or
    'Odsbobs!'

2*do* When asked out to dine by a Person of Quality,
Mind, and observe the most strict punctuality!
    For should you come late, And make
      dinner wait,
And the victuals get cold, you'll incur, sure as
    fate,
The Master's displeasure, the Mistress's hate.
And—though both may, perhaps, be too well-
    bred to swear—
They'll heartily *wish* you—I need not say *Where*.

3*tio* Look well to your Maid-servants!—say you
    expect them
To see to the children, and not to neglect
    them!
And if you're a widower, just throw a cursory
Glance in, at times, when you go near the
    Nursery.
—Perhaps it's as well to keep children from
    plums,
And from pears in the season,—and sucking their
    thumbs!

4*to* To sum up the whole with a 'Saw' of much use,
Be *just* and be *generous*,—don't be *profuse!*—

Pay the debts that you owe,—keep your word to
 your friends,
But—DON'T SET YOUR CANDLES ALIGHT AT BOTH
 ENDS ! !—
For of this be assured, if you 'go it' too fast,
 You'll be 'dish'd' like Sir Guy, And like
 him, perhaps, die
A poor, old, half-starved, Country Parson at
 last !

46.

. . . IT was broken. Then he commanded each
of the warriors to leave his horse, to drive it away
and to go forth, to think of his hands and of good
courage. Then the kinsmen of Offa first found
out that the earl was not minded to suffer cowardice.
Then he let the loved hawk fly from his hands to
the wood, and went forward to the battle.

47. THE WHALE

IT was in the year of ninety-four, in March the
 twentieth day,
Our gallant tars their anchors weigh'd, and for
 sea they bore away,
 Brave boys,
 And for sea they bore away.

Speedicut was our captain's name, our ship was
 the *Lyon* bold,
And we have gone to sea, brave boys, to face the
 storm and cold,
 To face the storm and the cold.

When that we came to the cold country where the
    frost and the snow did lie,
Where the frost, and the snow, and the whale-fish
    so blue, and the daylight's never gone,
        Brave boys,
     And the daylight's never gone.

Our boatswain went to topmast high, with his
    spy-glass in his hand,
"A whale, a whale, a whale," he did cry, "and
    she blows at every span,
        Brave boys,
     She blows at every span."

Our captain stood on the quarter-deck, and a clever
    little man was he,
"Overhaul, overhaul, let the wind-tackle fall, and
    to launch your boats so free,
        Brave boys,
     And to launch your boats so free!"

There's harpooneers, and line coilers, and line
    colecks also,
There's boat-steerers and sailors brave,
To the whale, to where she blows, to the whale,
    to where she blows,
        Brave boys,
     To the whale, to where she blows.

We struck the whale, and away she went, casts
    a flourish with her tail,
But, oh, and alas, we've lost one man, and we
    did not kill that whale,
        Brave boys,
     And we did not kill that whale.

When that the news to our captain it did come,
    a sorrowful man was he,
For the losing of his 'prentice boy, and down his
    colours drew he,
        Brave boys,
        And down his colours drew he.

Now, my lads, don't be amazed for the losing of
    one man;
For fortune it will take its place, let a man do all
    he can,
        Brave boys,
        Let a man do all he can.

48. THE GIPSY LADDIE

It was late in the night when the Squire came home
Enquiring for his lady.
His servant made a sure reply:
She's gone with the gipsum Davy.
        Rattle tum a gipsum gipsum
        Rattle tum a gipsum Davy.

O go catch up my milk-white steed,
The black one's not so speedy,
I'll ride all night till broad daylight,
Or overtake my lady.

He rode and he rode till he came to the town,
He rode till he came to Barley.
The tears came rolling down his cheeks,
And then he spied his lady.

It's come go back, my dearest dear,
Come go back, my honey;
It's come go back, my dearest dear,
And you never shall lack for money.

I won't go back, my dearest dear,
I won't go back, my honey;
For I wouldn't give a kiss from gipsum's lips
For you and all your money.

It's go pull off those snow-white gloves,
A-made of Spanish leather,
And give to me your lily-white hand,
And bid farewell for ever.

It's she pulled off those snow-white gloves,
A-made of Spanish leather,
And gave to him her lily-white hand,
And bade farewell for ever.

She soon ran through her gay clothing,
Her velvet shoes and stockings;
Her gold ring off her finger's gone,
And the gold plate off her bosom.

O once I had a house and land,
Feather-bed and money;
But now I've come to an old straw pad
With the gipsies dancing round me.

49. THE MARRIAGE OF THE FROG AND THE MOUSE

IT was the frog in the well,
    Humbledum, humbledum,
And the merry mouse in the mill,
      Tweedle, tweedle, twino.

The frog would a-wooing ride
Sword and buckler by his side.

When he upon his high horse set,
His boots they shone as black as jet.

When he came to the merry mill-pin,—
"Lady Mouse, been you within?"

Then came out the dusty mouse:
"I am Lady of this house:

Hast thou any mind of me?"
"I have e'en great mind of thee?"

"Who shall this marriage make?"
"Our Lord which is the rat."

"What shall we have to our supper?"
"Three beans in a pound of butter?"

When supper they were at,
The frog, the mouse, and e'en the rat;

Then came in Gib our cat,
And catched the mouse e'en by the back.

Then did they separate,
And the frog leaped on the floor so flat.

Then came in Dick our drake,
And drew the frog e'en to the lake.

The rat ran up the wall,
    Humbledum, humbledum;
A goodly company, the Devil go with all!
    Tweedle, tweedle twino.

50.

Julius Cæsar Pompey Green
Wore a jacket of velveteen.

51. THE BATTLE OF SLUYS

Lithes,[1] and the batail I sal bigyn
Of Inglisch-men & Normandes in the Swyn

Minot with mowth had menid to make
Suth sawes [2] and sad for sum mens sake;
The wordes of sir Edward makes me to wake,
Wald he salve us sone mi sorow suld slake;
War mi sorow slaked sune wald I sing:
When God will sir Edward sal us bute[3] bring.

Sir Philip the Valas cast was in care,
And said sir Hugh Kyret to Flandres suld fare,
And have Normondes inogh to leve [4] on his lare,[5]
All Flandres to brin, and mak it all bare;

---

[1] listen.   [2] wise sayings.   [3] help.
[4] believe.   [5] teaching.

Bot, unkind coward, wo was him thare,
When he sailed in the Swin it sowed him sare;
Sare it tham smerted that ferd out of France,
Thare lered [1] Inglis-men tham a new daunce.

The burjase of Bruge ne war noght to blame,
I pray Jhesu save tham fro sin and fro schame;
For thai war sone at the Sluse all by a name,
Whare many of the Normandes tok mekill grame. [2]

When Bruges and Ipyre hereof herd tell,
Thai sent Edward to wit, that was in Arwell;
Than had he no liking langer to dwell,
He hasted him to the Swin with sergantes snell, [3]
To mete with the Normandes that fals war and fell,
That had ment, if thai might, al Flandres to quell.

King Edward unto sail was ful sune dight
With erles and barons, and many kene knight;
Thai come byfor Blankebergh on Saint Jons night,
That was to the Normondes a well sary sight;
Zhit trumped thai and daunced, with torches ful
    bright
In the wilde waniand [4] was thaire hertes light.

Opon the morn efter, if I suth say,
A meri man, sir Robard out of Morlay,
A half eb in the Swin soght he the way,
Thare lered men the Normandes at bukler to play;
Helpid tham no prayer that thai might pray,
The wreches es wonnen, thaire wapin es oway.
The Erle of Norhamton helpid at that nede,

    [1] taught.   [2] harm.   [3] quickly.   [4] waning moon.

76

Als wise man of wordes, and worthli in wede,[1]
Sir Walter the Mawnay, God gif him mede!
Was bold of body in batayle to bede.[2]
The duc of Lankaster was dight for to drive,
With mani mody [3] man that thoght for to thrive;
Wele and stalworthly stint he that strive,
That few of the Normandes left thai olive;
Fone left thai olive, bot did tham to lepe,
Men may find by the flode a hundred on hepe.

Sir Wiliam of Klinton was eth for to knaw,
Mani stout bachilere broght he on raw;
It semid with thaire schoting als it war snaw,
The bost of the Normandes broght thai ful law;
Thaire bost was abated, and thaire mekil pride,
Fer might thai noght fle, bot thare bud tham bide.

The gude Erle of Glowceter, God mot him glade!
Broght many bold men with bowes ful brade;
To biker with the Normandes baldely thai bade,
And in middes the flode did tham to wade;
To wade war tho wretches casten in the brim,
The kaitefs come out of France at lere tham to swim.

I prays John Badding als one of the best;
Faire come he sayland out of the suthwest,
To prove of tha Normandes was he ful prest,
Till he had foghten his fill he had never rest.

John of Aiie of the Sluys with scheltron full schene,
Was comen into Cagent, cantly and kene;

<hr />

[1] armour.   [2] offer.   [3] proud.

77

Bot sone was his trumping turned to tene,[1]
Of him had sir Edward his will, als I wene.

The schipmen of Ingland sailed ful swith,
That none of the Normandes fro tham might skrith:
Whoso kouth wele his craft thare might it kith:
Of al the gude that thai gat gaf thai no tithe.

Two hundreth and mo schippes in the sandes
Had oure Inglis-men won with thaire handes;
The kogges [2] of Ingland war broght out of bandes,
And also the Cristofir, that in the streme standes;
In that stound [3] thai stode with stremers ful stil,
Till thai wist ful wele sir Edwardes will.

Sir Edward, oure gude king, wurthi in wall,
Faght wele on that flude, faire mot him fall!
Als it es custom of king to confort tham all,
So thanked he gudely the grete and the small;
He thanked tham gudely, God gif him mede!
Thus come our king in the Swin till that gude dede.

This was the bataile that fell in the Swin,
Whare many Normandes made mekill din;
Wele war thai armed up to the chin,
Bot God and sir Edward gert thaire boste blin [4];
Thus blinned thaire boste, als we wele ken:
God assoyle [5] thaire sawls! sais all Amen.

[1] grief.   [2] a broadly built ship usually used for trading.
[3] time.   [4] cease.   [5] absolve.

52.

LONDON BRIDGE is broken down,
  Dance o'er my Lady Lee,
London Bridge is broken down,
  With a gay lady.

How shall we build it up again?
  Dance o'er my Lady Lee,
How shall we build it up again?
  With a gay lady.

Silver and gold will be stole away,
  Dance o'er my Lady Lee,
Silver and gold will be stole away,
  With a gay lady.

Build it up again with iron and steel,
  Dance o'er my Lady Lee,
Build it up with iron and steel,
  With a gay lady.

Iron and steel will bend and bow,
  Dance o'er my Lady Lee,
Iron and steel will bend and bow,
  With a gay lady.

Build it up with wood and clay,
  Dance o'er my Lady Lee,
Build it up with wood and clay,
  With a gay lady.

Wood and clay will wash away,
    Dance o'er my Lady Lee,
Wood and clay will wash away,
    With a gay lady.

Build it up with stone so strong,
    Dance o'er my Lady Lee,
Huzza! 'twill last for ages long,
    With a gay lady.

53. THE WINNING OF CALES

LONG the proud Spaniards had vaunted to conquer
    us,
    Threatening our country with fyer and sword;
Often preparing their navy most sumptuous
    With as great plenty as Spain could afford.
        Dub a dub, dub a dub, thus strike their drums:
        Tantara, tantara, the Englishman comes.

To the seas presently went our lord admiral,
    With knights courageous and captains full good;
The brave Earl of Essex, a prosperous general,
    With him prepared to pass the salt flood.
        Dub a dub, etc.

At Plymouth speedilye, took they ship valiantlye,
    Braver ships never were seen under sayle,
With their fair colours spread, and streamers ore
        their head,
    Now bragging Spaniards, take heed of your tayle.
        Dub a dub, etc.

Unto Cales cunninglye, came we most speedilye,
  Where the kinges navy securelye did ryde;
Being upon their backs, piercing their butts of
      sacks,
  Ere any Spaniards our coming descryde.
    Dub a dub, etc.

Great was the crying, the running and ryding,
  Which at that season was made in that place;
The beacons were fyred, as need then required;
  To hyde their great treasure they had little space.
    Dub a dub, etc.

There you might see their ships, how they were
      fyred fast,
  And how their men drowned themselves in the
      sea;
There might you hear them cry, wayle and wccp
      piteously,
  When they saw no shift to scape thence away.
    Dub a dub, etc.

The great *St. Phillip*, the pryde of the Spaniards,
  Was burnt to the bottom, and sunk in the sea;
But the *St. Andrew*, and eke the *St. Matthew*,
  Wee took in fight manfullye and brought away.
    Dub a dub, etc.

The Earl of Essex, most valiant and hardye,
  With horsemen and footmen marched up to the
      town;

The Spaniards, which saw them, were greatly
  alarmed,
    Did fly for their savegard, and durst not come
    down.
      Dub a dub, etc.

"Now," quoth the noble Earl, "courage my
  soldiers all,
    Fight and be valiant, the spoil you shall have;
And be well rewarded all from the great to the
  small;
    But looke that the women and children you
    save."
      Dub a dub, etc.

The Spaniards at that sight, thinking it vain to fight,
    Hung upp flags of truce and yielded the towne;
Wee marched in presentlye, decking the walls on
  hye,
    With English colours which purchase renowne.
      Dub a dub, etc.

Entering the houses then, of the most richest men,
    For gold and treasure we searched eche day;
In some places we did find, pyes baking left behind,
    Meate at fire rosting, and folkes run away.
      Dub a dub, etc.

Full of rich merchandize, every top catched our
  eyes,
    Damasks and sattens and velvets full fayre;

Which soldiers measur'd out by the length of their
    swords;
  Of all commodities eche had a share.
    Dub a dub, etc.

Thus Cales was taken, and our brave general
  March'd to the market-place, where he did
    stand:
There many prisoners fell to our several shares,
  Many crav'd mercye, and mercye they fannd.
    Dub a dub, etc.

When our brave General saw they delayed all,
  And wold not ransome their towne as they said,
With their fair wanscots, their presses and bed-
    steads,
  Their joint-stools and tables a fire we made;
    And when the town burned all in flame,
    With tara, tantara, away we all came.

54.

  Lord Lundy from his earliest years
  Was far too freely moved to Tears.
  For instance, if his Mother said,
  "Lundy! It's time to go to Bed!"
  He bellowed like a Little Turk.
  Or if his father, Lord Dunquerque
  Said, "Hi!" in a Commanding Tone,
  "Hi, Lundy! Leave the Cat alone!"

Lord Lundy, letting go its tail,
Would raise so terrible a wail
As moved
His Grandpapa the Duke
To utter the severe rebuke:
"When I, Sir! was a little Boy,
An Animal was not a Toy!"
His father's Elder Sister, who
Was married to a Parvenoo,
Confided to Her Husband, "Drat!
The Miserable, Peevish Brat!
Why don't they drown the Little Beast?"
Suggestions which, to say the least,
Are not what we expect to hear
From Daughters of an English Peer.
His grandmamma, His Mother's Mother,
Who had some dignity or other,
The Garter, or no matter what,
I can't remember all the Lot!
Said, "Oh! that I were Brisk and Spry
To give him that for which to cry!"
(An empty wish, alas! for she
Was Blind and nearly ninety-three.)
The Dear Old Butler thought—but there!
I really neither know nor care
For what the Dear Old Butler thought!
In my opinion, Butlers ought
To know their place, and not to play
The Old Retainer night and day
I'm getting tired and so are you,
Let's cut the Poem into two!

Second Canto

It happened to Lord Lundy then,
As happens to so many men:
Towards the age of twenty-six,
They shoved him into politics;
In which profession he commanded
The income that his rank demanded
In turn as Secretary for
India, the Colonies, and War.
But very soon his friends began
To doubt if he were quite the man:
Thus, if a member rose to say
(As members do from day to day),
"Arising out of that reply . . .!"
Lord Lundy would begin to cry.
A Hint at harmless little jobs
Would shake him with convulsive sobs.
While as for Revelations, these
Would simply bring him to his knees,
And leave him whimpering like a child.
It drove his Colleagues raving wild!
They let him sink from Post to Post,
From fifteen hundred at the most
To eight, and barely six—and then
To be Curator of Big Ben! . . .
And finally there came a Threat
To oust him from the Cabinet!

The Duke—his aged grand sire—bore
The shame till he could bear no more.
He rallied his declining powers,
Summoned the youth to Brackley Towers,

And bitterly addressed him thus—
"Sir! you have disappointed us!
We had intended you to be
The next Prime Minister but three:
The stocks were sold; the Press was squared;
The Middle Class was quite prepared.
But as it is! . . . My language fails!
Go out and govern New South Wales!"

. . . . .

The Aged Patriot groaned and died:
And gracious! how Lord Lundy cried!

55. THE MAID OF THE MOOR

MAIDEN in the moor lay,
    In the moor lay,
Seven nights full, seven nights full,
Maiden in the moor lay,
    In the moor lay,
Seven nights full and a day.

Well was her meat;
  What was her meat?
  The primrose and the,—
  The primrose and the,—
Well was her meat;
What was her meat?
  The primrose and the violet.

Well was her drink;
   What was her drink?
   The cold water of,—
   The cold water of,—
Well was her drink;
What was her drink?
   The cold water of the well-spring.

Well was her bower;
   What was her bower?
   The red rose and the,—
   The red rose and the,—
Well was her bower;
What was her bower?
   The red rose and the lily flower.

56. THE SAILING OF THE PILGRIMS

MEN may leve all gamys
That saylen to Sent Jamys;
For many a man hit gramys;
   When they begyn to sayle.

For when they have take the see,
At Sandwyche, or at Wynchylsee,
At Bristow, or where that hyt bee,
   Theyr herts begyn to fayle.

Anone the mastyr commaundeth fast
To hys shyp-men in all the hast,
To dresse hem sone about the mast,
   Theyr takelyng to make.

With "howe! hissa!" then they cry,
"What, hoist! mate thow stondst to ny,
Thy felow may nat hale the by;"
　　Thus they begyn to crake.

A boy or tweyne anone up-styen,
And overthwarte the sayle-yerde lyen;—
"Y how! taylia!" the remenaunte cryen,
　　And pull with all theyr myght.

"Bestowe the boote, bote-swayne, anon,
That our pylgryms may pley thereon;
For som ar lyke to cowgh and grone,
　　Or hit be full mydnyght."

"Hale the bowelyne! now, vere the shete!
Cooke, mak redy anoone our mete,
Our pylgryms have no lust to ete,
　　I pray God yeve him rest."

"Go to the helm! what, howe! no nere?
Steward, felow! a pot of bere!"
"Ye shall have, sir, with good chere,
　　Anone all of the best."

"Y howe! trussa! hale in the brayles!
Thow halest nat, be God, thow fayles,
O se how well owre good shyp sayles!"
　　And thus they say among.

"Hale in the Wartake!" "Hit shall be done."
"Steward! cover the boorde anone,
And set bred and salt thereone,
　　And tarry nat to long."

Then cometh oone and seyth, "Be mery;
Ye shall have a storme or a pery."
"Hold thow thy pese! thow canst no whery,
    Thow medlyst wondyr sore."

Thys menewhyle the pylgryms ly,
And have theyr bowlys fast them by,
And cry afthyr hote malvesy,
    "Thow helpe for to restore."

And som wold have a saltyd tost,
For they myght ete neyther sode ne rost
A man myght sone pay for theyr cost,
    As for oo day or twayne.

Som layde theyr bookys on theyr kne,
And rad so long they myght nat se;—
"Allas! myne hede woll cleve on thre!"
    Thus seyth another certayne.

Then commeth oure owner lyke a lorde,
And speketh many a royall worde,
And dresseth hym to the hygh borde
    To see all thyng be well.

Anone he calleth a carpentere,
And biddyth hym bryng with hym hys gere,
To make the cabans here and there,
    With many a febyl cell.

A sak of strawe werr there rygth good
For som must lyg them in theyr hood,
I had as lefe be in the wood,
    Without mete or drynk.

For when that we shall go to bedde,
The pumpe was nygh our bedde hede,
A man were as good to be dede,
　　As smell thereof the stynk.

57.

My clothing was once of the linsey woolsey fine,
My tail it grew at length, my coat did likewise shine;
But now I'm growing old; my beauty does decay,
My master frowns upon me; one day I heard him
　　say,
　　　　　　Poor old horse: poor old horse.

Once I was kept in the stable snug and warm,
To keep my tender limbs from any cold or harm;
But now, in open fields, I am forced for to go,
In all sorts of weather, let it be hail, rain, freeze,
　　or snow.
　　　　　　Poor old horse: poor old horse.

Once I was fed on the very best corn and hay
That ever grew in yon fields, or in yon meadows
　　gay;
But now there's no such doing can I find at all,
I'm glad to pick the green sprouts that grow behind
　　yon wall.
　　　　　　Poor old horse: poor old horse.

"You are old, you are cold, you are deaf, dull,
　　dumb and slow,
You are not fit for anything, or in my team to draw.

You have eaten all my hay, you have spoiled all
　　my straw,
So hang him, whip, stick him, to the huntsman let
　　him go."
　　　　　　　Poor old horse: poor old horse.

My hide unto the tanners then I would freely give,
My body to the hound dogs, I would rather die
　　than live,
Likewise my poor old bones that have carried you
　　many a mile,
Over hedges, ditches, brooks, bridges, likewise gates
　　and stiles.
　　　　　　　Poor old horse: poor old horse.

58.

My Mammy was a wall-eyed goat,
My Old Man was an ass,
And I feed myself off leather boots
And dynamite and grass;
For I'm a mule, a long-eared fool
And I ain't never been to school—
　　Mammeee! Ma-ha-mam-hee!
　　Heee-haw! Mamaah!
　　Ma-ha-mee!

59.

My mother said that I never should
Play with the gypsies in the wood,
The wood was dark; the grass was green;
In came Sally with a tambourine.

I went to the sea—no ship to get across;
I paid ten shillings for a blind white horse;
I up on his back and was off in a crack,
Sally, tell my Mother I shall never come back.

60.

"My plaid awa', my plaid awa',
　And ore the hill and far awa',
　And far awa' to Norrowa,
My plaid shall not be blown awa'."

The elphin knight sits on yon hill,
　Ba, ba, bella, ba,
He blowes it east, he blowes it west,
He blowes it where he lyketh best . . .
"My plaid awa', my plaid awa',
And ore the hill and far awa'."

61.

Nay, Ivy, nay,
　Hyt shal not be, I wys;
Let Holy hafe the maystry,
　As the maner ys.

Holy stond in the halle,
　Fayre to behold;
Ivy stond wythout the dore,
　She ys ful sore a-cold.
　　Nay, Ivy, nay . . .

Holy and hys mery men,
   They dawnsyn and they syng;
Ivy and hur maydenys,
   They wepyn and they wryng.
     Nay, Ivy, nay . . .

Ivy hath a kybe,[1]
   She kaght yt wyth the colde,
So mot thay all haf ae,
   That wyth Ivy hold.
     Nay, Ivy, nay . . .

Holy hath berys,
   As rede as any rose,
The foster and the hunter
    Kepe hem fro the doos.
     Nay, Ivy, nay . . .

Ivy hath berys,
   As blake as any slo,
Ther com the oulė,
    And ete hym as she goo.
     Nay, Ivy, nay . . .

Holy hath byrdys,
   A ful fayre flok,
The nyghtyngale, the poppynguy,
   The gayntyl lavyrok.[2]
     Nay, Ivy, nay . . .

Gode Ivy [tell me]
   What byrdys ast thu?
Non but the howlat,[3]
    That kreye how, how!

[1] chilblain.   [2] lark.   [3] owl.

Nay, Ivy, nay,
Hyt shal not be, I wys,
Let Holy hafe the maystry,
As the maner ys.

62.

Now Israel
   may say, and that truly,
If that the Lord
   had not our cause maintain'd;
If that the Lord
   had not our right sustain'd,
When cruel men
   against us furiously
Rose up in wrath,
   to make of us their prey;

Then certainly
   they had devour'd us all,
And swallow'd quick,
   for ought that we could deem;
Such was their rage,
   as we might well esteem.
And as fierce floods
   before them all things drown,
So had they brought
   our soul to death quite down.

The raging streams,
   with their proud swelling waves,
Had then our soul
   o'erwhelmed in the deep.

But bless'd be God,
   who doth us safely keep,
And hath not giv'n
   us for a living prey
Unto their teeth,
   and bloody cruelty.

Ev'n as a bird
   out of the fowler's snare
Escapes away,
   so is our soul set free:
Broke are their nets,
   and thus escaped we.
Therefore our help
   is in the Lord's great name,
Who heav'n and earth
   by his great pow'r did frame.

63. THE CROCODILE

Now listen you landsmen unto me, to tell you the
   truth I'm bound,
What happened to me by going to sea, and the
   wonders that I found;
Shipwrecked I was once off Perouse and cast upon
   the shore,
So then I did resolve to roam, the country to
   explore.
   Tomy rit fal lal li bollem tit, tomy rit fal lal li dee!
   Tomy rit fal lal li bollem tit, tomy rit fal lal li dee!

'Twas far I had not scouted out, when close alongside the ocean,
I saw something move which at first I thought was
  all the world in motion;
But steering up close alongside, I found 'twas a
  crocodile,
And from his nose to the tip of his tail he measured
  five hundred mile.
  Tomy rit, &c.

While up aloft the wind was high, it blew a gale
  from the south,
I lost my hold and away did fly right into the
  crocodile's mouth,
He quickly closed his jaws on me and thought he'd
  got a victim,
But I ran down his throat, d'ye see, and that's the
  way I tricked him.
  Tomy rit, &c.

I travelled on for a month or two, till I got into his
  maw,
Where I found of rum-kegs not a few, and a thousand
  fat bullocks in store,
Of life I banished all my care, for of grub I was not
  stinted,
And in this crocodile I lived ten years, and very well
  contented.
  Tomy rit, &c.

This crocodile being very old, one day, alas, he died;
He was ten long years a-getting cold, he was so long
  and wide.

His skin was eight miles thick, I'm sure, or very near
    about,
For I was full ten years or more a-cutting my way
    out.
  Tomy rit, &c.

And now I've once more got on earth, I've vow'd
    no more to roam,
In a ship that passed I got a berth, and now I'm
    safe at home.
And if my story you should doubt, should you ever
    travel the Nile,
It's ten to one you'll find the shell of the wonderful
    crocodile.
  Tomy rit, &c.

64.

Nurse oh My Love is slain, I saw him go
Ocr the white alps alone.

65. THE SICK ROSE

O Rose, thou art sick!
  The invisible worm
That flies in the night,
  In the howling storm,

Has found out thy bed
  Of crimson joy,
And his dark secret love
  Does thy life destroy.

66. THE TWO MAGICIANS

O SHE looked out of the window,
  As white as any milk;
But He looked into the window,
  As black as any silk.

Hulloa, hulloa, hulloa, hulloa, you coal black smith!
  O what is your silly song?
You never shall change my maiden name
  That I have kept so long;
I'd rather die a maid, yes, but then she said,
And be buried all in my grave,
Than I'd have such a nasty, husky, dusky, musty,
    fusky,
  Coal black smith
                    A maiden I will die.

Then She became a duck,
  A duck all on the stream;
And He became a water dog,
  And fetched her back again.
        Hulloa, etc.

Then She became a hare,
  A hare all on the plain;
And He became a greyhound dog,
  And fetched her back again.
        Hulloa, etc.

Then She became a fly
  A fly all in the air;
And He became a spider,
  And fetched her to his lair.
        Hulloa, etc.

67. THE FAUSE KNICHT UPON THE ROAD

"O WHARE are ye gaun?"
  Quo' the fause knicht upon the road;
"I'm gaun to the scule,"
  Quo' the wee boy, and still he stude.

"What is that upon your back?"
  Quo' the fause knicht upon the road;
"Atweel it is my bukes,"
  Quo' the wee boy, and still he stude.

"What's that ye've got in your arm?"
  Quo' the fause knicht upon the road;
"Atweel it is my peit,"
  Quo' the wee boy, and still he stude.

"Wha's aucht they sheep?"
  Quo' the fause knicht upon the road;
"They're mine and my mither's,"
  Quo' the wee boy, and still he stude.

"How monie o' them are mine?"
  Quo' the fause knicht upon the road;
"A' they that hae blue tails,"
  Quo' the wee boy, and still he stude.

"I wiss ye were on yon tree:"
  Quo' the fause knicht upon the road;
"And a gude ladder under me,"
  Quo' the wee boy, and still he stude.

"And the ladder for to break,"
  Quo' the fause knicht upon the road;
"And you for to fa' down,"
  Quo' the wee boy, and still he stude.

"I wiss ye were in yon sie,"
  Quo' the fause knicht upon the road;
"And a gude bottom under me,"
  Quo' the wee boy, and still he stude.

"And the bottom for to break,"
  Quo' the fause knicht upon the road;
"And ye to be drowned,"
  Quo' the wee boy, and still he stude.

68.

O WHAT if the fowler my blackbird has taken?
  The roses of dawn blossom over the sea;
Awaken, my blackbird, awaken, awaken,
  And sing to me out of my red fuchsia tree!

O what if the fowler my blackbird has taken?
  The sun lifts his head from the lap of the sea—
Awaken, my blackbird, awaken, awaken,
  And sing to me out of my red fuchsia tree!

O what if the fowler my blackbird has taken?
  The mountain grows white with the birds of the
    sea;
But down in my garden forsaken, forsaken,
  I'll weep all the day by my red fuchsia tree!

69. LORD RANDAL

'O WHERE hae ye been, Lord Randal, my son?
O where hae ye been, my handsome young man?'
'I hae been to the wild wood; mother, make my
    bed soon,
For I'm weary wi hunting, and fain wald lie down.'

'Where gat ye your dinner, Lord Randal, my son?
Where gat ye your dinner, my handsome young
    man?'
'I dined wi my true-love; mother, make my bed
    soon,
For I'm weary wi hunting, and fain wald lie down.'

'What gat ye to your dinner, Lord Randal, my son?
What gat ye to your dinner, my handsome young
    man?'
'I gat eels boiled in broth; mother, make my bed
    soon,
For I'm weary wi hunting, and fain wald lie down.'

'What became of your bloodhounds, Lord Randal,
    my son?
What became of your bloodhounds, my handsome
    young man?'
'O they swelld and they died; mother, make my
    bed soon,
For I'm weary wi hunting, and fain wald lie down.'

'O I fear ye are poisond, Lord Randal, my son!
O I fear ye are poisond, my handsome young man!'
'O yes! I am poisond; mother, make my bed soon,
For I'm sick at the heart and I fain wald lie down.'

70. THE DAEMON LOVER

"O where have you been, my long, long love,
  This long seven years and more?"
"O I'm come to seek my former vows
  Ye granted me before."

"O hold your tongue of your former vows,
  For they will breed sad strife;
 O hold your tongue of your former vows,
  For I am become a wife."

He turned him right and round about,
  And the tear blinded his ee:
"I wad never hae trodden on Irish ground,
  If it had not been for thee.

"I might hae had a king's daughter,
  Far, far beyond the sea;
 I might have had a king's daughter,
  Had it not been for love o thee."

"If ye might have had a king's daughter,
  Yersel ye had to blame;
 Ye might have taken the king's daughter,
  For ye kend that I was nane.
      .   .   .   .   .   .

"If I was to leave my husband dear,
  And my two babes also,
 O what have you to take me to,
  If with you I should go?"

"I hae seven ships upon the sea—
  The eighth brought me to land—
With four-and-twenty bold mariners,
  And music on every hand."

She has taken up her two little babes,
  Kissd them baith cheek and chin:
"O fair ye weel, my ain two babes,
  For I'll never see you again."

She set her foot upon the ship,
  No mariners could she behold;
But the sails were o' the taffetie,
  And the masts o' the beaten gold.

She had not sailed a league, a league,
  A league but barely three,
When dismal grew his countenance,
  And drumlie grew his ee.

· · · · · ·

They had not sailed a league, a league,
  A league but barely three,
Until she espied his cloven foot,
  And she wept right bitterlie.

"O hold your tongue of your weeping," says he,
  "Of your weeping now let me be;
I will shew you how the lilies grow
  On the banks of Italy."

"O what hills are yon, yon pleasant hills,
  That the sun shines sweetly on?"
"O yon are the hills of heaven," he said,
  "Where you will never win."

"O whaten a mountain is yon," she said,
  "All so dreary wi frost and snow?"
"O yon is the mountain of hell," he cried,
  "Where you and I will go."

      .   .   .   .   .

He strack the tap-mast wi his hand,
  The fore-mast wi his knee,
And he brake that gallant ship in twain,
  And sank her in the sea.

71. THE TWA BROTHERS

"O will ye gae to the school, brother?
  Or will ye gae to the ba?
Or will ye gae to the wood a-warslin,
  To see whilk o's maun fa?"

"It's I winna gae to the school, brother;
  Nor will I gae to the ba;
But I will gae to the wood a-warslin,
  And it is you maun fa'."

They warstled up, they warstled down,
  The lee-lang simmer's day;
[And nane was near to part the strife,
  That raise atween them tway,
Till out and Willie's drawn his sword,
  And did his brother slay.]

"O lift me up upon your back;
  Tak me to yon wall fair;
You'll wash my bluidy wounds o'er and o'er,
  And syne they'll bleed nae mair."

"And ye'll tak aff my Hollin sark,
    And riv't frae gair to gair;
Ye'll stap it in my bluidy wounds,
    And syne they'll bleed nae mair."

He's liftit his brother upon his back,
    Ta'en him to yon wall fair;
He's washed his bluidy wounds o'er and o'er,
    But ay they bled mair and mair.

And he's ta'en aff his Hollin sark,
    And riven't frae gair to gair;
He's stappit it in his bluidy wounds;
    But ay they bled mair and mair.

"Ye'll lift me up upon your back,
    Tak me to Kirkland fair;
Ye'll mak my greaf baith braid and lang,
    And lay my body there.

"Ye'll lay my arrows at my head,
    My bent bow at my feet;
My sword and buckler at my side,
    As I was wont to sleep.

"When ye gae hame to your father,
    He'll speer for his son John:—
Say, ye left him into Kirkland fair,
    Learning the school alone.

"When ye gae hame to my sister,
    She'll speer for her brother John:—
Ye'll say, ye left him in Kirkland fair,
    The green grass growin aboon.

"When ye gae hame to my true love,
    She'll speer for her lord John:—
Ye'll say, ye left him in Kirkland fair,
    But hame ye fear he'll never come."—

He's gane hame to his father;
    He speered for his son John:
"It's I left him into Kirkland fair,
    Learning the school alone."

And whan he gaed home to his sister,
    She speered for her brother John:—
"It's I left him into Kirkland fair,
    The green grass growin aboon."

And when he gaed home to his true love,
    She speer'd for her lord John:
"It's I left him into Kirkland fair,
    And hame I fear he'll never come."

"But whaten bluid's that on your sword, Willie?
    Sweet Willie, tell to me."
"O it is the bluid o' my grey hounds;
    They wadna rin for me."

"It's nae the bluid o' your hounds, Willie;
    Their bluid was never so red;
But it is the bluid o' my true love,
    That ye hae slain indeed."

That fair may wept, that fair may mourn'd
    That fair may mourn'd and pin'd;
"When every lady looks for her love,
    I ne'er need look for mine."

"O whaten a death will ye die, Willie?
    Now, Willie, tell to me."
"Ye'll put me in a bottomless boat,
    And I'll gae sail the sea."

"Whan will ye come hame again, Willie?
    Now Willie, tell to me."
"Whan the sun and moon dance on the green,
    And that will never be."

72.

OLD JOE is dead, and gone to hell,
    O we say so and we hope so;
Old Joe is dead, and gone to hell,
    O poor old Joe.

The ship did sail, the winds did roar,
    O we say so, and we hope so;
The ship did sail, the winds did roar,
    O poor old Joe.

He's as dead as a nail in the lamp-room door,
    O we say so, and we hope so;
He's as dead as a nail in the lamp-room door,
    O poor old Joe.

He won't come hazing us no more,
    O we say so, and we hope so;
He won't come hazing us no more,
    O poor old Joe.

73.

OLD ROGER (or: Poor Robin) is dead and gone to
  his grave,
He, Hi, gone to his grave.
They planted an apple-tree over his head,
He, Hi, over his head.
The apple grew ripe and ready to drop,
He, Hi, ready to drop.
There came an old woman of Hipertihop,
He, Hi, Hipertihop,
She began a picking them up,
He, Hi, picking them up,
Old Roger got up and gave her knock,
He, Hi, gave her a knock,
Which made the old woman go hipertihop,
He, Hi, Hipertihop.

74. THE REBEL SOLDIER

ONE morning, one morning, one morning in May,
I heard a poor soldier lamenting and say,
I heard a poor soldier lamenting and mourn:
I am a rebel soldier and far from my home.

It's grape-shot and musket and the cannons lumber
  loud.
There's a many a mangled body, a blanket for their
  shroud,
There's a many a mangled body left on the field
  alone.
I am a rebel soldier and far from my home.

I'll eat when I'm hungry and drink when I am dry.
If the Yankees don't kill me I'll live until I die,
If the Yankees don't kill me and cause me to mourn.
I am a rebel soldier and far from my home.

I'll build me a castle on some green mountain high,
Where the wild geese can see me as they do pass me
    by,
Where the wild geese can see me and hear my sad
    mourn:
I am a rebel soldier and far from my home.

75.

OUR journey had advanced;
Our feet were almost come
To that odd fork in Being's road,
Eternity by term.

Our pace took sudden awe,
Our feet reluctant led.
Before were cities, but between,
The forest of the dead.

Retreat was out of hope,—
Behind, a sealed route,
Eternity's white flag before,
And God at every gate.

76. HENRY BEFORE AGINCOURT

. . . OUR King went up upon a hill high
And looked down to the valleys low:
He saw where the Frenchmen came hastily
As thick as ever did hail or snow.

Then kneeled our King down, in that stound,
And all his men on every side:
Every man made a cross and kissed the ground,
And on their feet fast gan abide.

Our King said, "Sirs, what time of the day?"
"My Liege," they said, "it is nigh Prime."
"Then go we to our journey,
By the grace of JESU, it is good time:
For saints that lie in their shrine
To GOD for us be praying.
All the Religious of England, in this time,
Ora pro nobis for us they sing."

ST. GEORGE was seen over the host:
Of very truth this sight men did see.
Down was he sent by the HOLY GHOST,
To give our King the victory. . . .

77. TONY O

OVER the bleak and barren snow
A voice there came a-calling;
"Where are you going to, Tony O!
Where are you going this morning?"

"I am going where there are rivers of wine,
The mountains bread and honey;
There Kings and Queens do mind the swine,
And the poor have all the money."

78. PARIPACE AND PARIPALE

PARIPALE and Paripace
Lived on the borders of Chimborace.
Paripale
Had a ridiculous face.
And a most ridiculous tail.
Paripace
Had a ridiculous tail.
And a most ridiculous face.
Said Paripace
To Paripale:
"I like your face,
But I really cannot abide your tail."
Said Paripale
To Paripace:
"I adore your tail,
But I can't put up with so plain a face."
So they fought and fratched
And struggled and scratched
And bit and tore
Till never-no-more
Where the forest clambers up Chimborace
Will you see the face
Of Paripace
Or the tail
Of pitiful perished Paripale!

QUOTH John to Joan, will thou have me:
I prithee now, wilt? and I'll marry thee,
My cow, my calf, my house, my rents,
And all my lands and tenements:
    Oh, say, my Joan, will not that do?
    I cannot come every day to woo.

I've corn and hay in the barn hard-by,
And three fat hogs pent up in the sty,
I have a mare and she is coal black,
I ride on her tail to save my back.
    Then, say, my Joan, will not that do?
    I cannot come every day to woo.

I have a cheese upon the shelf,
And I cannot eat it all myself;
I've three good marks that lie in a rag,
In a nook of the chimney, instead of a bag.
    Then, say, my Joan, will not that do?
    I cannot come every day to woo.

To marry I would have thy consent,
But faith I never could compliment;
I can say nought but "Hoy, gee ho!"
Words that belong to the cart and the plough.
    Oh, say, my Joan, will not that do?
    I cannot come every day to woo.

80. FURRY DAY CAROL

REMEMBER us poor Mayers all!
  And thus we do begin-a
To lead our lives in righteousness,
  Or else we die in sin-a:

>   *With Holan-to, sing merry, O,*
>   *With Holan-to, sing merry,*
>   *With Holan-to, sing merry, O,*
>   *With Holan-to, sing merry!*

We have been rambling half the night,
  And almost all the day-a,
And now, returnèd back again,
  We've brought you a branch of May-a:

O, we were up as soon as day,
  To fetch the summer home-a;
The summer is a coming-on,
  And winter is a gone-a:

Then let us all most merry be,
  And sing with cheerful voice-a;
For we have good occasion now
  This time for to rejoice-a:

Saint George he next shall be our song:
  Saint George, he was a knight-a;
Of all the men in Christendom
  Saint George he was the right-a:

God bless our land with power and might,
     God send us peace in England;
Pray send us peace both day and night,
     For ever in merry England:

81.

     SALLY go round the moon, Sally,
     Sally go round the sun.
     Sally go round the ominlebus
     On a Sunday afternoon.

82.

SIR EGLAMOUR, that worthy knight,
He took his sword and went to fight:
And as he rode both hill and dale,
Armëd upon his shirt of mail,
A dragon came out of his den,
Had slain, God knows how many men!

When he espied Sir Eglamour,
Oh, if you had but heard him roar,
And seen how all the trees did shake,
The knight did tremble, horse did quake,
The birds betake them all to peeping—
It would have made you fall a weeping!

But now it is in vain to fear,
Being come unto, "fight dog! fight bear!"

To it they go and fiercely fight
A live-long day from morn till night.
The dragon had a plaguy hide,
And could the sharpest steel abide.

No sword will enter him with cuts,
Which vexed the knight unto the guts;
But, as in choler he did burn,
He watched the dragon a good turn;
And, as a yawning he did fall,
He thrust his sword in, hilts and all.

Then, like a coward, he to fly
Unto his den that was hard by;
And there he lay all night and roared.
The knight was sorry for his sword,
But, riding thence, said, "I forsake it,
He that will fetch it, let him take it!"

83.

SIR FRANCIS, Sir Francis, Sir Francis is come;
Sir Robert, and eke Sir William his son,
And eke the good Earl of Huntington
Marched gallantly on the road.

Then came the Lord Chamberlain with his white
    staff,
And all the people began to laugh;
And then the Queen began to speak,
"You're welcome home, Sir Francis Drake."

You gallants all o' the British blood,
Why don't you sail o' the ocean flood?
I protest you're not all worth a filbert
If once compared to Sir Humphry Gilbert.

For he went out on a rainy day,
And to the new-found land found out his way,
With many a gallant both fresh and green,
And he ne'er came home again.   God bless the
    Queen!

84. HAWKING FOR THE PARTRIDGE

[*The separate names should be spoken by separate voices, and the groups
of names by separate groups.*]

SITH sickles and the shearing scythe
    Hath shorn the fields of late,
Now shall our hawks and we be blithe.
    Dame Partridge ware your pate!
        Our murdering kites
        In all their flights
        Will seld or never miss
To truss you ever and make your bale our bliss.

Whurr ret	Duty	Wurr ret	Beauty
	Quando		Timble
	Travel		Trover
	Jew		Damsel

Hey dogs hey!

Ware haunt hey	Wanton	ret	Sugar	ret	Mistress
	Sempster		Faver		Minx
	Callis		Dover		Sant
	Dancer		Jerker		Quoy

116

ret	Tricker	ret	Crafty	ret	Minion
	Dido		Civil		Lemmon
	Cherry		Carver		Courtier
	Stately		Ruler		German whurr! let fly!

O well flown, eager kite, mark!
We falconers thus make sullen kites
    Yield pleasure fit for kings,
And sport with them in those delights,
    And oft in other things.

85.

SOME years of late, in eighty-eight
    As I do well remember,
It was, some say, the tenth of May,
    And, some say, in September,
    And, some say, in September.

The Spanish train launch'd forth amain,
    With many a fine bravado,
Their (as they thought, but it proved not)
    Invincible Armado,
    Invincible Armado.

There was a little man, that dwelt in Spain,
    Who shot well in a gun-a,
Don Pedro hight, as black a wight
    As the Knight of the Sun-a,
    As the Knight of the Sun-a.

King Philip made him Admiral,
  And bid him not to stay-a,
But to destroy both man and boy,
  And so to come away-a,
  And so to come away-a.

Their navy was well victualled
  With biscuit, pease, and bacon;
They brought two ships, well fraught with whips,
  But I think they were mistaken,
  But I think they were mistaken.

Their men were young, munition strong,
  And, to do us more harm-a,
They thought it meet to join the fleet,
  All with the Prince of Parma,
  All with the Prince of Parma.

They coasted round about our land,
  And so came in by Dover;
But we had men set on them then
  And threw the rascals over,
  And threw the rascals over.

The Queen was then at Tilbury,
  What more could we desire-a?
And Sir Francis Drake, for her sweet sake,
  Did set them all on fire-a,
  Did set them all on fire-a.

Then, straight, they fled, by sea and land,
  That one man killed threescore-a;

And had not they all ran away,
     In truth he had killed more-a,
In truth he had killed more-a.

Then let them neither brag nor boast,
     But if they come agen-a,
Let them take heed, they do not speed
     As they did, you know when-a.
As they did, you know when-a.

86. THE BLACKSMITHS

SWART swarthy smiths besmattered with smoke
Drive me to death with din of their dints.
Such noise on nights heard noone never;
What knavish cry and clattering of knocks!
The snub nosed changelings cry after 'col, col!'
And blow their bellows till all their brains burst:
'Huf, puf!' saith one; 'haf paf' another.
They spit and sprawl and spell many spells;
They grind teeth and gnash them, and groan
     together,
And hold them hot with their hard hammers.
Of bull's hide are their leather aprons.
Their shanks are shielded from the fierce sparks:
Heavy hammers they have; that are hard handled,
Stark strokes they strike on an anvil of steel
Lus, bus! Las, das! they strike in rotation
The Devil destroy such an doleful noise.

The master lengthens a little piece, belabours a
  smaller,
Twines the two together, strikes a treble note
Tik, tak! Hic, hac! ticket, taket! tyk, tak!
Lus, bus! Las das! such lives they lead
All horseshoers: Christ give them sorrow
For none for these waterburners at night may rest.

87.

THAN Margery Mylkeducke
Her kyrtell she did uptucke
An ynche above her kne,
Her legges that ye myght se;
But they were sturdy and stubbed,
Myghty pestels and clubbed,
As fayre and as whyte
As the fote of a kyte:
She was somwhat foule,
Crokenecked lyke an oule;
And yet she brought her fees,
A cantell of Essex chese
Was well a fote thycke,
Full of maggottes quycke;
It was huge and greate,
And myghty stronge meate
For the devyll to eate;
It was tart and punyete.

88.

THE animals came in two by two,
Vive la compagnie.
The centipede with the kangaroo,
Vive la compagnie.
One more river, and that's the river of Jordan,
One more river, there's one more river to cross.

The animals came in three by three,
Vive la compagnie.
The elephant on the back of the flea,
Vive la compagnie.
One more river, etc.

The animals came in four by four,
Vive la compagnie.
The camel, he got stuck in the door,
Vive la compagnie.
One more river, etc.

The animals came in five by five,
Vive la compagnie.
Some were dead, and some were alive,
Vive la compagnie.
One more river, etc.

The animals came in six by six,
Vive la compagnie.
The monkey he was up to his tricks,
Vive la compagnie.
One more river, etc.

The animals came in seven by seven,
    Vive la compagnie.
Some went to Hell, and some went to Heaven,
    Vive la compagnie.
        One more river, etc.

The animals came in eight by eight,
    Vive la compagnie.
The worm was early, the bird was late,
    Vive la compagnie.
        One more river, etc.

The animals came in nine by nine,
    Vive la compagnie.
Some had water and some had wine,
    Vive la compagnie.
        One more river, etc.

The animals came in ten by ten,
    Vive la compagnie.
If you want any more you must sing it again,
    Vive la compagnie.
        One more river, etc.

89.   1390–91

THE axe was sharp, the stock was hard,
In the thirteenth year of King Richard.

90.

THE common cormorant or shag
Lays eggs inside a paper bag
The reason you will see no doubt
It is to keep the lightning out
But what these unobservant birds
Have never noticed is that herds
Of wandering bears may come with buns
And steal the bags to hold the crumbs.

91. SIR FRANCIS DRAKE

THE Dragon that our Seas did raise his Crest
And brought back heapes of gold unto his nest,
Unto his Foes more terrible than Thunder,
Glory of his age, After-ages' wonder,
Excelling all those that excelled before;
It's feared we shall have none such any more;
Effecting all he sole did undertake,
Valiant, just, wise, milde, honest, Godly *Drake*.
This man when I was little I did meete
As he was walking up Totnes' long street.
He asked me whose I was?   I answered him.
He asked me if his good friend were within?
A faire red Orange in his hand he had,
He gave it me whereof I was right glad,
Takes and kist me, and prayes *God blesse my boy*:
Which I record *with comfort* to this day.
Could he on me have breathèd with his breath,
His gifts, Elias-like, after his death,

Then had I beene enabled for to doe
Many brave things I have a heart unto.
I have as great desire as e're had *hee*
To joy, annoy, friends, foes; but 'twill not be.

92. A STORM

THE fifth day fiercely fell at the noon,
Suddenly the soft wind unsoberly blew;
A mist and a mirkness mingled together;
A thunder and a thick rain troubled the clouds
With an ugsome noise, noy for to hear;
All flashed in a fire the firmanent over;
With no light but lightning that launched from
    above:
It skirmished in the skies with a shimmering flame
Through the clattering clouds close to the heaven,
As the welkyn should falter for fury of heat
With blasts full big of the breme winds,
Walt up the waves upon wan hills.
Stout was the storm, stirred all the ships,
Hopped on high with the haste of the floods.
The sea was unsober, sundered the navy,
Walt over waves, and no way held,
Departed the people, pine to behold,
In coasts unknowing cut down their sails,
Ropes rent to shreds, rent up the hatches,
Topcastle overturned, tackles were lost.
The night came anon, noy was the more.

93.

THE first day of Christmas,
My true love sent to me
A partridge in a pear-tree.

The second day of Christmas,
Two turtle doves and
A partridge in a pear-tree.

The third day of Christmas,
My true love sent to me
Three French hens,
Two turtle doves, and
A partridge in a pear-tree.

The fourth day of Christmas,
My true love sent to me
Four colly birds,
Three French hens,
Two turtle doves, and
A partridge in a pear-tree.

The fifth day of Christmas,
My true love sent to me
Five gold rings,
Four colly birds,
Three French hens,
Two turtle doves, and
A partridge in a pear-tree.

The sixth day of Christmas,
My true love sent to me
Six geese a laying,
Five gold rings,
Four colly birds,
Three French hens,
Two turtle doves, and
A partridge in a pear-tree.

The seventh day of Christmas,
My true love sent to me
Seven swans a swimming,
Six geese a laying,
Five gold rings,
Four colly birds,
Three French hens,
Two turtle doves, and
A partridge in a pear-tree.

The eighth day of Christmas,
My true love sent to me
Eight maids a milking
Seven swans a swimming,
Six geese a laying,
Five gold rings,
Four colly birds,
Three French hens,
Two turtle doves, and
A partridge in a pear-tree.

The ninth day of Christmas,
My true love sent to me

Nine drummers drumming,
Eight maids a milking,
Seven swans a swimming,
Six geese a laying,
Five gold rings,
Four colly birds,
Three French hens,
Two turtle doves, and
A partridge in a pear-tree.

The tenth day of Christmas,
My true love sent to me
Ten pipers piping,
Nine drummers drumming,
Eight maids a milking,
Seven swans a swimming,
Six geese a laying,
Five gold rings,
Four colly birds,
Three French hens,
Two turtle doves, and
A partridge in a pear-tree.

The eleventh day of Christmas,
My true love sent to me
Eleven ladies dancing,
Ten pipers piping,
Nine drummers drumming,
Eight maids a milking,
Seven swans a swimming,
Six geese a laying,
Five gold rings,

Four colly birds,
Three French hens,
Two turtle doves, and
A partridge in a pear-tree.

The twelfth day of Christmas,
My true love sent to me
Twelve lords a leaping,
Eleven ladies dancing,
Ten pipers piping,
Nine drummers drumming,
Eight maids a milking,
Seven swans a swimming,
Six geese a laying,
Five gold rings,
Four colly birds,
Three French hens,
Two turtle doves, and
A partridge in a pear-tree.

94. HORATIAN ODE UPON CROMWELL'S RETURN FROM IRELAND

THE forward youth that would appear,
Must now forsake his Muses dear,
Nor in the shadows sing
His numbers languishing:

'Tis time to leave the books in dust,
And oil the unused armour's rust;
Removing from the wall
The corslet of the hall.

So restless Cromwell could not cease
In the inglorious arts of peace,
     But through adventurous war
     Urgéd his active star;

And like the three-forked lightning first,
Breaking the clouds where it was nurst,
     Did through his own side
     His fiery way divide:

(For 'tis all one to courage high,
The emulous, or enemy;
     And with such, to enclose,
     Is more than to oppose;)

Then burning through the air he went,
And palaces and temples rent;
     And Cæsar's head at last
     Did through his laurels blast.

'Tis madness to resist or blame
The face of angry heaven's flame;
     And if we would speak true,
     Much to the man is due,

Who from his private gardens, where
He lived reservéd and austere
     (As if his highest plot
     To plant the bergamot;)

Could by industrious valour climb
To ruin the great work of Time,
     And cast the kingdoms old,
     Into another mould;

Though Justice against Fate complain,
And plead the ancient rights in vain;
    (But those do hold or break,
    As men are strong or weak.)

Nature that hateth emptiness,
Allows of penetration less,
    And therefore must make room
    Where greater spirits come.

What field of all the civil war,
Where his were not the deepest scar?
    And Hampton shows what part
    He had of wiser art;

Where, twining subtle fears with hope,
He wove a net of such a scope
    That Charles himself might chase
    To Carisbrook's narrow case,

That thence the royal actor borne,
The tragic scaffold might adorn;
    While round the arméd bands
    Did clap their bloody hands.

He nothing common did, or mean,
Upon that memorable scene,
    But with his keener eye
    The axe's edge did try;

Nor called the Gods with vulgar spite
To vindicate his helpless right;
    But bowed his comely head
    Down, as upon a bed.

This was that memorable hour,
Which first assured the forcéd power;
    So, when they did design
    The Capitol's first line,

A bleeding head, where they begun,
Did fright the architects to run;
    And yet in that the state
    Foresaw its happy fate.

And now the Irish are ashamed
To see themselves in one year tamed;
    So much one man can do,
    That does both act and know.

They can affirm his praises best,
And have, though overcome, confessed
    How good he is, how just,
    And fit for highest trust.

Nor yet grown stiffer with command,
But still in the republic's hand—
    How fit he is to sway,
    That can so well obey!

He to the Commons' feet presents
A kingdom for his first year's rents;
    And, what he may, forbears
    His fame, to make it theirs;

And has his sword and spoils ungirt,
To lay them at the public's skirt:
    So, when the falcon high
    Falls heavy from the sky,

She, having killed, no more doth search,
But on the next green bough to perch;
      Where, when he first does lure,
      The falconer has her sure.

What may not then our isle presume,
While victory his crest does plume?
      What may not others fear,
      If thus he crowns each year?

As Cæsar he, ere long, to Gaul,
To Italy an Hannibal,
      And to all states not free,
      Shall climacteric be.

The Pict no shelter now shall find
Within his parti-coloured mind,
      But, from this valour sad
      Shrink underneath the plaid;

Happy, if in the tufted brake,
The English hunter him mistake,
      Nor lay his hounds in near
      The Caledonian deer.

But thou, the war's and fortune's son,
March indefatigably on;
      And for the last effect,
      Still keep the sword erect:

Besides the force it has to fright
The spirits of the shady night,
      The same arts that did gain
      A power, must it maintain.

95. THE MIDNIGHT SKATERS

The hop-poles stand in cones,
   The icy pond lurks under,
The pole-tops steeple to the thrones
   Of stars, sound gulfs of wonder;
But not the tallest there, 'tis said,
Could fathom to this pond's black bed.

Then is not death at watch
   Within those secret waters?
What wants he but to catch
   Earth's heedless sons and daughters?
With but a crystal parapet
Between, he has his engines set.

Then on, blood shouts, on, on,
   Twirl, wheel and whip above him,
Dance on this ball-floor thin and wan,
   Use him as though you love him;
Court him, elude him, reel and pass,
And let him hate you through the glass.

96.

The Miller was a stout carl for the nones,
Ful big he was of braun, and eek of bones;
That proved wel, for overal there he cam,
At wrestling he wolde have alwey the ram.[1]
He was schort schuldred, brood, a thicke knarre,[2]
Ther nas no dore that he nolde [3] heve of harre,[4]
Or breke it, at a rennyng with his heed.

[1] prize for wrestling.   [2] stout man.   [3] would not.   [4] hinge.

His berd as ony sowe or fox was reed,
And therto brood, as though it were a spade.
Upon the cop[1] right of his nose he hade
A werte, and theron stood a tuft of heres,
Reede as the berstles of a sowes eeres.
His nose-thurles blake were and wyde.
A swerd and a bocler baar he by his side,
His mouth as wyde was as a gret forneys.[2]
He was a jangler and a golyardeys,[3]
And that was most of synne and harlotries.
Wel cowde he stele corn, and tollen thries;[4]
And yet he hadde a thombe of gold, pardee.
A whit cote and a blewe hood wered he.
A baggepipe wel cowde he blowe and sowne.
And therwithal he broughte us out of Towne.

97. TOM O' BEDLAM

THE moon's my constant mistress,
    And the lovely owl my marrow;
      The flaming drake,
      And the night-crow, make
Me music to my sorrow.

I know more than Apollo;
    For oft, when he lies sleeping,
      I behold the stars
      At mortal wars,
And the rounded welkin weeping.

[1] top.
[2] furnace.
[3] jester, or buffoon.
[4] charge thrice his fees.

The moon embraces her shepherd,
  And the Queen of Love her warrior;
    While the first does horn
    The stars of the morn,
  And the next the heavenly farrier.

With a heart of furious fancies,
  Whereof I am commander:
    With a burning spear,
    And a horse of air,
  To the wilderness I wander;

With a Knight of ghosts and shadows,
  I summoned am to Tourney:
    Ten leagues beyond
    The wide world's end;
  Methinks it is no journey.

98. THE HIGH TIDE ON THE COAST OF LINCOLNSHIRE (1571)

THE old mayor climbed the belfry tower,
  The ringers ran by two, by three;
'Pull, if ye never pulled before;
  Good ringers, pull your best,' quoth he.
'Play up, play up, O Boston bells!
Ply all your changes, all your swells,
  Play up "The Brides of Enderby."'

Men say it was a stolen tide—
 The Lord that sent it, He knows all;
But in mine ears doth still abide
 The message that the bells let fall:
And there was nought of strange, beside
The flights of mews and peewits pied
 By millions crouched on the old sea wall.

I sat and spun within the door,
 My thread brake off, I raised mine eyes;
The level sun, like ruddy ore,
 Lay sinking in the barren skies,
And dark against day's golden death
She moved where Lindis wandereth,
My son's fair wife, Elizabeth.

'Cusha! Cusha! Cusha!' calling,
Ere the early dews were falling,
Far away I heard her song.
'Cusha! Cusha!' all along
Where the reedy Lindis floweth,
 Floweth, floweth;
From the meads where melick groweth
Faintly came her milking song—

'Cusha! Cusha! Cusha!' calling,
'For the dews will soon be falling;
Leave your meadow grasses mellow,
 Mellow, mellow;
Quit your cowslips, cowslips yellow;
Come up Whitefoot, come up Lightfoot
Quit the stalks of parsley hollow,
 Hollow, hollow;

Come up Jetty, rise and follow,
From the clovers lift your head;
Come up Whitefoot, come up Lightfoot,
Come up Jetty, rise and follow,
Jetty, to the milking shed.'

If it be long, ay, long ago,
   When I begin to think how long,
Again I hear the Lindis flow,
   Swift as an arrow, sharp and strong;
And all the air, it seemeth me,
Bin full of floating bells (saith she),
That ring the tune of Enderby.

All fresh the level pasture lay,
   And not a shadow might be seen,
Save where full five good miles away
   The steeple towered from out the green;
And lo! the great bell far and wide
Was heard in all the country side
That Saturday at eventide.

The swanherds where their sedges are
   Moved on in sunset's golden breath,
The shepherd lads I heard afar,
   And my son's wife, Elizabeth;
Till floating o'er the grassy sea
Came down that kindly message free,
The 'Brides of Mavis Enderby.'

Then some looked up into the sky,
And all along where Lindis flows

To where the goodly vessels lie,
And where the lordly steeple shows.
They said, 'And why should this thing be?
What danger lowers by land or sea?
They ring the tune of Enderby!

'For evil news from Mablethorpe,
   Of pirate galleys warping down;
For ships ashore beyond the scorpe,
   They have not spared to wake the town;
But while the west bin red to see,
And storms be none, and pirates flee,
Why ring "The Brides of Enderby"?'

I looked without, and lo! my son
   Came riding down with might and main:
He raised a shout as he drew on,
   Till all the welkin rang again,
'Elizabeth! Elizabeth!'
(A sweeter woman ne'er drew breath
   Than my son's wife Elizabeth.)

'The old sea wall (he cried) is down,
   The rising tide comes on apace,
And boats adrift in yonder town
   Go sailing up the market-place.'
He shook as one that looks on death:
'God save you, mother!' straight he saith;
'Where is my wife, Elizabeth?'

'Good son, where Lindis winds away,
   With her two bairns I marked her long;

138

And ere yon bells began to play
  Afar I heard her milking song.'
He looked across the grassy lea,
To right, to left, 'Ho, Enderby!'
They rang 'The Brides of Enderby!'

With that he cried and beat his breast;
  For lo! along the river's bed
A mighty eygre reared his crest,
  And up the Lindis raging sped.
It swept with thunderous noises loud;
Shaped like a curling snow-white cloud,
Or like a demon in a shroud.

And rearing Lindis backward pressed
  Shook all her trembling banks amain;
Then madly at the eygre's breast
  Flung up her weltering walls again.
Then banks came down with ruin and rout—
Then beaten foam flew round about—
Then all the mighty floods were out.

So far, so fast the eygre drave,
  The heart had hardly time to beat,
Before a shallow seething wave
  Sobbed in the grasses at our feet:
The feet had hardly time to flee
Before it broke against the knee,
And all the world was in the sea.

Upon the roof we sat that night,
  The noise of bells went sweeping by;

I marked the lofty beacon light
  Stream from the church tower, red and high—
A lurid mark and dread to see;
And awesome bells they were to me,
That in the dark rang 'Enderby.'

They rang, the sailor lads to guide
  From roof to roof who fearless rowed;
And I—my son was at my side,
  And yet the ruddy beacon glowed;
And yet he moaned beneath his breath,
'O come in life, or come in death!
O lost! my love, Elizabeth.'

And didst thou visit him no more?
  Thou didst, thou didst, my daughter dear;
The waters laid thee at his door,
  Ere yet the early dawn was clear.
Thy pretty bairns in fast embrace,
The lifted sun shone on thy face,
Down drifted to thy dwelling-place.

That flow strewed wrecks about the grass,
  That ebb swept out the flocks to sea;
A fatal ebb and flow, alas!
  To many more than mine and me;
But each will mourn his own (she saith),
And sweeter woman ne'er drew breath
Than my son's wife, Elizabeth.

    I shall never hear her more
    By the reedy Lindis shore,

'Cusha! Cusha! Cusha!' calling,
Ere the early dews be falling;
I shall never hear her song,
'Cusha! Cusha!' all along
Where the sunny Lindis floweth,
    Goeth, floweth;
From the meads where melick groweth,
When the water winding down,
Onward floweth to the town.

I shall never see her more
Where the reeds and rushes quiver,
    Shiver, quiver;
Stand beside the sobbing river,
Sobbing, throbbing, in its falling
To the sandy lonesome shore;
I shall never hear her calling,

'Leave your meadow grasses mellow,
    Mellow, mellow;
Quit your cowslips, cowslips yellow;
Come up Whitefoot, come up Lightfoot;
Quit your pipes of parsley hollow,
    Hollow, hollow;
Come up Lightfoot, rise and follow;
    Lightfoot, Whitefoot,
From your clovers lift the head;
Come up Jetty, follow, follow,
Jetty, to the milking shed.'

99. THE POPLAR FIELD

THE poplars are felled;—farewell to the shade,
And the whispering sound of the cool colonnade!
The winds play no longer and sing in the leaves,
Nor Ouse on his bosom their image receives.

Twelve years have elapsed since I last took a view
Of my favourite field, and the bank where they
    grew;
And now in the grass behold they are laid,
And the tree is my seat, that once lent me a shade.

The blackbird has fled to another retreat,
Where the hazels afford him a screen from the heat,
And the scene where his melody charmed me before,
Resounds with his sweet-flowing ditty no more. . . .

100. AUTUMN

THE thistle down's flying, though the winds are all
    still,
On the green grass now lying, now mounting the
    hill,
The spring from the fountain now boils like a pot;
Through stones past the counting it bubbles red-
    hot.

The ground parched and cracked is like overbaked
    bread,
The greensward all wracked is, bents dried up and
    dead.
The fallow fields glitter like water indeed,
And gossamers twitter, flung from weed unto weed.

142

Hill tops like hot iron glitter bright in the sun,
And the rivers we're eying burn to gold as they run;
Burning hot is the ground, liquid gold is the air;
Whoever looks round sees Eternity there.

<h2 style="text-align:center">101.</h2>

THEN sang Moses and the children of Israel this song unto the Lord, and spake, saying, I will sing unto the Lord, for he hath triumphed gloriously: the horse and his rider hath he thrown into the sea.

The Lord is my strength and song, and he is become my salvation: he is my God, and I will prepare him an habitation; my father's God, and I will exalt him.

The Lord is a man of war: the Lord is his name.

Pharaoh's chariots and his host hath he cast into the sea: his chosen captains also are drowned in the Red sea.

The depths have covered them: they sank into the bottom as a stone.

Thy right hand, O Lord, is become glorious in power: thy right hand, O Lord, hath dashed in pieces the enemy.

And in the greatness of thine excellency thou hast overthrown them that rose up against thee: thou sentest forth thy wrath, which consumed them as stubble.

And with the blast of thy nostrils the waters were

gathered together, the floods stood upright as an heap, and the depths were congealed in the heart of the sea.

The enemy said, I will pursue, I will overtake, I will divide the spoil; my lust shall be satisfied upon them; I will draw my sword, my hand shall destroy them.

Thou didst blow with thy wind, the sea covered them: they sank as lead in the mighty waters.

Who is like unto thee, O Lord, among the gods? who is like thee, glorious in holiness, fearful in praises, doing wonders?

Thou stretchedst out thy right hand, the earth swallowed them.

Thou in thy mercy hast led forth the people which thou hast redeemed: thou hast guided them in thy strength unto thy holy habitation.

The people shall hear, and be afraid: sorrow shall take hold on the inhabitants of Palestina.

Then the dukes of Edom shall be amazed; the mighty men of Moab, trembling shall take hold upon them; all the inhabitants of Canaan shall melt away.

Fear and dread shall fall upon them; by the greatness of thine arm they shall be as still as a stone; till thy people pass over, O Lord, till the people pass over, which thou hast purchased.

Thou shalt bring them in, and plant them in the mountain of thine inheritance, in the place,

O Lord, which thou hast made for thee to dwell in; in the Sanctuary, O Lord, which thy hands have established.

The Lord shall reign for ever and ever.

For the horse of Pharaoh went in with his chariots and with his horsemen into the sea, and the Lord brought again the waters of the sea upon them; but the children of Israel went on dry land in the midst of the sea.

102.

THERE's a Black Ball barque coming down the
        river,
        Blow, bullies, blow;
There's a Black Ball barque coming down the river,
        Blow, my bully boys, blow.

And who d'ye think is Captain of her?
        Blow, bullies, blow;
O who d'ye think is Captain of her?
        Blow, my bully boys, blow.

Why, bully Hains is the Captain of her,
        Blow, bullies, blow;
Why, bully Hains is the Captain of her,
        Blow, my bully boys, blow.

He'll make you wish you was dead and buried,
Blow, bullies, blow;
He'll make you wish you was dead and buried,
Blow, my bully boys, blow.

You'll brighten brass, and you'll scrape the cable,
Blow, bullies, blow;
You'll brighten brass, and you'll scrape the cable,
Blow, my bully boys, blow.

And who d'ye think is mate aboard her?
Blow, bullies, blow;
O who d'ye think is mate aboard her?
Blow, my bully boys, blow.

Santander James is the mate aboard her,
Blow, bullies, blow;
Santander James is the mate aboard her,
Blow, my bully boys, blow.

He'll ride you down like you ride the spanker,
Blow, bullies, blow;
He'll ride you down like you ride the spanker,
Blow, my bully boys, blow.

And who d'ye think is the second mate of her?
Blow, bullies, blow;
O who d'ye think is the second mate of her?
Blow, my bully boys, blow.

Some ugly case what hates poor sailors,
Blow, bullies, blow;
Some ugly case what hates poor sailors,
Blow, my bully boys, blow.

103

THERE came a wind like a bugle;
It quivered through the grass,
And a green chill upon the heat
So ominous did pass
We barred the windows and the doors
As from an emerald ghost;
The doom's electric moccason
That very instant passed.
On a strange mob of panting trees,
And fences fled away,
And rivers where the houses ran
The living looked that day.
The bell within the steeple wild
The flying tidings whirled.
How much can come
And much can go,
And yet abide the world!

104. THE GOLDEN VANITY

THERE was a gallant ship, and a gallant ship was she,
   Eck iddle du, and the Lowlands low;
And she was called The Goulden Vanitie.
   As she sailed to the Lowlands low.

She had not sailed a league, a league but only three,
When she came up with a French gallee.
   As she sailed to the Lowlands low.

Out spoke the little cabin-boy, out spoke he;
"What will you give me if I sink that French gallee?
  As ye sail to the Lowlands low."

"I'll give thee gold, and I'll give thee fee,
And my eldest daughter thy wife shall be
  If you sink her off the Lowlands low."

"Then row me up ticht in a black bull's skin,
And throw me oer deck-buird, sink I or swim.
  As ye sail to the Lowlands low."

So they've rowed him up ticht in a black bull's skin,
And have thrown him oer deck-buird, sink he or
    swim.
  As they sail to the Lowlands low.

About, and about, and about went he,
Until he cam up with the French gallee.
  As they sailed to the Lowlands low.

O some were playing cards, and some were playing
    dice,
The boy he had an auger bored holes two at twice;
He let the water in, and it dazzled in their eyes,
  As they sailed to the Lowlands low.

Then some they ran with cloaks, and some they ran
    with caps,
To try if they could stap the saut-water draps.
  As they sailed to the Lowlands low.

About, and about, and about went he,
Until he cam back to The Goulden Vanitie.
As they sailed to the Lowlands low.

"Now throw me oer a rope and pu me up on buird,
And prove unto me as guid as your word.
As ye sail to the Lowlands low."

"We'll no throw ye oer a rope, nor pu you up on
buird,
Nor prove unto you as guid as our word.
As we sail to the Lowlands low."

"You promised me gold, and you promised me fee,
Your eldest daughter my wife she should be.
As ye sail to the Lowlands low."

"You shall have gold, and you shall have fee,
But my eldest daughter your wife shall never be.
As we sail to the Lowlands low."

Out spoke the little cabin-boy, out spoke he;
"Then hang me, I'll sink ye as I sunk the French
gallee.
As ye sail to the Lowlands low."

The boy he swam round all by the starboard side,
When they pu'd him up on buird it's there he soon
died;
They threw him o'er deck-buird to go down with the
tide,
And sink off the Lowlands low.

105

THERE was a knicht riding frae the east,
   Jennifer gentle an' rosemaree.
Who had been wooing at monie a place,
   As the doo flies owre the mulberry tree.

He cam' unto a widow's door,
And speird whare her three dochters were.

"The auldest ane's to a washing gane,
The second's to a baking gane."

"The youngest ane's to a wedding gane,
And it will be nicht or she be hame."

He sat him doun upon a stane,
Till thir three lasses cam' tripping hame.

The auldest ane she let him in,
And pinned the door wi' a siller pin.

The second ane she made his bed,
And laid saft pillows unto his head.

The youngest ane was bauld and bricht,
And she tarried for words wi' this unco knicht.—

"Gin ye will answer me questions ten,
The morn ye sall be made my ain:—

"O what is higher nor the tree?
And what is deeper nor the sea?

"Or what is heavier nor the lead?
And what is better nor the bread?

"Or what is whiter nor the milk?
Or what is safter nor the silk?

"Or what is sharper nor a thorn?
Or what is louder nor a horn?

"Or what is greener nor the grass?
Or what is waur nor a woman was?"

"O heaven is higher nor the tree,
And hell is deeper nor the sea.

"O sin is heavier nor the lead,
The blessing's better nor the bread.

"The snaw is whiter nor the milk,
And the down is safter nor the silk.

"Hunger is sharper nor a thorn,
And shame is louder nor a horn.

"The pies are greener nor the grass,
And Clootie's waur nor a woman was."

As sune as she the fiend did name,
    Jennifer gentle an' rosemaree,
He flew awa' in a blazing flame,
    As the doo flies owre the mulberry tree.

106

THERE was a man of double deed
Who sowed his garden full of seed;
And when the seed began to grow,
'Twas like a garden full of snow;
And when the snow began to fall,
Like birds it was upon the wall;
And when the birds began to fly,
'Twas like a shipwreck in the sky;
And when the sky began to crack,
'Twas like a stick upon my back;
And when my back began to smart,
'Twas like a pen-knife in my heart;
And when my heart began to bleed,
Then I was dead—and dead indeed.

107.

THERE was a robber met a robber
On a rig of beans;
Says a robber to a robber
"Can a robber tell a robber
What a robber means?"

108. KING HEROD AND THE COCK

THERE was a star in David's land,
In David's land appeared:
And in King Herod's chamber
So bright it did shine there.

The Wise Men they soon spied it,
    And told the King a-nigh
That a princely babe was born that night,
    No King shall e'er destroy.

'If this be the truth,' King Herod said,
    'That thou hast told to me,
The roasted cock that lies in the dish
    Shall crow full senses three.'

O the cock soon thrustened and feathered well,
    By the work of God's own hand,
And he did crow full senses three,
    In the dish where he did stand.

109. JOHN BARLEYCORN

THERE was three kings into the east,
    Three kings both great and high,
And they hae sworn a solemn oath
    John Barleycorn should die.

They took a plough and plough'd him down,
    Put clods upon his head,
And they hae sworn a solemn oath
    John Barleycorn was dead.

But the cheerfu' Spring came kindly on,
    And show'rs began to fall;
John Barleycorn got up again,
    And sore surpris'd them all.

The sultry suns of Summer came,
   And he grew thick and strong,
His head weel arm'd wi' pointed spears,
   That no one should him wrong.

The sober Autumn enter'd mild,
   When he grew wan and pale;
His bending joints and drooping head
   Show'd he began to fail.

His colour sicken'd more and more,
   He faded into age;
And then his enemies began
   To show their deadly rage.

They've ta'en a weapon, long and sharp,
   And cut him by the knee;
Then tied him fast upon a cart,
   Like a rogue for forgerie.

They laid him down upon his back,
   And cudgell'd him full sore;
They hung him up before the storm,
   And turn'd him o'er and o'er.

They fillèd up a darksome pit
   With water to the brim,
They heavèd in John Barleycorn,
   There let him sink or swim.

They laid him out upon the floor,
   To work him farther woe;
And still, as signs of life appear'd,
   They toss'd him to and fro.

They wasted, o'er a scorching flame,
    The marrow of his bones;
But a miller us'd him worst of all,
    For he crush'd him between two stones.

And they hae ta'en his very heart's blood,
    And drank it round and round;
And still the more and more they drank,
    Their joy did more abound.

John Barleycorn was a hero bold,
    Of noble enterprise;
For if you do but taste his blood,
    'Twill make your courage rise;

'Twill make a man forget his woe;
    'Twill heighten all his joy:
'Twill make the widow's heart to sing
    Tho' the tear were in her eye. . . .

110. THE THREE HUNTSMEN

THERE were three jovial Welshmen,
    As I have heard men say,
And they would go a-hunting, boys,
    Upon St. David's Day.
And all the day they hunted,
    But nothing could they find,
Except a ship a-sailing,
    A sailing with the wind.
        And a-hunting they did go.

One said it surely was a ship,
    The second he said, Nay;
The third declared it was a house
    With the chimney blown away.
Then all the night they hunted,
    And nothing could they find,
Except the moon a-gliding,
    A-gliding with the wind.
        And a-hunting they did go.

One said it surely was the moon,
    The second he said, Nay;
The third declared it was a cheese
    The half o't cut away.
Then all next day they hunted,
    And nothing could they find,
Except a hedgehog in a bush,
    And that they left behind.
        And a-hunting they did go.

One said it was a hedgehog,
    The second he said, Nay;
The third, it was a pincushion,
    The pins stuck in wrong way.
Then all next night they hunted,
    And nothing could they find,
Except a hare in a turnip field,
    And that they left behind.
        And a-hunting they did go.

One said it surely was a hare,
    The second he said, Nay;

The third, he said it was a calf,
    And the cow had run away.
Then all next day they hunted,
    And nothing could they find,
But one owl in a holly-tree
    And that they left behind.
        And a-hunting they did go.

One said it surely was an owl,
    The second he said, Nay;
The third said t'was an aged man
    Whose beard was growing grey.
Then all three jovial Welshmen
    Came riding home at last,
"For three days we have nothing killed,
    And never broke our fast!"
        And a-hunting they did go.

III. THE TWA SISTERS

THERE were twa sisters liv'd in a bowr;
    Binnorie, O Binnorie!
There came a knight to be their wooer,
    By the bonny mill-dams of Binnorie.

He courted the eldest wi' glove an ring,
    Binnorie, O Binnorie!
But he lov'd the youngest aboon a' thing,
    By the bonny mill-dams of Binnorie.

He courted the eldest wi' broach an knife,
  Binnorie, O Binnorie!
But he lov'd the youngest as his life,
  By the bonny mill-dams of Binnorie.

The eldest she was vexèd sair,
  Binnorie, O Binnorie!
And sair envied her sister fair,
  By the bonny mill-dams of Binnorie.

Intill her bower she couldna rest,
  Binnorie, O Binnorie!
Wi' grief an spite she maistlie brast,
  By the bonny mill-dams of Binnorie.

Upon a morning fair and clear,
  Binnorie, O Binnorie!
She cried upon her sister dear,
  By the bonny mill-dams of Binnorie.

"O sister, come to yon sea strand,
  Binnorie, O Binnorie!
And see our father's ships come to land,"
  By the bonny mill-dams of Binnorie.

She's ta'en her by the milk-white hand,
  Binnorie, O Binnorie!
And led her down to yon sea strand,
  By the bonny mill-dams of Binnorie.

The youngest stood upon a stane,
  Binnorie, O Binnorie!
The eldest came an threw her in,
  By the bonny mill-dams of Binnorie.

She tooke her by the middle sma',
  Binnorie, O Binnorie!
And dashed her bonny back to the jaw,
  By the bonny mill-dams of Binnorie.

"O sister, sister, tak my hand,
  Binnorie, O Binnorie!
And I'se mack ye heir to a' my land,
  By the bonny mill-dams of Binnorie.

"O sister, sister, tak my middle,
  Binnorie, O Binnorie!
And yes get my goud and my gouden girdle,
  By the bonny mill-dams of Binnorie.

"O sister, sister, save my life,
  Binnorie, O Binnorie!
And I swear I'se never be nae man's wife,"
  By the bonny mill-dams of Binnorie.

"Foul fa' the hand that I should tak,
  Binnorie, O Binnorie!
It twin'd me an my warldes mak,
  By the bonny mill-dams of Binnorie.

"Your cherry cheeks and yellow hair
  Binnorie, O Binnorie!
Gars me gang maiden for evermair,"
  By the bonny mill-dams of Binnorie.

Sometimes she sank, sometimes she swam,
  Binnorie, O Binnorie!
Till she came to the mouth o' yon mill-dam,
  By the bonny mill-dams of Binnorie.

O out it came the miller's son,
  Binnorie, O Binnorie!
An' saw the fair maid soummin in,
  By the bonny mill-dams of Binnorie.

"O father, father, draw your dam,
  Binnorie, O Binnorie!
Here's either a mermaid or a swan,"
  By the bonny mill-dams of Binnorie.

The miller quickly drew the dam,
  Binnorie, O Binnorie!
An there he found a drown'd woman.
  By the bonny mill-dams of Binnorie.

"And sair and lang mat their teen last
  Binnorie, O Binnorie!
That wrought thee sic a dowie cast,"
  By the bonny mill-dams of Binnorie.

You coudna see her yellow hair
  Binnorie, O Binnorie!
For goud and pearl that were sae rare,
  By the bonny mill-dams of Binnorie.

You couldna see her middle sma',
  Binnorie, O Binnorie!
For gouden girdle that was sae braw,
  By the bonny mill-dams of Binnorie.

You coudna see her fingers white,
  Binnorie, O Binnorie!
For gouden rings that was sae gryte,
  By the bonny mill-dams of Binnorie.

And by there came a harper fine,
  Binnorie, O Binnorie!
That harpèd to the king at dine,
  By the bonny mill-dams of Binnorie.

When he did look that lady upon,
  Binnorie, O Binnorie!
He sigh'd and made a heavy moan,
  By the bonny mill-dams of Binnorie.

He's taen three locks o' her yellow hair,
  Binnorie, O Binnorie!
And wi' them strung his harp sae fair,
  By the bonny mill-dams of Binnorie.

The first tune he did play and sing,
  Binnorie, O Binnorie!
Was, "Fareweel to my father the king,"
  By the bonny mill-dams of Binnorie.

The nexten tune that it play'd seen,
  Binnorie, O Binnorie!
Was, "Fareweel to my mither the queen,"
  By the bonny mill-dams of Binnorie.

The thirden tune that it play'd then,
  Binnorie, O Binnorie!
Was, "Wae to my sister, fair Ellen,"
  By the bonny mill-dams of Binnorie.

112. THE JUMBLES

I

They went to sea in a Sieve, they did,
  In a Sieve they went to sea:
In spite of all their friends could say,
On a winter's morn, on a stormy day,
  In a Sieve they went to sea!
And when the Sieve turned round and round,
And every one cried, "You'll all be drowned!"
They called aloud, "Our Sieve ain't big,
But we don't care a button! we don't care a fig!
  In a Sieve we'll go to sea!"
    Far and few, far and few,
      Are the lands where the Jumblies live;
      Their heads are green, and their hands are blue,
      And they went to sea in a Sieve.

II

They sailed away in a Sieve, they did,
  In a Sieve they sailed so fast,
With only a beautiful pea-green veil
Tied with a riband by way of a sail,
  To a small tobacco-pipe mast;
And every one said, who saw them go,
"O won't they be soon upset, you know!
For the sky is dark, and the voyage is long,
And happen what may, it's extremely wrong
  In a Sieve to sail so fast!"
    Far and few, far and few,
      Are the lands where the Jumblies live;
      Their heads are green, and their hands are blue,
      And they went to sea in a Sieve.

III

The water it soon came in, it did,
   The water it soon came in;
So to keep them dry, they wrapped their feet
In a pinky paper all folded neat,
   And they fastened it down with a pin.
And they passed the night in a crockery-jar,
And each of them said, "How wise we are!
Though the sky be dark, and the voyage be long,
Yet we never can think we were rash or wrong,
   While round in our Sieve we spin!"
     Far and few, far and few,
      Are the lands where the Jumblies live;
      Their heads are green, and their hands are blue,
       And they went to sea in a Sieve.

And all night long they sailed away;
   And when the sun went down,
They whistled and warbled a moony song
To the echoing sound of a coppery gong,
   In the shade of the mountains brown.
"O Timballo! How happy we are,
When we live in a sieve and a crockery-jar,
And all night long in the moonlight pale,
We sail away with a pea-green sail,
   In the shade of the mountains brown!"
     Far and few, far and few,
      Are the lands where the Jumblies live;
      Their heads are green, and their hands are blue,
       And they went to sea in a Sieve.

They sailed to the Western Sea, they did,
   To a land all covered with trees,
And they bought an Owl, and a useful Cart,
And a pound of Rice, and a Cranberry Tart,
   And a hive of silvery Bees.
And they bought a Pig, and some green Jack-daws,
And a lovely Monkey with lollipop paws,
And forty bottles of Ring-Bo-Ree,
   And no end of Stilton Cheese.
     Far and few, far and few,
      Are the lands where the Jumblies live;
     Their heads are green and their hands are blue,
      And they went to sea in a Sieve.

VI

And in twenty years they all came back,
   In twenty years or more,
And every one said, "How tall they've grown!
For they've been to the Lakes, and the Terrible Zone,
   And the hills of the Chankly Bore";
And they drank their health, and gave them a feast
Of dumplings made of beautiful yeast;
And every one said, "If we only live,
We too will go to sea in a Sieve,—
   To the hills of the Chankly Bore!"
     Far and few, far and few,
      Are the lands where the Jumblies live;
     Their heads are green, and their hands are blue,
      And they went to sea in a Sieve.

THIS is the Key of the Kingdom:
In that Kingdom is a city;
In that city is a town;
In that town there is a street;
In that street there winds a lane;
In that lane there is a yard;
In that yard there is a house;
In that house there waits a room;
In that room an empty bed;
And on that bed a basket—
A Basket of Sweet Flowers:
Of Flowers, of Flowers;
A Basket of Sweet Flowers.

Flowers in a Basket;
Basket on the bed;
Bed in the chamber;
Chamber in the house;
House in the weedy yard;
Yard in the winding lane;
Lane in the broad street;
Street in the high town;
Town in the city;
City in the Kingdom—
This is the Key of the Kingdom.
Of the Kingdom this is the Key.

THIS saying good-bye on the edge of the dark
And the cold to an orchard so young in the bark
Reminds me of all that can happen to harm
An orchard away at the end of the farm
All winter, cut off by a hill from the house.
I don't want it girdled by rabbit and mouse,
I don't want it dreamily nibbled for browse
By deer, and I don't want it budded by grouse.
(If certain it wouldn't be idle to call
I'd summon grouse, rabbit and deer to the wall
And warn them away with a stick for a gun.)
I don't want it stirred by the heat of the sun.
(We made it secure against being, I hope,
By setting it out on a northerly slope.)
No orchard's the worse for the wintriest storm;
But one thing about it, it mustn't get warm.
'How often already you've had to be told,
Keep cold, young orchard. Good-bye and keep cold.
Dread fifty above more than fifty below.'
I have to be gone for a season or so.
My business awhile is with different trees,
Less carefully nurtured, less fruitful than these,
And such as is done to their wood with an axe—
Maples and birches and tamaracks.
I wish I could promise to lie in the night
And think of an orchard's arboreal plight
When slowly (and nobody comes with a light)
Its heart sinks lower under the sod.
But something has to be left to God.

115.

THREE little children sitting on the sand,
All, all a-lonely,
Three little children sitting on the sand,
All, all a-lonely,
Down in the green wood shady—
There came an old woman, said Come on with me,
All, all a-lonely,
There came an old woman, said Come on with me,
All, all a-lonely,
Down in the green wood shady—
She stuck her pen-knife through their heart,
All, all a-lonely,
She stuck her pen-knife through their heart,
All, all a-lonely,
Down in the green wood shady.

116.

THREE wise men of Gotham
Went to sea in a bowl,
If the bowl had been stronger
My story had been longer.

117.

'TIS the voice of the Lobster; I heard him declare,
'You have baked me too brown, I must sugar my
hair.'

As a duck with its eyelids, so he with his nose
Trims his belt and his buttons, and turns out his
toes.
When the sands are all dry, he is gay as a lark,
And will talk in contemptuous tones of the Shark:
But, when the tide rises and sharks are around,
His voice has a timid and tremulous sound.

I passed by his garden, and marked, with one eye,
How the Owl and the Panther were sharing a pie:
The Panther took pie-crust, and gravy, and meat,
While the Owl had the dish as its share of the treat.
When the pie was all finished, the Owl, as a boon,
Was kindly permitted to pocket the spoon:
While the Panther received knife and fork with a
growl,
And concluded the banquet——

118.

To *my*,
Ay,
And we'll *furl*,
Ay,
And pay Paddy Doyle for his boots.

We'll *sing*,
Ay,
And we'll *heave*,
Ay,
And pay Paddy Doyle for his boots.

We'll *heave*,
　　Ay,
With a *swing*,
　　Ay,
And pay Paddy Doyle for his boots.

119. JABBERWOCKY

'Twas brillig, and the slithy toves
　　Did gyre and gimble in the wabe;
All mimsy were the borogoves,
　　And the mome raths outgrabe.

"Beware the Jabberwock, my son!
　　The jaws that bite, the claws that catch!
Beware the Jubjub bird, and shun
　　The frumious Bandersnatch!"

He took his vorpal sword in hand:
　　Long time the manxome foe he sought—
So rested he by the Tumtum tree,
　　And stood awhile in thought.

And as in uffish thought he stood,
　　The Jabberwock, with eyes of flame,
Came whiffling through the tulgey wood,
　　And burbled as it came!

One, two! One, two! And through and
　　through
　　The vorpal blade went snicker-snack!
He left it dead, and with its head
　　He went galumphing back.

"And hast thou slain the Jabberwock?
    Come to my arms, my beamish boy!
O frabjous day! Callooh! Callay!"
    He chortled in his joy.

'Twas brillig, and the slithy toves
    Did gyre and gimble in the wabe;
All mimsy were the borogoves,
    And the mome raths outgrabe.

120. TO THE VIRGINIAN VOYAGE

You brave heroic minds,
Worthy your country's name,
That honour still pursue,
    Whilst loit'ring hinds
Lurk here at home, with shame.
    Go, and subdue.

Britons, you stay too long,
Quickly abroad bestow you,
And with a merry gale
    Swell your stretched sail,
    With vows as strong,
As the winds that blow you.

Your course securely steer,
West and by south forth keep,
Rocks, lee-shores, nor shoals,
    When Eolus scowls,
    You need not fear,
So absolute the deep.

And cheerfully at sea,
Success you still entice,
To get the pearl and gold,
    And ours to hold
    Virginia,
Earth's only Paradise.

Where Nature hath in store
Fowl, venison, and fish,
And the fruitful'st soil,
    Without your toil,
    Three harvests more
All greater than your wish.

And the ambitious vine
Crowns with his purple mass,
The cedar reaching high
    To kiss the sky;
    The cypress, pine,
And useful sassafras.

To whose, the golden age
Still Nature's laws doth give,
No other cares that tend,
    But them to defend,
    From winter's rage
That long there doth not live.

When as the luscious smell
Of that delicious land,
Above the seas that flows,

The clear wind throws,
Your hearts to swell
Approaching the dear strand.

In kenning of the shore
(Thanks to God first given)
O you, the happiest men,
Be frolic then,
Let cannons roar
Frighting the wide heaven.

And in regions far
Such heroes bring ye forth,
As those from whom we came,
And plant our name
Under that star
Not known unto our north.

And as there plenty grows
Of laurel everywhere,
Apollo's sacred tree,
You it may see,
A poet's brows
To crown, that may sing there.

Thy voyages attend,
Industrious Hakluyt,
Whose reading shall inflame
Men to seek fame,
And much commend
To after-times thy wit.

121. TO CHRISTOPHER NORTH

You did late review my lays,
    Crusty Christopher;
You did mingle blame and praise,
    Rusty Christopher.
When I learnt from whom it came,
I forgave you all the blame,
    Musty Christopher;
I could *not* forgive the praise,
    Fusty Christopher.

122. WATER BOY[1]

WATER Boy where are you hiding;
If you don't-a come
Gwine tell-a yoh Mammy.

There ain't no hammer
That's on-a this mountain
That ring-a like mine, boys,
That ring-a like mine.

Done bus' this rock, boys,
From hyeh to Macon
All th' way to th' jail, boys,
Yes back to th' jail.

You Jack-o-Di'monds,
Yo Jack-o-Di'monds

[1] The boy who brought water to the convicts working on the roads.

Ah know yeh of old, boys,
Yes, know yeh of ol'.

You robbed my pocket,
Yes robba my pocket
Done a-robba my pocket,
Of silver an gol'.

123.

WEEP you no more, sad fountains;
    What need you flow so fast?
Look how the snowy mountains
    Heaven's sun doth gently waste.
        But my sun's heavenly eyes
            View not your weeping,
            That now lies sleeping
        Softly, now softly lies
            Sleeping.

Sleep is a reconciling,
    A rest that peace begets:
Doth not the sun rise smiling
    When fair at even he sets?
        Rest you then, rest, sad eyes,
            Melt not in weeping,
            While she lies sleeping
        Softly, now softly lies
            Sleeping.

124

We're all in the dumps
For diamonds are trumps
The kittens are gone to St. Paul's
The babies are bit
The moon's in a fit
And the houses are built without walls.

125. THE DONG WITH A LUMINOUS NOSE

When awful darkness and silence reign
Over the great Gromboolian plain,
  Through the long, long, wintry nights;—
    When the angry breakers roar
    As they beat on the rocky shore;—
  When Storm-clouds brood on the towering heights
    Of the Hills of the Chankly Bore:—

Then, through the vast and gloomy dark,
There moves what seems a fiery spark,
  A lonely spark with silvery rays
    Piercing the coal-black night,—
    A meteor strange and bright:—
  Hither and thither the vision strays,
    A single lurid light.

Slowly it wanders,—pauses,—creeps,—
Anon it sparkles,—flashes and leaps;
And ever as onward it gleaming goes
A light on the Bong-tree stems it throws.

And those who watch at that midnight hour
From Hall or Terrace, or lofty Tower,
Cry, as the wild light passes along,—
    "The Dong!—the Dong!
  "The wandering Dong through the forest goes!
    "The Dong! the Dong!
  "The Dong with a luminous Nose!"

    Long years ago
  The Dong was happy and gay,
Till he fell in love with a Jumbly Girl
  Who came to those shores one day.
For the Jumblies came in a Sieve, they did,—
Landing at eve near the Zemmery Fidd
    Where the Oblong Oysters grow,
  And the rocks are smooth and gray.
And all the woods and the valleys rang
With the Chorus they daily and nightly sang,—
  "*Far and few, far and few,*
    Are the lands where the Jumblies live;
    Their heads are green, and their hands are blue,
    And they went to sea in a sieve."

Happily, happily passed those days!
  While the cheerful Jumblies staid;
  They danced in circlets all night long,
  To the plaintive pipe of the lively Dong,
    In moonlight, shine or shade.
For day and night he was always there
By the side of the Jumbly Girl so fair,
With her sky-blue hands, and her sea-green hair.

Till the morning came of that hateful day
When the Jumblies sailed in their sieve away,
And the Dong was left on the cruel shore
Gazing—gazing for evermore,—
Ever keeping his weary eyes on
That pea-green sail on the far horizon,—
Singing the Jumbly Chorus still
As he sate all day on the grassy hill,—
 "*Far and few, far and few,*
  Are the lands where the Jumblies live;
  Their heads are green, and their hands are blue,
  And they went to sea in a sieve."

But when the sun was low in the West,
 The Dong arose and said,—
 "What little sense I once possessed
 Has quite gone out of my head!"
And since that day he wanders still
By lake and forest, marsh and hill,
Singing—"O somewhere, in valley or plain
Might I find my Jumbly Girl again!
For ever I'll seek by lake and shore
Till I find my Jumbly Girl once more!"

  Playing a pipe with silvery squeaks,
  Since then his Jumbly Girl he seeks.
  And because by night he could not see,
  He gathered the bark of the Twangum Tree
   On the flowery plain that grows.
   And he wove him a wondrous Nose,—
  A Nose as strange as a Nose could be!

Of vast proportions and painted red,
And tied with cords to the back of his head.
   —In a hollow rounded space it ended
   With a luminous lamp within suspended,
      All fenced about
      With a bandage stout
      To prevent the wind from blowing it out;—
   And with holes all round to send the light,
   In gleaming rays on the dismal night.

And now each night, and all night long,
Over those plains still roams the Dong;
And above the wail of the Chimp and Snipe
You may hear the squeak of his plaintive pipe
While ever he seeks, but seeks in vain
To meet with his Jumbly Girl again;
Lonely and wild—all night he goes,—
The Dong with a luminous Nose!
And all who watch at the midnight hour,
From Hall or Terrace, or lofty Tower,
Cry, as they trace the Meteor bright,
Moving along through the dreary night,—
   " This is the hour when forth he goes,
   The Dong with a luminous Nose!
   Yonder—over the plain he goes;
      He goes!
      He goes;
   The Dong with a luminous Nose!"

126. I DO LIKE TO BE BESIDE THE SEA-SIDE

WHEN
> Don

Pasquito arrived at the seaside
Where the donkey's hide tide brayed, he
Saw the banditto Jo in a black cape
Whose slack shape waved like the sea—
Thetis wrote a treatise noting wheat is silver like the
    sea; the lovely cheat is sweet as foam; Erotis
    notices that she
> Will
> Steal
> The

Wheat-king's luggage, like Babel
Before the League of Nations grew—
So Jo put the luggage and the label
In the pocket of Flo the Kangaroo.
Through trees like rich hotels that bode
Of dreamless ease fled she,
Carrying the load and goading the road
Through the marine scene to the sea.
"Don Pasquito, the road is eloping
With your luggage, though heavy and large;
You must follow and leave your moping
Bride to my guidance and charge!"

When
> Don

Pasquito returned from the road's end
Where vanilla-coloured ladies ride

From Sevilla, his mantilla'd bride and young friend
Were forgetting their mentor and guide.
For the lady and her friend from Le Touquet
In the very shady trees upon the sand
Were plucking a white satin bouquet
Of foam, while the sand's brassy band
Blared in the wind.   Don Pasquito
Hid where the leaves drip with sweet . . .
But a word stung him like a mosquito . . .
For what they hear, they repeat!

127.   LAUGHING SONG

WHEN the green woods laugh with the voice of joy,
And the dimpling stream runs laughing by;
When the air does laugh with our merry wit,
And the green hill laughs with the noise of it;

When the meadows laugh with lively green,
And the grasshopper laughs in the merry scene;
When Mary and Susan and Emily
With their sweet round mouths sing "Ha, Ha, He!"

When the painted birds laugh in the shade,
Where our table with cherries and nuts is spread:
Come live, and be merry, and join with me,
To sing the sweet chorus of "Ha, Ha, He!"

WHERE Goodwife Gull broke her good man's pate
In came her man to make up the number,
Who had his nose shod with the steel of a scumber;
But in fine these three began to agree
And knit themselves up into one Trinity
And after they loved like brother and brother,
For very love they did kill one another
And they were buried I do remember
In Staunton's straw hat seven mile from December
Where they had not lyn the space of a day
But four of these three were thence run away
The Constable came with a back on his bill
And because they were gone he did them kill
I, Courage, so cleft their cushions asunder
To see how they bled it made me to wonder
I myself was twice smitten to the ground
I was very sore hurt but had not a wound.

129. THE AKOND OF SWAT

WHO, or why, or which, or *what*, Is the Akond of
                                    SWAT?

Is he tall or short, or dark or fair?
Does he sit on a stool or a sofa or chair,   or SQUAT,
                              The Akond of Swat?

Is he wise, or foolish, young or old?
Does he drink his soup and his coffee cold,   or HOT,
                              The Akond of Swat?

Does he sing or whistle, jabber or talk,
And when riding abroad does he gallop or walk,
                              or TROT,
                    The Akond of Swat?

Does he wear a turban, a fez, or a hat?
Does he sleep on a mattress, a bed, or a mat,
                              or a COT,
                    The Akond of Swat?

When he writes a copy in round-hand size,
Does he cross his T's and finish his I's   with a DOT,
                    The Akond of Swat?

Can he write a letter concisely clear
Without a speck or a smudge or a smear,   or BLOT,
                    The Akond of Swat?

Do his people like him extremely well?
Or do they, whenever they can, rebel,   or PLOT,
                    At the Akond of Swat?

If he catches them then, either old or young,
Does he have them chopped in pieces or hung,
                              or *shot*
                    The Akond of Swat?

Do his people prig in the lanes or park?
Or even at times, when days are dark,   GAROTTE?
                    O the Akond of Swat!

Does he study the wants of his own dominion?
Or doesn't he care for public opinion   a JOT,
                    The Akond of Swat?

To amuse his mind do his people show him
Pictures, or anyone's last new poem,   or WHAT,
                    For the Akond of Swat?

At night if he suddenly screams and wakes,
Do they bring him only a few small cakes,   or a LOT,
                    For the Akond of Swat?

Does he live on turnips, tea, or tripe?
Does he like his shawl to be marked with a stripe,   or
                              a DOT,
                    The Akond of Swat?

Does he like to lie on his back in a boat
Like the lady who lived in that isle remote,
                              SHALLOTT,
                    The Akond of Swat?

Is he quiet, or always making a fuss?
Is his steward a Swiss or a Swede or a Russ,   or
                              a SCOT,
                    The Akond of Swat?

Does he like to sit by the calm blue wave?
Or to sleep and snore in a dark green cave,   or
                              a GROTT,
                    The Akond of Swat?

Does he drink small beer from a silver jug?
Or a bowl? or a glass? or a cup? or a mug?   or
                              a POT,
                    The Akond of Swat?

Does he beat his wife with a gold-topped pipe,
When she lets the gooseberries grow too ripe,
                                or ROT,
                    The Akond of Swat?

Does he wear a white tie when he dines with friends,
And tie it neat in a bow with ends,   or a KNOT,
                    The Akond of Swat?

Does he like new cream, and hate mince-pies?
When he looks at the sun does he wink his eyes,
                                or NOT,
                    The Akond of Swat?

Does he teach his subjects to roast and bake?
Does he sail about on an inland lake,   in a YACHT,
                    The Akond of Swat?

Someone, or nobody, knows I wot
Who or which or why or what
                    Is the Akond of Swat!

Note.—For the existence of this potentate see Indian news-papers, *passim*. The proper way to read the verses is to make an immense emphasis on the monosyllabic rhymes, which indeed ought to be shouted out by a chorus.

130. THE SONG OF THE MAD PRINCE

   WHO said, 'Peacock Pie'?
     The old King to the sparrow:
   Who said, 'Crops are ripe'?
     Rust to the harrow:

Who said, 'Where sleeps she now?
   Where rests she now her head,
Bathed in eve's loveliness'?—
   That's what I said.

Who said, 'Ay, mum's the word';
   Sexton to willow:
Who said, 'Green dusk for dreams,
   Moss for a pillow'?
Who said, 'All Time's delight
   Hath she for narrow bed;
Life's troubled bubble broken'?—
   That's what I said.

131.

"Will you walk a little faster?" said a
     whiting to a snail.
"There's a porpoise close behind us, and he's
     treading on my tail.
See how eagerly the lobsters and the turtles
     all advance!
They are waiting on the shingle—will you
     come and join the dance?
Will you, won't you, will you, won't you,
     will you join the dance?
Will you, won't you, will you, won't you,
     won't you join the dance?

"You can really have no notion how delightful
    it will be,
When they take us up and throw us, with the
    lobsters, out to sea!"
But the snail replied, "Too far, too far!" and
    gave a look askance—
Said he thanked the whiting kindly, but
    he would not join the dance.
Would not, could not, would not, could not,
    would not join the dance.
Would not, could not, would not, could not,
    could not join the dance.

"What matters it how far we go?" his scaly
    friend replied.
"There is another shore, you know, upon the
    other side.
The further off from England the nearer is to
    France—
Then turn not pale beloved snail, but come and
    join the dance.
Will you, won't you, will you, won't you,
    will you join the dance?
Will you, won't you, will you, won't you,
    won't you join the dance?"

[*Enter the Presenter*]

Presenter.   I open the door, I enter in;
I hope your favour we shall win.
Stir up the fire and strike a light,
And see my merry boys act to-night.
Whether we stand or whether we fall,
We'll do our best to please you all.

[*Enter the actors, and stand in a clump*]

Presenter.   Room, room, brave gallants all,
Pray give us room to rhyme;
We're come to show activity,
This merry Christmas time;
Activity of youth,
Activity of age,
The like was never seen
Upon a common stage.
And if you don't believe what I say,
Step in St. George—and clear the way.

[*Enter St. George*]

St. George.   In come I, Saint George,
The man of courage bold;
With my broad axe and sword
I won a crown of gold.
I fought the fiery dragon,
And drove him to the slaughter,

187

And by these means I won
    The King of Egypt's daughter.
Show me the man that bids me stand;
I'll cut him down with my courageous hand.

Presenter.   Step in, Bold Slasher.

[*Enter Bold Slasher*]

Slasher.   In come I, the Turkish Knight,
    Come from the Turkish land to fight.
I come to fight St. George,
    The man of courage bold;
And if his blood be hot,
    I soon will make it cold.

St. George.   Stand off, stand off, Bold Slasher,
    And let no more be said,
For if I draw my sword,
    I'm sure to break thy head.
Thou speakest very bold,
    To such a man as I;
I'll cut thee into eyelet holes,
    And make thy buttons fly.

Slasher.   My head is made of iron,
    My body is made of steel,
My arms and legs of beaten brass;
    No man can make me feel.

St. George.   Then draw thy sword and fight,
    Or draw thy purse and pay;
For satisfaction I must have,
    Before I go away.

Slasher.   No satisfaction shalt thou have,
   But I will bring thee to thy grave.

St. George.   Battle to battle with thee I call,
   To see who on this ground shall fall.

Slasher.   Battle to battle with thee I pray,
   To see who on this ground shall lay.

St. George.   Then guard thy body and mind thy
      head,
   Or else my sword shall strike thee dead.

Slasher.   One shall die and the other shall live;
   This is the challenge that I do give.

[*They fight.   Slasher falls*]

133. THE REVESBY PLAY

THE PLOW BOYS, OR MORRIS DANCERS

Enter Fool.

You gentle Lords of honour,
    Of high and low, I say,
We all desire your favour
    For to see our pleasant play.

Our play it is the best, kind sirs,
    That you would like to know;
And we will do our best, sirs,
    And think it well bestowd.

Tho' some of us be little,
    And some of a middle sort,
We all desire your favour
    To see our pleasant sport.

You must not look on our actions,
    Our wits they are all to seek,
So I pray take no exceptions
    At what I am a-going to speak.

We are come over the mire and moss;
We dance an Hobby Horse;
A Dragon you shall see,
And a wild Worm for to flee.
Still we are all brave, jovial boys
And takes delight in Christmas toys.

We are come both for bread and beer,
And hope for better cheer
And something out of your purse sir,
Which I hope you will be never the worse, sir.
Still we are all brave, jovial boys
And takes delight in Christmas toys.

Come now, Mr. Musick Man, play me my
delight.

Fidler. What is that, old father?

Fool. Ah! boy, times is hard! I love to have
money in both pockets.

Fid. You shall have it, old father.

Fool. Let me see it.

> *The Fool then calls in his five sons: first
> Pickle Herring, then Blue Britches, then
> Ginger Britches, Pepper Britches, and last
> calls out:*

Come now, you Mr. Allspice!

> *They foot it once round the room, and the man that
> is to ride the Hobby Horse goes out, and the rest sing
> the following song:*

Come in, come in, thou Hobby Horse,
And bring thy old fool in thy course!
Sing tanter a day, sing tanter a day,
Sing heigh down, down, with a derry down a!

> *Then the Fool and the Horse fights about the room,
> whilst the following song is singing by the rest:*

Come in, come in, thou bonny wild Worm!
For thou hast ta'en many a lucky turn.
Sing tanteraday, sing tanteraday,
Sing heigh down, down, with a derry down!

> *The wild Worm is only sprung three or four times,
> as the man walks round the room, and then goes out,
> and the Horse and The Fool fights again, whilst the
> following song is sung:*

Come in, come in, thou Dragon stout,
And take thy compass round about!
Sing tanteraday, sing tanteraday,
Sing heigh down, down, with a derry down!

Now you shall see a full fair fight
Between our old Fool and his right.
Sing tanteraday, sing tanteraday,
Sing heigh down, down, with a derry down!

Now our scrimage is almost done;
Then you shall see more sport soon.
Sing tanteraday, sing tanteraday,
Sing heigh down, down, with a derry down!

Fool.—Up well hark, and up well hind!
Let every man then to his own kind.
Sing tanteraday, sing tanteraday,
Sing heigh down, down, with a derry down!

Come, follow me, merry men all!
Tho' we have made bold for to call,
It is only once by the year
That we are so merry here.
Still we are all brave, jovial boys,
And takes delight in Christmas toys.

*Then they all foot it round the room and follows The
Fool out. They all re-enter, and lock their swords to
make the glass, The Fool running about the room.*

Pickle Herring. What is the matter now, father?
Fool. Why, I tell thee what, Pickle Herring.
As a I was a-looking round about me
through my wooden spectacles made of a
great, huge, little tiney bit of leather,
placed right behind me, even before me,
I thought I saw a feat thing—
P. H. You thought you saw a feat thing? What
might this feat thing be, think you,
father?
Fool. How can I tell, boy, except I see it again?
P. H. Would you know it if you see it again?
Fool. I cannot tell thee, boy. Let me get it
looked at.

Pickle Herring, holding up the glass, says:

P. H. Is this it, father?

The Fool, looking round, says:

Fool. Why, I protest, Pickle Herring, the very
same thing! But what might thou call
this very pretty thing?

P. H. What might you call it? You are older than I am.

Fool. How can that be, boy, when I was born before you?

P. H. That is the reason that makes you older.

Fool. Well, what dost thou call this very pretty thing?

P. H. Why, I call it a fine large looking-glass.

Fool. Let me see what I can see in this fine large looking-glass. Here's a hole through it, I see. I see, and I see!

P. H. You see and you see? and what do you see?

Fool. Marry, e'en a fool, just like thee!

P. H. It is only your own face in the glass.

Fool. Why, a fool may be mistain sometimes, Pickle Herring. But what might this fine large looking-glass cost thee?

P. H. That fine large looking-glass cost me a guinea.

Fool. A guinea, boy? Why, I could have bought as good a one at my own door for three half-pence.

The Fool keeping the glass all the while in his hands, says:

Fool. Why was thou such a ninnie, boy, to go to ware a guinea to look for thy beauty where it never was? But I will show thee, boy, how foolish thou has wared a deal of good money.

Then The Fool flings the glass upon the floor, jumps upon it; then the dancers every one

194

drawing out his own sword, and The Fool
dancing about the room, Pickle Herring takes
him by the collar and says:

P. H. Father, father, you are so merrylly disposed
this good time there is no talking to you!
Here is very bad news.

Fool. Very good news? I am glad to hear it; I do
not hear good news every day.

P. H. It is very bad news!

Fool. Why, what is the matter now, boy?

P. H. We have all concluded to cut off your head.

Fool. Be mercyfull to me, a sinner! If you should
do as you have said, there is no such thing.
I would not lose my son Pickle Herring for
fifty pounds.

P. H. It is your son Picklc Herring that must lose
you. It is your head we desire to take off.

Fool. My head? I never had my head taken off in
all my life!

P. H. You both must and shall.

Fool. Hold, hold, boy! thou seem'st to be in good
earnest; but I'll tell thee where I'll be
buryed.

P. H. Why, where will you be buried but in the
churchyard, where other people are buried?

Fool. Churchyard? I never was buried there in all
my life!

P. H. Why, where will you be buried?

Fool. Ah! boy, I am often dry; I will be buried in
Mr Mirfin's ale-celler.

P. H. It is such a place as I never heard talk off in
all my life.

Fool. No, nor nobody else, boy.

P. H. What is your fancy to be buried there?

Fool. Ah! boy, I am oftens dry, and, when they come to fill the quart, I'll drink it off, and they will wonder what is the matter.

P. H. How can you do so when you will be dead? We shall take your head from your body, and you will be dead.

Fool. If I must die, I will dye with my face to the light, for all you!

> *Then The Fool, kneeling down, with the swords round his neck, says:*

Fool. Now gentlemen, you see how ungratefull my children is grown! When I had them all at home, small, about as big as I am, I put them out to good learning: I put them to Coxcomb Colledge, and then to the University of Loggerheads; and I took them home again this good time of Christmas, and I examin'd them all one by one, altogether for shortness. And now they are grown so proud and presumptious they are a-going to kill their old father for his little means. So I must dye for all this?

P. H. You must dye, father.

Fool. And I will die for all the tother. But I have a little something, I will give it amongst you as far as it goes, and then I shall dye quietly.

P. H. I hope you will.

Fool. So, to my first son, Pickle Herring,—
        I'll give him the roaned nag,
        And that will make the rogue brag.
    And to my second son,—
        I'll give him the brindled cow.
    And to my third son,—
        I'll give him the sanded sow;
        And hope I shall please you all enow.
    And to my fourth son,—
        I'll give him the great ruff dog,
        For he always lives like a hog.
    And to my fifth son,—
        I'll give him the ram,
        And I'll dye like a lamb.

> *Then they draw their swords, and The Fool falls on the floor, and the dancers walk once round The Fool; and Pickle Herring stamps with his foot and The Fool rises on his knees again; and Pickle Herring says:*

P. H. How now, father?
Fool. How now, then, boy?   I have another squeak
    for my life?
P. H. You have a many.

> *Then, the dancers puting their swords round the Fool's neck again,*

Fool. So I must dye?
P. H. You must dye, father.
Fool. Hold! I have yet a little something more
    to leave amongst you, and then I hope I

shall dye quietly. So to my first son, Pickle Herring,—

I'll give him my cap and my coat,—
A very good sute, boy.
And to my second son,—
I'll give him my purse and apparel,
But be sure, boys, you do not quarrel.

As to my other three,
My executors they shall be.

Then, Pickle Herring puting his hand to his sword,

Fool. Hold, hold, boy! Now I submit my soul to God.
P. H. A very good thought, old father!
Fool. Mareham churchyard, I hope, shall have my bones.

Then the dancers walk round The Fool with their swords in their hands, and Pickle Herring stamps with his foot and says:

P. H. Heigh, old father!
Fool. Why, boy, since I have been out of this troublesome world I have heard so much musick of fiddles playing and bells ringing that I have a great fancy to go away singing. So, prithee, Pickle Herring, let me have one of thy best songs.
P. H. You shall have it, old father.
Fool. Let me see it.

They sing.

Good people all, I pray you now behold,
Our old Fool's bracelet is not made of gold,
But it is made of iron and good steel,
And unto death we'll make this old Fool yield.

Fool. I pray, forbear, my children small;
For, as I am lost as parent to you all,
O, let me live a while your sport for to advance,
That I may rise again and with you have a dance.

The Sons sing.

Now, old father, that you know our will,
That for your estate we do your body kill,
Soon after death the bell for you shall toll,
And wish the Lord he may receive your soul.

*Then The Fool falls down, and the dancers with
their swords in their hands, sings the following song.*

Good people all, you see what we have done:
We have cut down our father like ye evening sun,
And here he lies all in his purple gore,
And we are afraid he never will dance more.

Fool rises from the floor and says:

Fool. No, no, my children! by chance you are all
      mistaen!
   For here I find myself, I am not slain;
   But I will rise, your sport then to advance,
   And with you all, brave boys, I'll have a dance.

199

> *Then the Foreman and Cicely dances down and the other two couple stand their ground, After a short dance called 'Jack, the brisk young Drummer,' they all go out but The Fool, Fidler, and Cicely.*

Fool.　Hear you, do you please to hear the sport of a fool?

Cicely.　A fool? for why?

Fool.　Because I can neither leap, skip, nor dance, but cut a caper thus high. [*He capers*] Sound, music! I must be gon; the Lord of Pool draws nigh.

Enter Pickle Herring.

P. H.　I am the Lord of Pool,
　　　And here begins my measure,
　　　And after me a fool,
　　　　To dance a while for pleasure
　　　In Cupid's school.

Fool.　A fool, a fool, a fool,
　　　　A fool I heard thou say.
　　　　But more the other way.
　　　　I'll make a maid to play,
　　　Although in Cupid's school.
　　　　Come all away!

Enter Blue Britches.

Blue B.　I am the Knight of Lee,
　　　　And here I have a dagger,
　　　Offended not to be.
　　　　Come in, thou needy beggar,
　　　And follow me!

200

Enter Ginger Britches.

Ginger B.   Behold, behold, behold
             A man of poor estate!
         Not one penny to infold!

Enter Pepper Britches.

Pepper B.   My money is out at use, or else I would.

Enter Mr. Allspice.

Allspice.   With a hack, a hack, a hack,
           See how I will skip and dance
               For joys that we have found!
           Let each man take his chance,
               And we will all dance around.

> *Then they dance the sword dance which is
> called 'Nelly's Gig'; then they run under
> their swords, which is called 'Runing Battle';
> then three dancers dance with three swords,
> and the Foreman jumping over the swords;
> then The Fool goes up to Cicely.*

Fool.   Here comes I that never come yet,
        Since last time, lovy!
        I have a great head but little wit.
        Tho' my head be great and my wits be small,
        I can play the fool for a while as well as the
            best of ye all.
        My name is noble Anthony;
        I am as meloncholly as a mantle-tree.
        I am come to show you a little sport and
            activity,
               And soon, too!

Make room for noble Anthony
And all his good company!
Drive out all these proud rogues, and let my
lady and I have a parl!

Cicely. O, ye clown! what makes you drive out my
men so soon?

Fool.   O, pardon, madam, pardon! and I
Will never offend you more.
I will make your men come in as fast
As ever they did before.

Cicely. I pray you at my sight,
And drive it not till night,
That I may see them dance once more
So lovely in my sight.

Fool.   A-faith, madam, and so I will!
I will play the man
And make them come in
As fast as ever I can.—

But hold, gip! Mrs. Clagars,
How do you sell geese?

Cicely. Go, look, Mister Midgecock!
Twelve pence apiece.

Fool. Oh, the pretty pardon!
Cicely. A gip for a frown!
Fool. An ale-wife for an apparitor!
Cicely. A rope for a clown!
Fool. Why, all the devise in the country
Cannot pull this down!

I am a valiant knight just come from the seas:
    You do know me, do you?
I can kill you ten thousand, tho' they be but fleas.
I can kill you a man for an ounce of mustard,
Or I can kill you ten thousand for a good custard.
    I have an old sheep skin,
    And I lap it well in,
Sword and buckler by my side, all ready for to
    fight!
Come forth, you gluttons all! for, had it not been in
    this country, I should not have shewen my
    valour amongst you.   But sound, music! for
    I must be gone.

                                    [*Exit Fool.*]

                Enter Pickle Herring.

P. H.   In first and formost do I come,
              All for to lead this race,
          Seeking the country far and near
              So fair a lady to embrace.

          So fair a lady did I never see,
              So comely in my sight,
          Drest in her gaudy gold
              And silver shining bright.

          She has fingers long, and rings
              Of honor of beaten gold:
              My masters all, behold!
          It is now for some pretty dancing time,
          And we will foot it fine.

Blue B.   I am a youth of jollitree;
        Where is there one like unto me?
        My hair is bush'd very thick;
        My body is like an hasel stick;

        My legs they quaver like an eel;
        My arms become my body weel;
        My fingers they are long and small:
        Am not I a jolly youth, proper and tall?

        Therefore, Mister Musick Man,
          Whatsoever may be my chance,
        It is for my ladie's love and mine,
          Strike up the morris dance.

        Then they foot it once round.

Ginger B.   I am a jolly young man of flesh, **blood**
          and bone;
        Give eare, my masters all, each one!

        And especially you, my lady dear,
          I hope you like me well.
        Of all the gallants here
          It is I that doth so well.

        Therefore, Mister Musick Man,
          Whatsoever may be my chance,
        It is for my ladie's love and mine,
          Strike up the morris dance.

        Then they foot it round.

Pepper B.   I am my father's eldest son,
   And heir of all his land,
  And in a short time, I hope,
   It will fall into my hands.

  I was brought up at Lindsey Court
   All the days of my life.
  Here stands a fair lady,
   I wish she was my wife.

  I love her at my heart,
   And from her I will never start.
  Therefore, Mr. Musick Man, play up my
   part.
Fool (rushing in).   And mine, too!

   Enter Allspice, and they foot it round.
   Pickle Herring, suter to Cicely, takes her by
   the hand and walks about the room.

P. H.   Sweet Ciss, if thou wilt be my love,
  A thousand pounds I will give thee.
Cicely.   No, you're too old, sir, and I am too young,
  And alas! old man, that must not be.

P. H.   I'll buy thee a gown of violet blue,
  A petticoat imbroidered to thy knee;
  Likewise my love to thee shall be true.
Cicely.   But alas! old man, that must not be.

P. H.   Thou shalt walk at thy pleasure, love, all
   the day,
  If at night thou wilt but come home to me;
  And in my house bear all the sway.
Cicely.   Your children they'll find fault with me.

P. H.	I'll turn my children out of doors.
Cicely.	And so, I fear, you will do me.
P. H.	Nay, then, sweet Ciss, ne'er trust me more,
	For I never loved lass before like thee.

Enter Fool.

Fool.	No, nor behind, neither.
	Well met, sweet Cis, well over-ta'en !
Cicely.	You are kindly wellcome, sir, to me.
Fool.	I'll wipe my eyes, and I'll look again !
	Methinks, sweet Cis, I now thee see !

Cicely.	Raf, what has thou to pleasure me?
Fool.	Why, this, my dear, I will give thee,
	And all I have it shall be thine.
Cicely.	Kind sir, I thank you heartelly.

P. H. (*to The Fool*). Stand back, stand back, thou silly old swain !

This girl shall go with none but me.

Fool.	I will not !
P. H.	Stand back, stand back, or I'll cleave thy brain !

Then Pickle Herring goes up to Cis, and says:

O, now, sweet Cis, I am come to thee !

Cicely.	You are as wellcome as the rest,
	Wherein you brag so lustilly.
Fool.	For a thousand pounds she loves me best !
	I can see by the twinkling of her ee.

206

P. H.   I have store of gold, whereon I boast;
           Likewise my sword, love, shall fight for
             thee;
           When all is done, love, I'll scour the coast,
           And bring in gold for thee and me.

Cicely.   Your gold may gain as good as I,
           But by no means it shall tempt me;
           For youthfull years and frozen age
             Cannot in any wise agree.

           Then Blue Britches goes up to her and says:

Blue B. Sweet mistress, be advised by me:
             Do not let this old man be denyed,
           But love him for his gold in store;
             Himself may serve for a cloak, beside.

Cicely.   Yes, sir, but you are not in the right.   ·
             Stand back and do not council me!
           For I love a lad that will make me laugh,
           Not you but a youth shall pleasure me.

Fool.   Good wench!

P. H.   Love, I have a beard as white as milk.

Cicely. Ne'er better for that, thou silly old man!

P. H.   Besides, my skin, love, is soft as silk.

Fool.   And thy face shines like a dripping pan.

P. H.   Rafe, what has thou to pleasure her?

Fool.   Why a great deal more, boy, than there's
           in thee.

P. H.   Nay then, old rogue, I thee defye.

Cicely. I pray, dear friends, fall not out for me!

P. H.   Once I could skip, leap, dance, and sing;
           Why will you not give place to me?

Fool.   Nay, then, old rogue, I thee defye;
      For thy nose stands like a Maypole tree.

> *Then goes up Ginger Britches to Cicely and says:*

Ginger B.   Sweet mistress, mind what this man doth say,
      For he speaks nothing but the truth:
      Look on the soldier, now I pray;
      See, is not he a handsome youth?

Cicely.   Sir, I am engaged to one I love,
      And ever constant I will be,
      There is nothing that I prize above.

P. H.   For a thousand pounds, she's gone from me!

Fool.   Thou may lay two!

Cicely (*to Pickle Herring*).   Old father, for your reverend years,
      Stand you the next man unto me;
      Then he that doth the weapon bear;
      For I will have the hind man of the three!

Fool (*to Pickle Herring*).   Old father, a fig for your old gold!
      The soldier he shall bear no sway!
      But you shall see, and so shall we,
      'Tis I that carries the lass away.

> *Then the dancers takes hold of their swords, and foots it round the room; then every man makes his obeisance to the master of the house, and the whole concludes.*

FINIS

1. JOURNEY OF THE MAGI

'A COLD coming we had of it,
Just the worst time of the year
For a journey, and such a long journey:
The ways deep and the weather sharp,
The very dead of winter.'
And the camels galled, sore-footed, refractory,
Lying down in the melting snow.
There were times we regretted
The summer palaces on slopes, the terraces,
And the silken girls bringing sherbet.
Then the camel men cursing and grumbling
And running away, and wanting their liquor and
     women,
And the night-fires going out, and the lack of
     shelters,
And the cities hostile and the towns unfriendly
And the villages dirty and charging high prices:
A hard time we had of it.
At the end we preferred to travel all night,
Sleeping in snatches,
With the voices singing in our ears, saying
That this was all folly.
Then at dawn we came down to a temperate valley,
Wet, below the snow line, smelling of vegetation;
With a running stream and a water-mill beating
     the darkness,
And three trees on the low sky,
And an old white horse galloped away in the
     meadow.

Then we came to a tavern with vine-leaves over
    the lintel,
Six hands at an open door dicing for pieces of silver,
And feet kicking the empty wine-skins.
But there was no information, and so we continued
And arrived at evening, not a moment too soon
Finding the place; it was (you may say) satisfactory.

All this was a long time ago, I remember,
And I would do it again, but set down
This set down
This: were we led all that way for
Birth or Death? There was a Birth, certainly,
We had evidence and no doubt. I had seen birth
    and death,
But had thought they were different; this Birth was
Hard and bitter agony for us, like Death, our death.
We returned to our places, these kingdoms,
But no longer at ease here, in the old dispensation,
With an alien people clutching their gods.
I should be glad of another death.

2.

A SLUMBER did my spirit seal;
    I had no human fears:
She seemed a thing that could not feel
    The touch of earthly years.

No motion has she now, no force;
    She neither hears nor sees;
Rolled round in earth's diurnal course,
    With rocks, and stones, and trees.

3.

ALFRED DE MUSSET
Used to call his cat "pusset"
(His accent was affected—
That was to be expected.)

4.

'ALL, all of a piece without,
Thy chase had a beast in view,
Thy wars brought nothing about,
Thy lovers were all untrue;
'Tis well an old age is out
And time to begin a new.'

5.

AMPLE make this bed.
Make this bed with awe;
In it wait till judgment break
Excellent and fair.

Be its mattress straight,
Be its pillow round;
Let no sunrise' yellow noise
Interrupt this ground.

6.

AND now if e'er by chance I put,
 My fingers into glue,
Or madly squeeze a right-hand foot
 Into a left-hand shoe,
Or if I drop upon my toe
 A very heavy weight,
I weep, for it reminds me so
Of that old man I used to know—
Whose look was mild, whose speech was slow,
Whose hair was whiter than the snow,
Whose face was very like a crow,
With eyes, like cinders, all aglow,
Who seemed distracted with his woe,
Who rocked his body to and fro,
And muttered mumblingly and low,
As if his mouth were full of dough,
Who snorted like a buffalo—
That summer evening long ago
 A-sitting on a gate.

7. TO HIS MISTRESS' SKULL

AND now methinkes I could e'en chide myselfe
For doating on her beauty, tho' her death
Shall be reveng'd after no common action.
Does the silke-worme expend her yellow labours
For thee? for thee does she undoe herselfe?
Are Lordships sold to maintaine Ladyships
For the poore benefit of a bewildering minute?

4

Why does yon fellow falsify hie-waies
And put his life betweene the Judge's lippes
To refine such a thing, keepes horse and men
To beate their valours for her?

8.

AND now the salmon-fishers moist,
Their leathern boats begin to hoist;
And, like Antipodes in shoes,
Have shod their heads in their canoes.
How tortoise-like, but not so slow,
These rational amphibii go!
Let's in; for the dark hemisphere
Does now like one of them appear.

9. THE WHALE

AT every stroake his brazen finnes do take,
More circles in the broken sea they make
Then cannons voices, when the aire they teare:
His ribs are pillars, and his high arch'd roofe
Of barke that blunts best steele, is thunder-proofe:
Swimme in him swallow'd Dolphins, without feare,
And feele no sides, as if his vast wombe were
Some inland sea, and ever as hee went
Hee spouted rivers up, as if he ment
    To joyne our seas, with seas above the firmament.

He hunts not fish but as an officer,
Stayes in his court, at his owne net, and there
All suitors of all sorts themselves enthrall;

5

So on his backe lyes this whale wantoning,
And in his gulfe-like throat, sucks every thing
That passeth neare. Fish chaseth fish, and all,
Flyer and follower, in this whirlepoole fall;
O might not states of more equality
Consist? and is it of necessity
  That thousand guiltlesse smals, to make one great,
    must die?

Now drinkes he up seas, and he eates up flockes,
He justles Ilands, and he shakes firme rockes.
Now in a roomefull house this Soule doth float,
And like a Prince she sends her faculties
To all her limbes, distant as Provinces.
The Sunne hath twenty times both crab and goate
Parched, since first lanch'd forth this living boate;
'Tis greatest now, and to destruction
Nearest; There's no pause at perfection;
  Greatnesse a period hath, but hath no station. . . .

10.

At Timon's Villa let us pass a day,
Where all cry out, "What sums are thrown away!"
So proud, so grand; of that stupendous air,
Soft and Agreeable come never there.
Greatness, with Timon, dwells in such a draught
As brings all Brobdignag before your thought.
To compass this, his building is a town,
His pond an ocean, his parterre a down:
Who but must laugh, the master when he sees,
A puny insect, shiv'ring at a breeze!

6

Lo, what huge heaps of littleness around!
The whole, a labour'd quarry above ground:
Two Cupids squirt before: a lake behind
Improves the keenness of the northern wind.
His gardens next your admiration call,
On ev'ry side you look, behold the wall!
No pleasing intricacies intervene,
No artful wildness to perplex the scene:
Grove nods at grove, each alley has a brother,
And half the platform just reflects the other.
The suff'ring eye inverted Nature sees,
Trees cut to statues, statues thick as trees;
With here a fountain, never to be play'd;
And there a summer - house, that knows no
    shade:
Here Amphitrite sails thro' myrtle bow'rs;
There gladiators fight, or die, in flow'rs;
Unwatered see the drooping sea-horse mourn,
And swallows roost in Nilus' dusty urn.

My Lord advances with majestic mien,
Smit with the mighty pleasure, to be seen;
But soft—by regular approach—not yet—
First thro' the length of yon hot terrace sweat;
And when up ten steep slopes you've dragg'd your
    thighs,
Just at his study-door he'll bless your eyes.

His study! with what authors is it stor'd?
In books, not authors, curious is my Lord;
To all their dated backs he turns you round:
These Aldus printed, those Du Sueil has bound.
Lo, some are vellum, and the rest as good
For all his Lordship knows, but they are wood.

7

For Locke or Milton 'tis in vain to look,
These shelves admit not any modern book.
  And now the chapel's silver bell you hear,
That summons you to all the pride of pray'r:
Light quirks of music, broken and uneven,
Make the soul dance upon a jig to Heav'n.
On painted ceilings you devoutly stare,
Where sprawl the Saints of Verrio or Laguerre,
On gilded clouds in fair expansion lie,
And bring all Paradise before your eye.
To rest, the cushion and soft Dean invite,
Who never mentions Hell to ears polite.
  But hark! the chiming clocks to dinner call;
A hundred footsteps scrape the marble hall:
The rich buffet well-colour'd serpents grace,
And gaping Tritons spew to wash your face.
Is this a dinner? this a genial room?
No, 'tis a temple, and a hecatomb.
A solemn sacrifice, perform'd in state,
You drink by measure, and to minutes eat.
So quick retires each flying course, you'd swear
Sancho's dread doctor and his wand were there.
Between each act the trembling salvers ring,
From soup to sweet-wine, and God bless the King.
In plenty starving, tantaliz'd in state,
And complaisantly help'd to all I hate,
Treated, caress'd, and tir'd, I take my leave,
Sick of his civil pride from morn to eve;
I curse such lavish cost, and little skill,
And swear no day was ever past so ill.
  Yet hence the poor are cloth'd, the hungry fed;
Health to himself, and to his infants bread,

The lab'rer bears: What his hard heart denies,
His charitable Vanity supplies.
    Another age shall see the golden ear
Imbrown the slope, and nod on the parterre,
Deep harvests bury all his pride has plann'd,
And laughing Ceres re-assume the land.

11.

AVENGE O Lord thy slaughter'd saints, whose bones
    Lie scatter'd on the Alpine mountains cold;
    Ev'n them who kept thy truth so pure of old,
    When all our fathers worshipp'd stocks and stones,
Forget not: in thy book record their groans
    Who were thy sheep, and in their ancient fold
    Slain by the bloody Piedmontese that roll'd
    Mother with infant down the rocks.   Their moans
The vales redoubled to the hills, and they
    To Heav'n.   Their martyr'd blood and ashes sow
    O'er all th' Italian fields, where still doth sway
The triple tyrant; that from these may grow
    A hundred-fold, who having learn'd thy way
    Early may fly the Babylonian woe.

12.

DUKE: Be absolute for death; either death or life
Shall thereby be the sweeter. Reason thus with life—
If I do lose thee, I do lose a thing
That none but fools would keep: a breath thou art,

9

Servile to all the skiey influences,
That do this habitation, where thou keep'st,
Hourly afflict: merely, thou art death's fool;
For him thou labour'st by thy flight to shun,
And yet runn'st toward him still. Thou art not
    noble;
For all th' accommodations that thou bear'st
Are nurs'd by baseness. Thou'rt by no means
    valiant;
For thou dost fear the soft and tender fork
Of a poor worm. Thy best of rest is sleep,
And that thou oft provok'st; yet grossly fear'st
Thy death, which is no more. Thou art not thyself;
For thou exist'st on many a thousand grains
That issue out of dust. Happy thou art not;
For what thou hast not, still thou striv'st to get;
And what thou hast, forget'st. Thou art not
    certain;
For thy complexion shifts to strange affects,
After the moon. If thou art rich, thou art poor;
For, like an ass whose back with ingots bows,
Thou bear'st thy heavy riches but a journey,
And death unloads thee. Friend hast thou none;
For thine own bowels, which do call thee sire,
The mere effusions of thy proper loins,
Do curse the gout, serpigo, and the rheum,
For ending thee no sooner. Thou hast nor youth,
    nor age;
But, as it were, an after-dinner's sleep,
Dreaming on both; for all thy blessed youth
Becomes as aged, and doth beg the alms
Of palsied eld; and when thou art old, and rich,

Thou hast neither heat, affection, limb, nor beauty,
To make thy riches pleasant.   What's yet in this
That bears the name of life?   Yet in this life
Lie hid more thousand deaths; yet death we fear,
That makes these odds all even. . . .

CLAUDIO: Ay, but to die, and go we know not
   where;
To lie in cold obstruction, and to rot;
This sensible warm motion to become
A kneaded clod; and the delighted spirit
To bathe in fiery floods, or to reside
In thrilling region of thick-ribbed ice;
To be imprison'd in the viewless winds,
And blown with restless violence round about
The pendent world; or to be worse than worst
Of those that lawless and incertain thought
Imagine howling!—'tis too horrible!
The weariest and most loathed worldly life
That age, ache, penury, and imprisonment
Can lay on nature, is a paradise
To what we fear of death. . . .

13.

Be near me when my light is low,
   When the blood creeps, and the nerves prick
   And tingle; and the heart is sick,
And all the wheels of Being slow.

Be near me when the sensuous frame
   Is rack'd with pangs that conquer trust;
   And Time, a maniac scattering dust,
And Life, a Fury slinging flame.

Be near me when my faith is dry,
   And men the flies of latter spring,
   That lay their eggs, and sting and sing
And weave their petty cells and die.

Be near me when I fade away,
   To point the term of human strife,
   And on the low dark verge of life
The twilight of eternal day.

14.

BENEATH this stone, in hopes of Zion,
Doth lie the landlord of the Lion;
His son keeps on the business still,
Resigned unto the heavenly will.

15.

Bring us in good ale, and bring us in good ale;
For our blessed Lady sake bring us in good ale.

Bring us in no brown bread, for that is made of bran,
Nor bring us in no white bread, for therein is no gain,
   But bring us in good ale.

Bring us in no beef, for there is many bones,
But bring us in good ale, for that goth down at once;
   And bring us in good ale.

Bring us in no bacon, for that is passing fat,
But bring us in good ale, and give us enough of
  that;
  And bring us in good ale.

Bring us in no mutton, for that is often lean,
Nor bring us in no tripes, for they be seldom
  clean;
  But bring us in good ale.

Bring us in no eggs, for there are many shells,
But bring us in good ale, and give us nothing
  else;
  And bring us in good ale.

Bring us in no butter, for therein are many hairs;
Nor bring us in no pigges flesh, for that will make us
  bores;
  But bring us in good ale.

Bring us in no puddings, for therein is all God's
  good;
Nor bring us in no venison, for that is not for our
  blood;
  But bring us in good ale.

Bring us in no capon's flesh, for that is often dear;
Nor bring us in no duckes flesh, for they slobber in
  the mere;
  But bring us in good ale.

16.

But Lord Crist! whan that it remembreth me
Upon my youthe, and on my jolitee,
It tickleth me aboute myn herte rote
Unto this day it dooth myn herte bote
That I have had my world as in my tyme.

17.

Care-charming sleep, thou easer of all woes,
Brother to Death, sweetly thyself dispose
On this afflicted prince; fall like a cloud,
In gentle showers; give nothing that is loud,
Or painful to his slumbers; easy, light,
And as a purling stream, thou son of Night
Pass by his troubled senses; sing his pain,
Like hollow murmuring wind or silver rain;
Into this prince gently, oh, gently slide,
And kiss him into slumbers like a bride.

18.

Come, come, no time for lamentation now,
Nor much more cause: Samson hath quit himself
Like Samson, and heroicly hath finished
A life Heroic, on his Enemies
Fully reveng'd, hath left them years of mourning,
And lamentation to the Sons of Caphtor
Through all Philistian bounds; to Israel
Honour hath left, and freedom, let but them
Find courage to lay hold on this occasion;

To himself and Father's house eternal fame;
And which is best and happiest yet, all this
With God not parted from him, as was fear'd,
But favouring and assisting to the end.
Nothing is here for tears, nothing to wail
Or knock the breast, no weakness, no contempt,
Dispraise, or blame, nothing but well and fair,
And what may quiet us in a death so noble.

.   .   .   .

Chorus

All is best, though we oft doubt,
What th' unsearchable dispose
Of highest wisdom brings about,
And ever best found in the close.
Oft he seems to hide his face,
But unexpectedly returns
And to his faithful Champion hath in place
Bore witness gloriously: whence Gaza mourns
And all that band them to resist
His uncontroulable intent;
His servants he with new acquist
Of true experience from this great event
With peace and consolation hath dismist,
And calm of mind all passion spent.

19. A PUBLISHER TO HIS CLIENT

Dear Doctor, I have read your play,
Which is a good one in its way,—
Purges the eyes, and moves the bowels,
And drenches handkerchiefs like towels

With tears, that, in a flux of grief,
Afford hysterical relief
To shattered nerves and quickened pulses,
Which your catastrophe convulses.

I like your moral and machinery;
Your plot, too, has such scope for Scenery!
Your dialogue is apt and smart;
The play's concoction full of art;
Your hero raves, your heroine cries,
All stab, and every body dies.
In short, your tragedy would be
The very thing to hear and see:
And for a piece of publication,
If I decline on this occasion,
It is not that I am not sensible
To merits in themselves ostensible,
But—and I grieve to speak it—plays
Are drugs—mere drugs, sir—now-a-days.
I had a heavy loss by *Manuel*—
Too lucky if it prove not annual,—
And Sotheby, with his *Orestes*,
(Which, by the way, the old bore's best is),
Has lain so very long on hand,
That I despair of all demand;
I've advertised, but see my books,
Or only watch my Shopman's looks;—
Still *Ivan*, *Ina*, and such lumber,
My back-shop glut, my shelves encumber.

There's Byron too, who once did better,
Has sent me, folded in a letter,
A sort of—it's no more a drama
Than *Darnley*, *Ivan*, or *Kehama*:

So altered since last year his pen is,
I think he's lost his wits at Venice.

*   *   *   *   *   *   *   *

In short, Sir, what with one and t'other,
I dare not venture on another.
I write in haste; excuse each blunder;
The Coaches through the street so thunder!
My room's so full—we've Gifford here
Reading MS., with Hookham Frere,
Pronouncing on the nouns and particles
Of some of our forthcoming Articles.

    The *Quarterly*—Ah, sir, if you
Had but the genius to review!—
A smart Critique upon St. Helena,
Or if you only would but tell in a
Short compass what—but; to resume
As I was saying, sir, the Room—
The Room's so full of wits and bards,
Crabbes, Campbells, Crokers, Freres, and Wards
And others, neither bards nor wits:
My humble tenement admits
All persons in the dress of Gent.,
From Mr. Hammond to Dog Dent.

    A party dines with me to-day,
All clever men, who make their way:
Crabbe, Malcolm, Hamilton, and Chantrey
Are all partakers of my pantry.
They're at this moment in discussion
On poor De Staël's late dissolution.
Her book, they say, was in advance—
Pray Heaven she tell the truth of France!

Thus run our time and tongues away;—
But, to return, sir, to your play:
Sorry, sir, but I cannot deal,
Unless 'twere acted by O'Neill.
My hands are full—my head so busy,
I'm almost dead—and always dizzy;
And so, with endless truth and hurry,
Dear Doctor, I am yours   JOHN MURRAY.

20. IF WORDSWORTH HAD WRITTEN "THE EVERLASTING MERCY"

EVER since boyhood it has been my joy
To rove the hills and vales, the woods and streams,
To commune with the flowers, the beasts, the birds,
And all the humble messengers of God.
And so not seldom have my footsteps strayed
To that bare farm where Thomas Haythornthwaite
(Alas! 'tis now ten years the good old man
Is dead!) wrung turnips from the barren soil,
To keep himself and his good wife, Maria,
Whom I remember well, although 'tis now
Full twenty years since she deceased; and I
Have often visited her quiet grave
In summer and in winter, that I might
Place some few flowers upon it, and returned
In solemn meditation from the spot.
In the employment of this honest man
There was a hind, Saul Kane, I knew him well,
And oft-times 'twas my fortune to lament
The blackness of the youth's depravity.

For when I came to visit Haythornthwaite
The good old man, leaning upon his spade,
Would say to me, "Saul Kane is wicked, sir;
A wicked lad. Before he cut his teeth
He broke his poor old mother's heart in two.
For at the beer-house he is often seen
With ill companions, and at dead of night
We hear him loud blaspheming at the owls
That fly about the house. I oft have blushed
At deeds of his I could not speak about."
But yet so wondrous is the heart of man
That even Saul Kane repented of his sins—
A little maid, a little Quakermaid,
Converted him one day. "Saul Kane," she said,
"Dear Saul, I pray you will get drunk no more."
Nor did he; but embraced a sober life,
And married Mary Thorpe; and yesterday
I met him on my walk, and with him went
Up to the house where he and his do dwell.
And there I long in serious converse stayed,
Speaking of Nature and of politics,
And then turned homeward meditating much
About the single transferable vote.

21. SONG OF VENUS

FAIREST Isle, all Isles Excelling,
   Seat of Pleasures, and of Loves;
Venus here will chuse her Dwelling,
   And forsake her Cyprian Groves.

Cupid, from his Fav'rite Nation,
   Care and Envy will Remove;
Jealousy that poysons Passion,
   And Despair that dies for Love.

Gentle Murmurs, sweet complaining,
   Sighs that blow the Fire of Love;
Soft Repulses, kind Disdaining,
   Shall be all the Pains you prove.

Ev'ry Swain shall pay his Duty,
   Grateful ev'ry Nymph shall prove;
And as these Excel in Beauty,
   Those shall be Renown'd for love.

22. SPANISH LADIES

FAREWELL and adieu to you, Fair Spanish Ladies,
   Farewell and adieu to you, Ladies of Spain,
For we've received orders to sail for old England,
   But we hope in a short time to see you again.
      We'll rant and we'll roar, all o'er the wild
         ocean,
      We'll rant and we'll roar, all o'er the wild
         seas,
Until we strike soundings in the Channel of Old
   England,
From Ushant to Scilly is thirty-five leagues.

We hove our ship to, with the wind at sou'west, boys,
  We hove our ship for to strike soundings clear;
Then filled the main topsail and bore right away,
    boys,
  And straight up the Channel our course we did
    steer.
        We'll rant and we'll roar, etc.

The first land we made was a point called the
    Dodman,
  Next Rame Head off Plymouth, Start, Portland
    and Wight,
We sailed then by Beachy, by Fairlee and Dung'ness,
  Then bore straight away for the South Foreland
    Light.
        We'll rant and we'll roar, etc.

The signal was made for the Grand Fleet to anchor,
  We clewed up our topsails, stuck out tacks and
    sheets,
We stood by our stoppers, we brailed in our spanker,
  And anchored ahead of the noblest of fleets.
        We'll rant and we'll roar, etc.

Then let every man here toss off a full bumper,
  Then let every man here toss off his full bowl,
For we will be jolly and drown melancholy,
  With a health to each jovial and true-hearted
    soul.
        We'll rant and we'll roar, etc.

23. MACPHERSON'S FAREWELL

Farewell, ye dungeons dark and strong,
  The wretches destinie:
Macpherson's time will not be long
  On yonder gallows-tree.

  Sae rantingly,[1] sae wantonly,
    Sae dauntingly gaed he:
  He played a spring and danced it round,
    Below the gallows-tree.

Oh! what is death but parting breath?
  On mony a bloody plain
I've dared his face, and in this place
  I scorn him yet again!
    Sae rantingly, etc.

Untie these bands from off my hands,
  And bring to me my sword,
And there's no a man in all Scotland,
  But I'll brave him at a word.
    Sae rantingly, etc.

I've lived a life of sturt[2] and strife;
  I die by treacherie:
It burns my heart I must depart
  And not avengèd be.
    Sae rantingly, etc.

Now farewell light, thou sunshine bright,
  And all beneath the sky!
May coward shame distain his name,
  The wretch that dare not die!
    Sae rantingly, etc.

[1] joyously.   [2] trouble.

FROM all these events, from the slump, from the war, from the boom,
From the Italian holiday, from the skirring
Of the revolving light for an adventurer,
From the crowds in the square at dusk, from the shooting,
From the loving, from the dying, however we prosper in death
Whether lying under twin lilies and branched candles
Or stiffened on the pavement like a frozen sack, hidden
From night and peace by the lamps:
From all these events, Time solitary will emerge
Like a rocket bursting from mist: above the trouble
Untangled with our pasts, be sure Time will leave us.

At first growing up in us more nakedly than our own nature
Driving us beyond what seemed the final choking swamp,
Ruin, the all-covering illness, to a new and empty air;
Singling us from the war which killed ten millions;
Carrying us elate through the happy summer fields;
Nesting us in high rooms of a house where voices
Murmured at night from the garden, as if flowering from water;

Then sending us to lean days after the years of
    fulfilment;
At last dropping us into the hard, bright crater of
    the dead.

Our universal ally, but larger than our purpose,
    whose flanks
Stretch to planets unknown in our brief, particular
    battle,
To-morrow Time's progress will forget us even here,
When our bodies are rejected like the beetle's shard,
    to-day
Already, now, we are forgotten on those stellar
    shores.
Time's ambition, huge as space, will hang its flags
In distant worlds, and in years on this world as
    distant.

25. HYMN OF PAN

I

From the forests and highlands
    We come, we come;
From the river-girt islands,
    Where loud waves are dumb
      Listening to my sweet pipings.
The wind in the reeds and the rushes,
    The bees on the bells of thyme,
The birds on the myrtle bushes,
    The cicale above in the lime,
And the lizards below in the grass,
Were as silent as ever old Tmolus was
      Listening to my sweet pipings.

II

Liquid Peneus was flowing,
    And all dark Tempe lay
In Pelion's shadow, outgrowing
    The light of the dying day,
        Speeded by my sweet pipings
The Sileni, and Sylvans, and Fauns,
    And the Nymphs of the woods and waves,
To the edge of the moist river-lawns,
    And the brink of the dewy caves,
And all that did then attend and follow
Were silent with love, as you now, Apollo,
        With envy of my sweet pipings.

I sang of the dancing stars,
    I sang of the daedal Earth,
And of Heaven—and the giant wars,
    And Love, and Death, and Birth,—
        And then I changed my pipings,—
Singing how down the vale of Menalus
    I pursued a maiden and clasp'd a reed:
Gods and men, we are all deluded thus!
    It breaks in our bosom and then we bleed:
All wept, as I think both ye now would,
If envy or age had not frozen your blood,
        At the sorrow of my sweet pipings.

FROM the Gallows Hill to the Tineton Copse
There were ten ploughed fields, like ten full-stops,
All wet red clay, where a horse's foot
Would be swathed, feet thick, like an ash-tree root.
The fox raced on, on the headlands firm,
Where his swift feet scared the coupling worm;
The rooks rose raving to curse him raw,
He snarled a sneer at their swoop and caw.
Then on, then on, down a half-ploughed field
Where a ship-like plough drove glitter-keeled,
With a bay horse near and a white horse leading,
And a man saying "Zook," and the red earth
    bleeding.
He gasped as he saw the ploughman drop
The stilts and swear at the team to stop.
The ploughman ran in his red clay clogs,
Crying, "Zick un, Towzer; zick, good dogs!"
A couple of wire-haired lurchers lean
Arose from his wallet, nosing keen;
With a rushing swoop they were on his track,
Putting chest to stubble to bite his back.
He swerved from his line with the curs at heel,
The teeth as they missed him clicked like steel.
With a worrying snarl, they quartered on him,
While the ploughman shouted, "Zick; upon him."

   .   .   .   .   .   .

The fox raced on, up the Barton Balks,
With a crackle of kex in the nettle stalks,
Over Hammond's grass to the dark green line
Of the larch-wood smelling of turpentine.

Scratch Steven Larches, black to the sky,
A sadness breathing with one long sigh,
Grey ghosts of trees under funeral plumes,
A mist of twig over soft brown glooms.
As he entered the wood he heard the smacks,
Chip-jar, of the fir-pole feller's axe.
He swerved to the left to a broad green ride,
Where a boy made him rush for the farther side.
He swerved to the left, to the Barton Road,
But there were the timberers come to load—
Two timber-carts and a couple of carters
With straps round their knees instead of garters.
He swerved to the right, straight down the wood,
The carters watched him, the boy hallooed.
He leaped from the larch-wood into tillage,
The cobbler's garden of Barton village.

* * * * * * * *

The cobbler bent at his wooden foot,
Beating sprigs in a broken boot;
He wore old glasses with thick horn rim,
He scowled at his work, for his sight was dim.
His face was dingy, his lips were grey,
From primming sparrowbills day by day.
As he turned his boot he heard a noise
At his garden-end, and he thought, "It's boys."

. . . .

Like a rocket shot to a ship ashore
The lean red bolt of his body tore,
Like a ripple of wind running swift on grass;
Like a shadow on wheat when a cloud blows
    past,

27

Like a turn at the buoy in a cutter sailing
When the bright green gleam lips white at the
    railing,
Like the April snake whipping back to sheath,
Like the gannets' hurtle on fish beneath,
Like a kestrel chasing, like a sickle reaping,
Like all things swooping, like all things sweeping,
Like a hound for stay, like a stag for swift,
With his shadow beside like spinning drift.

    *   *   *   *   *   *   *   *

Past the gibbet-stock all stuck with nails,
Where they hanged in chains what had hung at
    jails,
Past Ashmundshowe where Ashmund sleeps,
And none but the tumbling peewit weeps,
Past Curlew Calling, the gaunt grey corner
Where the curlew comes as a summer mourner,
Past Blowbury Beacon, shaking his fleece,
Where all winds hurry and none brings peace;
Then down on the mile-long green decline,
Where the turf's like spring and the air's like wine,
Where the sweeping spurs of the downland spill
Into Wan Brook Valley and Wan Dyke Hill.

    *   *   *   *   *   *   *   *

On he went with a galloping rally
Past Maesbury Clump for Wan Brook Valley.
The blood in his veins went romping high,
"Get on, on, on, to the earth or die."
The air of the downs went purely past
Till he felt the glory of going fast,
Till the terror of death, though there indeed,
Was lulled for a while by his pride of speed.

He was romping away from hounds and hunt,
He had Wan Dyke Hill and his earth in front,
In a one mile more when his point was made
He would rest in safety from dog or spade;
Nose between paws he would hear the shout
Of the "Gone to earth!" to the hounds without,
The whine of the hounds, and their cat-feet gadding
Scratching the earth, and their breath pad-
    padding;
He would hear the horn call hounds away,
And rest in peace till another day.

   .   .   .   .

27. HYMN OF OUR LORD AT THE LAST SUPPER

GLORY be to thee, Word: Glory be to thee, Grace.
    Amen.
Glory be to thee, Spirit: Glory be to thee, Holy
    One:
Glory be to thy glory. Amen.
We praise thee, O Father; we give thanks to thee,
    O Light, wherein darkness dwelleth not. Amen.
Now wherefore we give thanks, I say:
I would be saved, and I would save. Amen.
I would be loosed, and I would loose. Amen.
I would be wounded, and I would wound. Amen.
I would be born, and I would bear. Amen.
I would eat, and I would be eaten. Amen.
I would hear, and I would be heard. Amen.
I would be thought, being wholly thought. Amen.

I would be washed, and I would wash. Amen.

Grace danceth. I would pipe; dance ye all. Amen.

I would mourn: lament ye all. Amen.

The number Eight singeth praise with us. Amen.

The number Twelve danceth on high. Amen.

The Whole on high hath part in *our* dancing. Amen.

Whoso danceth not, knoweth not what cometh to pass. Amen.

I would flee, and I would stay. Amen.

I would adorn, and I would be adorned. Amen.

I would be united, and I would unite. Amen.

A house I have not, and I have houses. Amen.

A place I have not, and I have places. Amen.

A temple I have not, and I have temples. Amen.

A lamp am I to thee that beholdest me. Amen.

A mirror am I to thee that perceivest me. Amen.

A door am I to thee that knockest at me. Amen.

A way am I to thee a wayfarer. Amen.

28. ALPHABETICAL SONG ON THE CORN LAW BILL

GOOD people draw near as you pass along
And listen awhile to my alphabetical song.
A is Prince Albert once buxome and keen
Who from Germany came and got spliced to the queen.

For they're all a spinning, their cause in triumph
    springing
And the poor man he is singing since the Corn bill
    is repailed.

B stands for Smith O Brien: he an Irishman so true
He hammered at coercion till he beat them black
    and blue
When he got out of prison that bill he did oppose
With the fright he gave old Wellington, he fell and
    broke his nose.

C is brave Cobden one night it is said
Threw a quarter loaf at old Buckingham's head
Concerning the Corn laws he laid it down strong
And he spun out yarn seventeen hour long.

D for the duncomb who helpt the plan
To give full and plenty to each in the land
E stands for Evans who would starve us again
Because he beat us 40 thousand old women in Spain.

F stands for Ferrand a protectioners Tool
He spoke seven hours and roared like a fool
G stands for Graham who is early and late
Breaking seals at the post office a repealer for to take.

H is old Hume he is clever do you see
He subtracted 2 from 1 and got the corn duty free
I is Bob Inglis aginst free trade Blewe a blast
He was seven hours in the stericks when the corn
    bill do pass.

J stands for Jerry who spoke till he was hoarse
In the middle of the fight his fair daughter he lost
She followed a soldier and off she went slap
With gun and a nap-sack slung over her back.

K is for Kelly, he kept up the jaw
Till he got the corn free and brought into law
L stands for Lindhurst with his Brushes, Paints, and
Pots
Guess how he was born or how that he was got.

M is Lord Morpeth who nobly fought
Each night in succession for the corn law
N is old nosey who opposes him its true
For to lose 15 thousand he is quite in the blues.

O is O connell to them told the law
And is still biding time for old Erin Gobraugh
P stands for Peel who is acting upright
As between you and me he has got a long sight.

Q is the question of coercion they say
So their stuck in the trap bob cut away
R is Lord Russell whos making all haste
To run down to Windsor to fill Bobby's place.

To ride in Peel's saddle he'll find it a job
For he shakes on his legs like a staggering bob.
S is Lord Stanley who shaking with fear
For his tenants payed him their rent with a bullet
this year.

And swore if they catch him he'll never elope
Till they well oil his body with flails of good oak
T is the teasel that comb them all down
U is for Uxbridge who wonders have done.

V stands for Villiers whom the farmers detest
For to slaughter the corn laws he did do his best
For free trade he struggled by day and by night
He is next in command to Cobden and Bright.

W stands for Wakley a doctor so bold
Who swore on the corn bill an Inquest to hold
When the jury he charged he let them all see
A verdict was returned for the corn to be free.

X is a letter which puts me in mind
Of a ship load of landlords that sailed against wind
Now over the ocean they must all away
To spend their last days in Botany Bay.

Y stands for York the archbishop so big
Who loves for to dine on a little tithe pig
Free trade on last Sunday did so him perplex
That he sang his Brittania and thought it the text.

Z is for Zetland an old English peer
Who swore he'd have bread and potatoes so dear
The corn bill is past the landlords are very bad
They must be muzzled in the dog days for fear they
        might go mad.

*HAIL thee, Festival Day! blest day that art hallowed for
    ever;*
*Day wherein God o'ercame hell and arose from the
    dead.*

Lo, the fair beauty of earth, from the death of the
    winter arising,
Every good gift of the year now with its Master
    returns.

He who was nailed to the Cross is God and the
    Ruler of all things;
All things created on earth worship the Maker
    of all.

God of all pity and power, let thy word be assured
    to the doubting;
Light on the third day returns: rise, Son of God,
    from the tomb!

.   .   .   .

Rise now, O Lord, from the grave and cast off the
    shroud that enwrapped thee;
Thou art sufficient for us: nothing without thee
    exists.

Mourning they laid thee to rest, who art Author of
    life and creation;
Treading the pathway of death, life thou bestowedst
    on man.

Show us thy face once more, that the ages may joy
    in thy brightness;
Give us the light of day, darkened on earth at thy
    death.

Out of the prison of death thou art rescuing number-
    less captives;
Freely they tread in the way whither their Maker
    has gone.

Jesus has harrowed hell; he has led captivity
    captive:
Darkness and chaos and death flee from the face
    of the light.

30. INSENSIBILITY

I

HAPPY are men who yet before they are killed
Can let their veins run cold.
Whom no compassion fleers
Or makes their feet
Sore on the alleys cobbled with their brothers.
The front line withers,
But they are troops who fade, not flowers
For poets' tearful fooling:
Men, gaps for filling:
Losses who might have fought
Longer; but no one bothers.

II

And some cease feeling
Even themselves or for themselves.
Dullness best solves
The tease and doubt of shelling,

35

And Chance's strange arithmetic
Comes simpler than the reckoning of their shilling.
They keep no check on armies' decimation.

III

Happy are those who lose imagination:
They have enough to carry with ammunition.
Their spirit drags no pack,
Their old wounds save with cold can not more ache.
Having seen all things red,
Their eyes are rid
Of the hurt of the colour of blood for ever.
And terror's first constriction over,
Their hearts remain small-drawn.
Their senses in some scorching cautery of battle
Now long since ironed,
Can laugh among the dying, unconcerned.

IV

Happy the soldier home, with not a notion
How somewhere, every dawn, some men attack,
And many sighs are drained.
Happy the lad whose mind was never trained:
His days are worth forgetting more than not.
He sings along the march
Which we march taciturn, because of dusk,
The long, forlorn, relentless trend
From larger day to huger night.

V

We wise, who with a thought besmirch
Blood over all our soul,

36

How should we see our task
But through his blunt and lashless eyes?
Alive, he is not vital overmuch;
Dying, not mortal overmuch;
Nor sad, nor proud,
Nor curious at all.
He cannot tell
Old men's placidity from his.

VI

But cursed are dullards whom no cannon stuns,
That they should be as stones;
Wretched are they, and mean
With paucity that never was simplicity.
By choice they made themselves immune
To pity and whatever moans in man
Before the last sea and the hapless stars;
Whatever mourns when many leave these shores;
Whatever shares
The eternal reciprocity of tears.

31. THE MANERE OF THE CRYING OF ANE PLAYE

HARRY, Harry, hobbillschowe! [1]
Se quha is cummyn nowe,
Bot I wait nevir howe,
      With the quhorle wynd?
A soldane owt of Seriand land,
A gyand strang for to stand,

[1] confused noise.

37

That with the strenth of my hand
  Beres may bynd.
Yit I trowe that I vary,
I am the nakit Blynd Hary,
That lang has bene in the fary [1]
  Farleis [2] to fynd:
And yit gif this be nocht I,
I wait [3] I am the spreit of Gy,
Or ellis go by the sky,
  Licht as the lynd.

 . . . .

My foregrantschir hecht [4] Fyn McKowle,
That dang the Devill and gart him yowle,
The skyis ranyd quhen he wald scowle
  And trublit all the aire:
He gat my grantschir Gog Magog;
Ay quhen he dansit, the warld wald schog; [5]
Five thousand ellis yeid in his frog [6]
  Of Hieland pladdis of haire.
Yit he was bot of tender youth;
Bot eftir he grewe mekle at fouth,
Ellevyne ell wyde met was his mouth,
  His teith was tene myle sqwaire.
He wald apone his tais stand,
And tak the sternis doune with his hand,
And set tham in a gold garland
  Abone his wyfis haire. . . .

[1] fairyland.   [2] wonder.   [3] know.
[4] was called. [5] shake.   [6] coat.

32. THE HOUSE OF SLEEP

HE, making speedy way through spersèd ayre,
And through the world of waters wide and deepe,
To Morpheus house doth hastily repaire.
Amid the bowels of the earth full steepe,
And low, where dawning day doth never peepe,
His dwelling is; there Tethys his wet bed
Doth ever wash, and Cynthia still doth steepe
In silver deaw his ever-drouping hed,
Whiles sad Night over him her mantle black doth
    spred.

Whose double gates he findeth lockèd fast,
The one faire fram'd of burnisht Yvory,
The other all with silver overcast;
And wakeful dogges before them farre doe lye,
Watching to banish Care their enimy,
Who oft is wont to trouble gentle Sleepe.
By them the Sprite doth passe in quietly,
And unto Morpheus comes, whom drownèd deepe
In drowsie fit he findes: of nothing he takes keepe.

And more to lulle him in his slumber soft,
A trickling streame from high rock tumbling downe,
And ever-drizling raine upon the loft,
Mixt with a murmuring winde, much like the
    sowne
Of swarming Bees, did cast him in a swowne.
No other noyse, nor peoples troublous cryes,
As still are wont t'annoy the wallèd towne,
Might there be heard; but carelesse Quiet lyes
Wrapt in eternall silence farre from enimyes.

33.

Her strong enchantments failing,
    Her towers of fear in wreck,
Her limbecks dried of poisons
    And the knife at her neck,

The Queen of air and darkness
    Begins to shrill and cry,
"O young man, O my slayer,
    To-morrow you shall die."

O Queen of air and darkness,
    I think 'tis truth you say,
And I shall die to-morrow;
    But you will die to-day.

34.

Here lie I, Martin Elginbrodde:
Ha'e mercy o' my soul, Lord God,
As I wad do, were I Lord God
And ye were Martin Elginbrodde.

35. CHARLES II

Here lies our sovereign Lord the King,
    Whose word no man relies on,
Who never said a foolish thing,
    Nor ever did a wise one.

36. THE GRAMMARIAN'S FUNERAL

(HERE's the town-gate reached: there's the market-
    place
        Gaping before us.)
Yea, this in him was the peculiar grace
        (Hearten our chorus!)
That before living he'd learn how to live—
        No end to learning:
Earn the means first—God surely will contrive
        Use for our earning.
Others mistrust and say, "But time escapes:
        "Live now or never!"
He said, "What's time?   Leave Now for dogs and
    apes!
        "Man has Forever."
Back to his book then: deeper drooped his head:
        Calculus racked him:
Leaden before, his eyes grew dross of lead:
        Tussis attacked him.

.   .   .   .

He ventured neck or nothing—heaven's success
        Found, or earth's failure:
"Wilt thou trust death or not?"   He answered
        "Yes:
        "Hence with life's pale lure!"
That low man seeks a little thing to do,
        Sees it and does it:
This high man, with a great thing to pursue,
        Dies ere he knows it.
That low man goes on adding one to one,
        His hundred's soon hit:

This high man, aiming at a million,
　　　　Misses an unit.

．　　．　　．　　．　　．　　．　　．　　．　　．

So, with the throttling hands of death at strife,
　　　　Ground he at grammar;
Still, thro' the rattle, parts of speech were rife:
　　　　While he could stammer
He settled *Hoti*'s business—let it be!—
　　　　Properly based *Oun*—
Gave us the doctrine of the enclitic *De*,
　　　　Dead from the waist down.
Well, here's the platform, here's the proper place:
　　　　Hail to your purlieus,
All ye highfliers of the feathered race,
　　　　Swallows and curlews!
Here's the top-peak; the multitude below
　　　　Live, for they can, there:
This man decided not to Live but Know—
　　　　Bury this man there?
Here—here's his place, where meteors shoot, clouds
　　　form,
　　　　Lightnings are loosened,
Stars come and go! Let joy break with the storm,
　　　　Peace let the dew send!
Lofty designs must close in like effects:
　　　　Loftily lying,
Leave him—still loftier than the world suspects,
　　　　Living and dying.

37. THE LEADEN ECHO

How to kéep—is there ány any, is there none such,
    nowhere known some, bow or brooch or braid
    or brace, láce, latch or catch or key to keep
Back beauty, keep it, beauty, beauty, beauty,
    . . . from vanishing away?
Ó is there no frowning of these wrinkles, rankèd
    wrinkles deep,
Dówn? no waving off of these most mournful
    messengers, still messengers, sad and stealing
    messengers of grey?
No there's none, there's none, O no there's none,
Nor can you long be, what you now are, called fair,
Do what you may do, what, do what you may,
And wisdom is early to despair:
Be beginning; since, no, nothing can be done
To keep at bay
Age and age's evils, hoar hair,
Ruck and wrinkle, drooping, dying, death's worst,
    winding sheets, tombs and worms and tumbling
    to decay;
So be beginning, be beginning to despair.
O there's none; no no no there's none:
Be beginning to despair, to despair,
Despair, despair, despair, despair.

38.

I CLIMB'D the roofs at break of day;
Sun-smitten Alps before me lay.
    I stood among the silent statues,
And statued pinnacles, mute as they.

43

How faintly-flush'd, how phantom-fair,
Was Monte Rosa, hanging there.
   A thousand shadowy-pencill'd valleys
And snowy dells in a golden air.

Remember how we came at last
To Como; shower and storm and blast
   Had blown the lake beyond his limit,
And all was flooded; and how we past

From Como, when the light was gray,
And in my head, for half the day,
   The rich Virgilian rustic measure
Of Lari Maxume, all the way,

Like ballad-burthen music, kept,
As on The Lariano crept
   To that fair port below the castle
Of Queen Theodolind, where we slept. . .

39. HOPE

I GAVE to Hope a Watch of mine: but he
   An Anchor gave to me.
Then a old Prayer-book I did present:
   And he an Optick sent.

With that I gave a Phial full of tears:
   But he a few green ears.
Ah, loiterer! I'll no more, no more I'll bring:
   I did expect a Ring.

I HAVE met them at close of day
Coming with vivid faces
From counter or desk among grey
Eighteenth-century houses.
I have passed with a nod of the head
Or polite meaningless words,
Or have lingered awhile and said
Polite meaningless words,
And thought before I had done
Of a mocking tale or a gibe
To please a companion
Around the fire at the club,
Being certain that they and I
But lived where motley is worn:
All changed, changed utterly:
A terrible beauty is born.

That woman's days were spent
In ignorant good will,
Her nights in argument
Until her voice grew shrill.
What voice more sweet than hers
When, young and beautiful,
She rode to harriers?
This man had kept a school
And rode our wingèd horse;
This other his helper and friend
Was coming into his force;
He might have won fame in the end,
So sensitive his nature seemed,
So daring and sweet his thought.

This other man I had dreamed
A drunken, vainglorious lout.
He had done most bitter wrong
To some who are near my heart,
Yet I number him in the song;
He, too, has resigned his part
In the casual comedy;
He, too, has been changed in his turn,
Transformed utterly:
A terrible beauty is born.

Hearts with one purpose alone
Through summer and winter seem
Enchanted to a stone
To trouble the living stream.
The horse that comes from the road,
The rider, the birds that range
From cloud to tumbling cloud,
Minute by minute they change;
A shadow of cloud on the stream
Changes minute by minute;
A horse-hoof slides on the brim,
And a horse plashes within it;
The long-legged moor-hens dive,
And hens to moor-cocks call;
Minute by minute they live:
The stone's in the midst of all.

Too long a sacrifice
Can make a stone of the heart.
O when may it suffice?

That is Heaven's part, our part
To murmur name upon name,
As a mother names her child
When sleep at last has come
On limbs that had run wild.
What is it but nightfall?
No, no, not night but death;
Was it needless death after all?
For England may keep faith
For all that is done and said.
We know their dream; enough
To know they dreamed and are dead;
And what if excess of love
Bewildered them till they died?
I write it out in a verse—
MacDonagh and MacBride
And Connolly and Pearse
Now and in time to be,
Wherever green is worn,
Are changed, changed utterly:
A terrible beauty is born.

41.

I HAVE no pain, dear mother, now,
But oh! I am so dry.
Connect me to a brewery
And leave me there to die.

42. TO FLAXMAN

I MOCK thee not, though I by thee am mockèd.
Thou call'st me madman, but I call thee
blockhead.

43. THE SUNLIT VALE

I SAW the sunlit vale, and the pastoral fairy-tale;
The sweet and bitter scent of the may drifted by;
And never have I seen such a bright bewildering
green,
But it looked like a lie,
Like a kindly meant lie.

When gods are in dispute, one a Sidney, one a
brute,
It would seem that human sense might not know,
might not spy;
But though nature smile and feign where foul
play has stabbed and slain,
There's a witness, an eye,
Nor will charms blind that eye.

Nymph of the upland song and the sparkling leafage
young,
For your merciful desire with these charms to
beguile,
For ever be adored; muses yield you rich reward;
But you fail, though you smile—
That other does not smile.

44. THE COLLAR

I STRUCK the board, and cried, 'No more;
    I will abroad.
What! shall I ever sigh and pine?
My lines and life are free; free as the road,
  Loose as the wind, as large as store.
    Shall I be still in suit?
  Have I no harvest but a thorn
  To let me blood, and not restore
What I have lost with cordial fruit?
      Sure there was wine
Before my sighs did dry it: there was corn
    Before my tears did drown it.
Is the year only lost to me?
    Have I no bays to crown it?
No flowers, no garlands gay? all blasted?
      All wasted?
Not so, my heart; but there is fruit,
      And thou hast hands.
  Recover all thy sigh-blown age
On double pleasures: leave thy cold dispute
Of what is *fit, and not*: forsake thy cage,
      Thy rope of sands,
Which petty thoughts have made, and made to
    thee
  Good cable, to enforce and draw,
      And be thy law,
  While thou didst wink and wouldst not see.
      Away; take heed:
      I will abroad.
Call in thy death's-head there: tie up thy fears.

He that forbears
To suit and serve his need,
Deserves his load.'
But as I raved and grew more fierce and wild
At every word,
Methought I heard one calling, 'Child':
And I replied, 'My Lord.'

45. LAMENT FOR THE MAKARIS [1]

I THAT in heill [2] wes and gladnes,
Am trublit now with gret seiknes,
And feblit with infermite;
Timor mortis conturbat me.

Our plesance heir is all vane glory,
This fals warld is bot transitory,
The flesche is brukle, the Fend is sle [3];
Timor mortis conturbat me.

The stait of man does change and vary,
Now sound, now seik, now blith, now sary,
Now dansand mery, now like to dee;
Timor mortis conturbat me.

. . . .

On to the ded gois all Estatis,
Princis, Prelotis, and Potestatis,
Baith riche and pur of al degre;
Timor mortis conturbat me.

. . . .

[1] poets.   [2] health.   [3] cunning.

He takis the campion in the stour,[1]
The capitane closit in the tour,
The lady in bour full of bewte;
   Timor mortis conturbat me.

He sparis no lord for his piscence,[2]
Na clerk for his intelligence;
His awfull strak may no man fle;
   Timor mortis conturbat me.

Art, magicianis, and astrologgis,
Rethoris, logicianis, and theologgis,
Thame helpis no conclusionis sle,
   Timor mortis conturbat me.

. . . .

He hes done petuously devour,
The noble Chaucer, of makaris flour,
The Monk of Bery, and Gower, all thre;
   Timor mortis conturbat me.

That scorpion fell hes done infek [3]
Maister Johne Clerk, and James Afflek,
Fra balat making and tragidie;
   Timor mortis conturbat me.

. . . .

He hes reft Merseir his endite,
That did in luf so lifly write,
So schort, so quyk, of sentence hie;
   Timor mortis conturbat me.

. . . .

[1] conflict.   [2] power.   [3] made incapable.

Sen he hes all my brether tane,
He will nocht lat me lif alane,
On forse I man his nyxt pray be;
    Timor mortis conturbat me.

Sen for the deid remeid is none,
Best is that we for dede dispone,
Eftir our deid that lif may we;
    Timor mortis conturbat me.

46. THE EVERLASTING PERCY
or Mr Masefield on the Railway Centenary

I USED to be a fearful lad,
The things I did were downright bad;
And worst of all were what I done
From seventeen to twenty-one
On all the railways far and wide
From sinfulness and shameful pride.

For several years I was so wicked
I used to go without a ticket,
And travelled underneath the seat
Down in the dust of people's feet,
Or else I sat as bold as brass
And told them 'Season,' in first-class.
In 1921, at Harwich,
I smoked in a non-smoking carriage;
I never knew what Life nor Art meant,
I wrote 'Reserved' on my compartment,
And once (I was a guilty man)
I swopped the labels in guard's van.

From 1922 to 4
I leant against the carriage door
Without a-looking at the latch;
And once, a-leaving Colney Hatch,
I put a huge and heavy parcel
Which I were taking to Newcastle,
Entirely filled with lumps of lead,
Up on the rack above my head;
And when it tumbled down, oh Lord!
I pulled communication cord.
The guard came round and said, 'You mule!
What have you done, you dirty fool?'
I simply sat and smiled, and said
'Is this train right for Holyhead?'
He said 'You blinking blasted swine,
You'll have to pay the five-pound fine.'
I gave a false name and address,
Puffed up with my vaingloriousness.
At Bickershaw and Strood and Staines
I've often got on moving trains,
And once alit at Norwood West
Before my coach had come to rest.
A window and a lamp I broke
At Chipping Sodbury and Stoke
And worse I did at Wissendine:
I threw out bottles on the line
And other articles as be
Likely to cause grave injury
To persons working on the line—
That's what I did at Wissendine.
I grew so careless what I'd do
Throwing things out, and dangerous too,

That, last and worst of all I'd done,
I threw a great sultana bun
Out of the train at Pontypridd—

*   *   *   *   *   *   *   *

It hit a platelayer, it did.
I thought that I should have to swing
And never hear the sweet birds sing.
The jury recommended mercy,
And that's how grace was given to Percy.

And now I have a motor-bike
And up and down the road I hike,
Seeing the pretty birds and flowers,
And windmills with their sails and towers,
And all the wide sweep of the downs,
And villages and country towns,
And hear the mowers mowing hay,
And smell the great sea far away!
And always keeping—cars be blowed!—
Well on the wrong side of the road,
And never heeding hoots nor warners,
Especially around the corners,
For even down the steepest hill
Redemption saves me from a spill.

I have a flapper on the carrier
And some day I am going to marry her.

I WAKE and feel the fell of dark, not day.
What hours, O what black hoürs we have spent
This night! what sights you, heart, saw; ways
    you went!
And more must, in yet longer light's delay.
  With witness I speak this. But where I say
Hours I mean years, mean life. And my lament
Is cries countless, cries like dead letters sent
To dearest him that lives alas! away.

  I am gall, I am heartburn. God's most deep
    decree
Bitter would have me taste: my taste was me;
Bones built in me, flesh filled, blood brimmed the
    curse.
  Selfyeast of spirit a dull dough sours. I see
The lost are like this, and their scourge to be
As I am mine, their sweating selves; but worse.

48. A POISON TREE

I WAS angry with my friend:
I told my wrath, my wrath did end.
I was angry with my foe:
I told it not, my wrath did grow.

And I water'd it in fears,
Night and morning with my tears;
And I sunnèd it with smiles,
And with soft deceitful wiles.

And it grew both day and night,
Till it bore an apple bright;
And my foe beheld it shine,
And he knew that it was mine,

And into my garden stole
When the night had veil'd the pole:
In the morning glad I see
My foe outstretch'd beneath the tree.

49. WISHES OF AN ELDERLY MAN

I WISH I loved the Human Race;
I wish I loved its silly face;
I wish I liked the way it walks;
I wish I liked the way it talks;
And when I'm introduced to one
I wish I thought *What Jolly Fun*!

50.

I WISH I weren't doing Divvers
It honestly gives me the shivers.
  I don't know the facts
  Of the Gospels and Acts
And to-morrow they'll drag all the rivers.

51. ODE TO EVENING

If aught of oaten stop, or pastoral song,
May hope, chaste Eve, to sooth thy modest ear,
   Like thy own solemn springs,
   Thy springs and dying gales;

O nymph reserved, while now the bright-haired sun
Sits in yon western tent, whose cloudy skirts,
   With brede ethereal wove,
   O'erhang his wavy bed:

Now air is hush'd, save where the weak-eyed bat
With short shrill shreak flits by on leathern wing,
   Or where the beetle winds
   His small but sullen horn,

As oft he rises, midst the twilight path
Against the pilgrim borne in heedless hum:
   Now teach me, maid composed,
   To breath some soften'd strain,

Whose numbers, stealing through thy darkening
     vale,
May not unseemly with its stillness suit,
   As, musing slow, I hail
   Thy genial loved return!

For when thy folding-star arising shows
His paly circlet, at his warning lamp
   The fragrant hours, and elves
   Who slept in buds the day,

And many a nymph who wreaths her brows with
    sedge,
And sheds the freshening dew, and, lovelier still,
    The pensive pleasures sweet,
    Prepare thy shadowy car:

Then lead, calm votaress, where some sheety lake
Cheers the lone heath, or sometime-hallowed pile,
    Or upland fallows grey
    Reflect its last cool gleam.

Or if chill blustering winds, or driving rain,
Prevent my willing feet, be mine the hut
    That from the mountain's side
    Views wilds and swelling floods,

And hamlets brown, and dim-discover'd spires,
And hears their simple bell, and marks o'er all
    Thy dewy fingers draw
    The gradual dusky veil.

While spring shall pour his show'rs, as oft he
    wont,
And bathe thy breathing tresses, meekest Eve!
    While Summer loves to sport
    Beneath thy lingering light;

While sallow Autumn fills thy lap with leaves,
Or Winter, yelling through the troublous air,
    Affrights thy shrinking train,
    And rudely rends thy robes:

So long, regardful of thy quiet rule,
Shall Fancy, Friendship, Science, rose-lipp'd Health,
  Thy gentlest influence own,
  And hymn thy favorite name!

52.

    If the man who turnips cries,
    Cry not when his father dies,
    'Tis a proof that he had rather
    Have a turnip than his father.

53. HALLO MY FANCY

    In melancholic fancy,
    Out of myself,
    In the vulcan dancy,
    All the world surveying,
    Nowhere staying,
  Just like a fairy elf;
Out o'er the tops of highest mountains skipping,
Out o'er the hill, the trees and valleys tripping,
Out o'er the ocean seas, without an oar or shipping,—
  Hallo my fancy, whither wilt thou go?

    Amidst the misty vapours
    Fain would I know
    What doth cause the tapers;
    Why the clouds benight us
    And affright us,
    While we travel here below;

Fain would I know what makes the roaring thunder,
And what these lightnings be that rend the clouds
      asunder,
And what these comets are on which we gaze and
      wonder—
  Hallo my fancy, whither wilt thou go?

      Fain would I know the reason,
      Why the little ant,
      All the summer season,
      Layeth up provision
      On condition
   To know no winter's want.
And how housewives, that are so good and painful,
Do unto their husbands prove so good and gainful;
And why the lazy drones to them do prove dis-
      dainful—
  Hallo my fancy, whither wilt thou go?

.   .   .   .

      Amidst the foamy ocean,
      Fain would I know
      What doth cause the motion,
      And returning
      In its journeying,
   And doth so seldom swerve?
And how the little fishes that swim beneath salt
      waters,
Do never blind their eye; methinks it is a matter
An inch above the reach of old Erra Pater!—
  Hallo my fancy, whither wilt thou go?

Fain would I be resolvèd
How things are done;
And where the bull was calvèd
Of bloody Phalaris,
And where the tailor is
  That works to the man i' the moon!
Fain would I know how Cupid aims so rightly;
And how the little fairies do dance and leap so
    lightly,
And where fair Cynthia makes her ambles nightly—
  Hallo my fancy, whither wilt thou go?

    In conceit like Phaeton
    I'll mount Phoebus' chair
    Having ne'er a hat on,
    All my hair a-burning
    In my journeying;
  Hurrying through the air.
Fain would I hear his fiery horses neighing
And see how they on foamy bits are playing,
All the stars and planets I will be surveying!—
  Hallo my fancy, whither wilt thou go?

    O from what ground of nature
    Doth the pelican,
    That self devouring creature
    Prove so froward
    And untoward,
  Her vitals for to strain!
And why the subtle fox, while in death's wounds
    a-lying,
Do not lament his pangs by howling and by crying,

And why the milk-swan doth sing when she's
    a-dying—
  Hallo my fancy, whither wilt thou go?

      Fain would I conclude this,
      At least make essay;
      What similitude is:
      Why fowls of a feather
      Flock and fly together,
    And lambs know beasts of prey;
How Nature's alchemists, these small laborious
    creatures,
Acknowledge still a prince in ordering their matters,
And suffer none to live who slothing lose their
    features—
  Hallo my fancy, whither wilt thou go?

  .   .   .   .

      To know this world's centre
      Height, depth, breadth and length,
      Fain would I adventure
      To search the hid attractions
      Of magnetic actions
    And adamantine strength.
Fain would I know, if in some lofty mountain,
Where the moon sojourns, if there be tree or fountain;
If there be beasts of prey, or yet be fields to hunt in—
  Hallo my fancy, whither wilt thou go? . . .

      Hallo my fancy, hallo,
      Stay, stay at home with me,
      I can no longer follow,

For thou hast betrayed me,
And bewrayed me;
It is too much for thee.
Stay, stay at home with me, leave off thy lofty
soaring;
Stay then at home with me, and on thy books be
poring;
For he that goes abroad, lays little up in storing—
Thou'rt welcome my fancy, welcome home to me.

54.

In that colde and frosty regioun,
Ther as Mars hath his sovereyn mancioun.
First on the wal was peynted a foreste,
In which ther dwellede neyther man ne beste,
With knotty knarry bareyn trees olde
Of stubbes scharpe and hidous to byholde;
In which ther ran a swymbul in a swough,[1]
As though a storme schulde bersten every bough:
And downward on an hil under a bent,
Ther stood the tcmpul of Marz armypotent,
Wrought al of burned steel, of which thentre
Was long and streyt, and gastly for to see.
And therout came a rage of suche a prise,
That it maad al the gates for to rise.
The northen light in at the dore schon,
For wyndow on the walle ne was ther noon,
Thorough the which men might no light discerne.
The dores wer alle ademauntz eterne,

[1] a soughing in the wind.

I-clenched overthward and endelong
With iren tough; and, for to make it strong,
Every piler the tempul to susteene
Was tonne greet, of iren bright and schene.
Ther saugh I furst the derk ymaginyng
Of felony, and al the compassyng;
The cruel ire, as reed as eny gleede [1];
The pikepurs, and eek the pale drede;
The smyler with the knyf under his cloke;
The schipne brennyng with the blake smoke;
The tresoun of the murtheryng in the bed;
The open werres, with woundes al bi-bled;
Contek with bloody knyf, and scharp manace.
Al ful of chirkyng [2] was that sory place.
The sleer of himself yet saugh I there,
His herte-blood hath bathed al his here;
The nayl y-dryve in the schode [3] a-nyght;
The colde deth, with mouth gapyng upright.
Amyddes of the tempul set meschaunce,
With sory comfort and evel contynaunce.
Yet I saugh woodnes [4] laughyng in his rage;
The hunte strangled with wilde bores corage.
The caraigne in the busche, with throte i-korve:
A thousand slayne, and not of qualme i-storve;
The tiraunt, with the pray bi force i-rafte;
The toune distroied, there was no thing lafte.
Yet saugh I brent the schippis hoppesteres [5];
The hunte strangled with the wilde beeres:
The sowe freten the child right in the cradel;
The cook i-skalded, for al his longe ladel.

---

[1] burning coal.   [2] hissing.   [3] head.   [4] madness.
[5] tossing ships.

Nought beth forgeten the infortune of Mart;
The carter over-ryden with his cart,
Under the whel ful lowe he lay adoun.
Ther wer also of Martz divisioun,
The barbour, and the bowcher, and the smyth
That forgeth scharpe swerdes on his stith.
And al above depeynted in a tour
Saw I conquest sittyng in gret honour,
With the scharpe swerd over his heed
Hangynge by a sotil twynes threed.

55.

In the first Rank of these did Zimri stand;
A man so various that he seem'd to be
Not one, but all Mankind's Epitome.
Stiff in opinions, always in the wrong;
Was everything by starts, and nothing long:
But, in the course of one revolving moon,
Was chymist, fiddler, statesman, and buffoon;
Then all for women, painting, rhyming, drinking,
Besides ten thousand freaks that died in thinking.
Blest madman, who could every hour employ
With something new to wish, or to enjoy!
Railing and praising were his usual themes,
And both (to show his judgment) in extremes:
So over violent, or over civil
That every man, with him, was God or Devil.
In squand'ring wealth was his peculiar art:
Nothing went unrewarded but desert.
Beggar'd by fools, whom still he found too late:
He had his jest, and they had his estate.

He laugh'd himself from court; then sought relief
By forming parties, but could ne'er be chief:
For, spite of him, the weight of business fell
On Absalom and wise Achitophel:
Thus, wicked but in will, of means bereft,
He left not faction, but of that was left.

56. THE NIGHT OF TRAFALGAR

I

In the wild October night-time, when the wind
    raved round the land,
And the Back-sea [1] met the Front-sea, and our doors
    were blocked with sand,
And we heard the drub of Dead-man's Bay, where
    bones of thousands are,
We knew not what the day had done for us at
    Trafalgár.
        (*All*) Had done,
             Had done,
        For us at Trafalgár!

II

"Pull hard, and make the Nothe, or down we go!"
    one says, says he.
We pulled; and bedtime brought the storm; but
    snug at home slept we.

[1] In those days the hind-part of the harbour adjoining this scene was so named, and at high tides the waves washed across the isthmus at a point called "The Narrows."

Yet all the while our gallants after fighting through
   the day,
Were beating up and down the dark, sou'-west of
   Cadiz Bay.
            The dark,
            The dark,
      Sou'-west of Cadiz Bay!

III

The victors and the vanquished then the storm it
   tossed and tore,
As hard they strove, those worn-out men, upon that
   surly shore;
Dead Nelson and his half-dead crew, his foes from
   near and far,
Were rolled together on the deep that night at
   Trafalgár!
            The deep,
            The deep,
      That night at Trafalgár!

57.

In valleys green and still
   Where lovers wander maying
They hear from over hill
   A music playing.

Behind the drum and fife,
   Past hawthornwood and hollow,
Through earth and out of life
   The soldiers follow.

The soldier's is the trade:
    In any wind or weather
He steals the heart of maid
    And man together.

The lover and his lass
    Beneath the hawthorn lying
Have heard the soldiers pass,
    And both are sighing.

And down the distance they
    With dying note and swelling
Walk the resounding way
    To the still dwelling.

58. ON THE MEETINGS OF THE SCOTCH COVENANTERS

INFORMER, art thou in the tree,
Take heed lest there thou hangèd be;
Look likewise to thy foothold well
Lest, if thou slip, thou fall to hell.

59. THE BARON OF BRACKLEY

INVEREY cam' doun Deeside, whistlin' and playin';
He was at brave Brackley's yates ere it was dawin'.

Says, 'Baron of Brackley, are ye within?
There's sharp swords at your yate will gar your blood spin.

Open the yate, Brackley, let us within,
Till on the green turf we gar your blood spin.'

68

The lady rase up, to the window she went;
She heard the kye lowin' o'er hill and o'er bent.

'O rise up, John,' she says, 'turn back your kye;
They're o'er the hills rinnin', they're skippin
    awye!'—

'Come to bed, Peggie, and let the kye rin:
For were I to gang out, I'd never get in.

For there is na gentlemen, not yet pretty lads,
But a curn[1] o' hired widdifu's,[2] wears belted plaids.'

Then she cry'd on her women, they quickly came
    ben:
'Tak' up your rocks, lasses, and fight a' like men!

Tho' I'm but a woman, to head you I'll try,
Nor let these vile Hielandmen steal a' our kye.'

Then up gat the Baron and cry'd for his graith[3];
Says, 'Lady, I'll gang, tho' to leave you I'm laith.

Come kiss me, my Peggie, and get me my gun;
For I well may gang out, but I'll never win in.'

When the Baron of Brackley he rade thro' the
    close
A gallanter gentleman ne'er mounted horse.

Tho' there cam' in with Inverey thirty and three,
There was nane wi' bold Brackley but his brither
    and he.

[1] small band.   [2] gallows birds.   [3] accoutrements.

69

Twa gallanter Gordons did never sword draw:
But against four and thirty, wae's me, what was
    twa?

Wi' swords and wi' daggers they did him surround,
And they've pierced the bold Brackley wi' mony a
    wound.

Frae the head o' the Dee to the banks o' the Spey
The Gordons may mourn him and ban Inverey.

'O cam' ye in by Brackley, and was ye in there?
Or saw ye his Peggy dear riving[1] her hair?'—

'O I cam' by Brackley, and I was in there,
But I saw-na his Peggy dear riving her hair'—

'O fye on ye, ladye! how could ye do sae?
You open'd your yate to the fause Inverey.'

She ate wi' him, drank wi' him, welcomed him in;
She's welcomed the villain that slew her Baròn.

She kept him till morning, syne bade him be
    gane,
And show'd him the road that he wouldna be ta'en.

'Thro' BirES and Aboyne,' she says, 'lyin' in a
    tour
O'er the hills o' Glentanor ye'll skip in an hour.'

There is dule in the kitchen, and mirth in the ha',
For the Baron of Brackley is dead and awa'.

But and up spak' the babe on his nourice's knee—
'Gin I live to be man, it's revenged I will be.'

[1] tearing.

60. ANIMULA

'Issues from the hand of God, the simple soul'
To a flat world of changing lights and noise,
To light, dark, dry or damp, chilly or warm;
Moving between the legs of tables and of chairs,
Rising or falling, grasping at kisses and toys,
Advancing boldly, sudden to take alarm,
Retreating to the corner of arm and knee,
Eager to be reassured, taking pleasure
In the fragrant brilliance of the Christmas tree,
Pleasure in the wind, the sunlight and the sea;
Studies the sunlit pattern on the floor
And running stags around a silver tray;
Confounds the actual and the fanciful,
Content with playing-cards and kings and queens,
What the fairies do and what the servants say.
The heavy burden of the growing soul
Perplexes and offends more, day by day;
Week by week, offends and perplexes more
With the imperatives of 'is and seems'
And may and may not, desire and control.
The pain of living and the drug of dreams
Curl up the small soul in the window seat
Behind the *Encyclopædia Britannica*.
Issues from the hand of time the simple soul
Irresolute and selfish, misshapen, lame,
Unable to fare forward or retreat,
Fearing the warm reality, the offered good,
Denying the importunity of the blood,
Shadow of its own shadows, spectre in its own
    gloom,

71

Leaving disordered papers in a dusty room;
Living first in the silence after the viaticum.

Pray for Guiterriez, avid of speed and power,
For Boudin, blown to pieces,
For this one who made a great fortune,
And that one who went his own way.
Pray for Floret, by the boarhound slain between the
     yew trees,
Pray for us now and at the hour of our birth.

61.

It is time that I wrote my will;
I choose upstanding men
That climb the streams until
The fountain leap, and at dawn
Drop their cast at the side
Of dripping stone; I declare
They shall inherit my pride,
The pride of people that were
Bound neither to Cause nor to State,
Neither to slaves that were spat on,
Nor to the tyrants that spat,
The people of Burke and of Grattan
That gave, though free to refuse—
Pride, like that of the morn,
When the headlong light is loose,
Or that of the fabulous horn,
Or that of the sudden shower
When all streams are dry,

Or that of the hour
When the swan must fix his eye
Upon a fading gleam,
Float out upon a long
Last reach of glittering stream
And there sing his last song.
And I declare my faith:
I mock Plotinus' thought
And cry in Plato's teeth,
Death and life were not
Till man made up the whole,
Made lock, stock and barrel
Out of his bitter soul,
Aye, sun and moon and star, all,
And further add to that
That, being dead, we rise,
Dream and so create
Translunar Paradise.
I have prepared my peace
With learned Italian things
And the proud stones of Greece,
Poet's imaginings
And memories of love,
Memories of the words of women,
All those things whereof
Man makes a superhuman
Mirror-resembling dream.

As at the loophole there
The daws chatter and scream,
And drop twigs layer upon layer.
When they have mounted up,

The mother bird will rest
On their hollow top,
And so warm her wild nest.

I leave both faith and pride
To young upstanding men
Climbing the mountain side,
That under bursting dawn
They may drop a fly;
Being of that metal made
Till it was broken by
This sedentary trade.

Now shall I make my soul,
Compelling it to study
In a learned school
Till the wreck of body,
Slow decay of blood,
Testy delirium
Or dull decrepitude,
Or what worse evil come—
The death of friends, or death
Of every brilliant eye
That made a catch in the breath—
Seem but the clouds of the sky
When the horizon fades;
Or a bird's sleepy cry
Among the deepening shades.

62.

IT's doon the Lang Stairs,
  And straight alang the Close,
All in Baker's Entry
  Adam Buckham knows.
O, Adam Buckham, O,
  O, Adam Buckham, O,
O, Adam Buckham, O,
  Wiv his bow legs.

Nanny carries water,
  Tommy cobbles shoes,
And Adam gans about,
  Geth'ring in the news.
      O, Adam Buckham, etc.

63. JUDAS

IT was upon a Maundy Thursday that our Lord
    arose;
Full mild were the words he spake to Judas:
'Judas, thou must to Jerusalem, our meat for to buy,
Thirty pieces of silver thou shalt take with thee.

Thou shalt come far into the broad street, far into
    the broad street;
Some of thy kinsmen there thou must meet.'

He has met with his sister, the wicked woman:
'Judas thou art *worthy* to be stoned with stone,
Judas, thou art worthy to be stoned with stone,
For the false prophet that thou believest on.'

'Be still, loved sister, lest thy heart break!
Wist my Lord Jesus, full well he would be wreke.'[1]

'Judas, go thou over rock, go thou over stone,
Lay thy head in my bosom, sleep thou anon.'

Soon as Judas from sleep was awake
Thirty pieces of silver from him were i-take.

He tore his hair, till his head was laved in blood;
The Jews in Jerusalem thought he was mad.

Towards him came the rich Jew that was called
    Pilatus:
'Wilt thou sell the Lord, that is called Jesus.'

'I wad sell my Lord for no kind of good
But it be for the thirty pieces that he entrust to me
    would.'

        .   .   .   .   .   .

In came our Lord, as his apostles sat at meat:
'Why sit ye, apostles, and why need ye eat.
Why sit ye apostles, and why need ye eat
I am bought and sold to-day for our meat.'

Up stood Judas 'Lord, is it I?
I was never in the place when thou spoke evil of me.'

Up stood Peter and spake with all his might:
'Though Pilatus came with ten hundred knights.
Though Pilatus came with ten hundred knights
Yet I will, Lord, for thy love fight.'

                [1] angry.

'Still be thou, Peter!   Well I thee know;
Thou will forsake me thrice ere the cock crow.'

64.

Jockie, thine horn pipe's dull;
Give wind, man, at full.
Fie on such a sad gull,
Like a hoody doody
　　All too moody.
　　Pipe it up thicker,
　　I'll tread it the quicker.
Why then about it roundly,
And I will foot it soundly,
I'll take my steps the shorter,
As if I trampled mortar.

Darité grows so grave,
I may not her have
In a round, when I crave.
　　With a hoop, sir, hoy day!
　　O you hurt me!
　　Set me thy work by,
　　And come to me smurkly.
Then if she chance to glance in,
Give us two room to dance in.
Though my green jerkin bare is,
Us two to all the parish!

65.

John the Miller hath ground small, small, small;
The King's son of heaven shall pay for all.
Be ware or you be woe;
Know your friend from your foe;
Have enough, and say 'Ho'[1];
And do well and better, and flee sin,
And seek peace, and hold thou therein.

66. LAPWING

Leaves, summer's coinage spent, golden are all
  together whirled,
sent spinning, dipping, slipping, shuffled by heavy-
  handed wind,
shifted sideways, sifted, lifted, and in swarms made to
  fly
spent sun-flies, gorgeous tatters, airdrift, pinions of
  trees.

Pennons of the autumn wind, flying the same loose
  flag,
minions of the rush of air, companions of draggled
  cloud,
tattered, scattered pell-mell, diving, with side-slip
  suddenly wailing
as they scale the uneasy sky flapping the lapwing
  fly.

[1] Pause!

Plover, with under the tail pine-red, dead leaf-
    wealth in down displayed,
crested with glancing crests, sheeny with seagreen,
    mirror of movement
of the deep sea horses plunging, restless, fretted by
    the whip of wind,
tugging green tons, wet waste, lugging a mass to
    Labrador.

See them fall wailing over high hill tops with hue and
    cry,
like uneasy ghosts slipping in the dishevelled air,
with ever so much of forlorn ocean and wastes of
    wind
in their elbowing of the air and in their lamentable
    call.

67.

LET the day perish wherein I was born, and the
night in which it was said, There is a man child
conceived.

Let that day be darkness; let not God regard it
from above, neither let the light shine upon it.

Let darkness and the shadow of death stain it;
let a cloud dwell upon it; let the blackness of the
day terrify it.

As for that night, let darkness seize upon it; let
it not be joined unto the days of the year, let it not
come into the number of the months.

Lo, let that night be solitary, let no joyful voice
come therein.

Let them curse it that curse the day, who are ready to raise up their mourning.

Let the stars of the twilight thereof be dark; let it look for light, but have none; neither let it see the dawning of the day:

Because it shut not up the doors of my mother's womb, nor hid sorrow from mine eyes.

Why died I not from the womb? why did I not give up the ghost when I came out of the belly?

Why did the knees prevent me? or why the breasts that I should suck?

For now should I have lain still and been quiet, I should have slept; then had I been at rest,

With kings and counsellors of the earth, which built desolate places for themselves;

Or with princes that had gold, who filled their houses with silver:

Or as an hidden untimely birth I had not been; as infants which never saw light.

There the wicked cease from troubling; and there the weary be at rest.

There the prisoners rest together; they hear not the voice of the oppressor.

The small and great are there; and the servant is free from his master.

Wherefore is light given to him that is in misery, and life unto the bitter in soul;

Which long for death, but it cometh not; and dig for it more than for hid treasures;

Which rejoice exceedingly, and are glad, when they can find the grave?

Why is light given to a man whose way is hid, and whom God hath hedged in?

For my sighing cometh before I eat, and my roarings are poured out like the waters.

For the thing which I greatly feared is come upon me, and that which I was afraid of is come unto me.

I was not in safety, neither had I rest, neither was I quiet; yet trouble came.

68. THE CITY IN THE SEA

Lo! Death has reared himself a throne
In a strange city lying alone
Far down within the dim West,
Where the good and the bad and the worst and the
    best
Have gone to their eternal rest.
There shrines and palaces and towers
(Time-eaten towers that tremble not!)
Resemble nothing that is ours.
Around, by lifting winds forgot,
Resignedly beneath the sky
The melancholy waters lie.
No rays from the Holy Heaven come down
On the long night-time of that town;
But light from out the lurid sea
Streams up the turrets silently—
Gleams up the pinnacles far and free—
Up domes—up spires—up kingly halls—
Up fanes—up Babylon-like walls—
Up shadowy long-forgotten bowers
Of sculptured ivy and stone flowers—

Up many and many a marvellous shrine
Whose wreathéd friezes intertwine
The viol, the violet, and the vine.
Resignedly beneath the sky
The melancholy waters lie.
So blend the turrets and shadows there
That all seem pendulous in air,
While from a proud tower in the town
Death looks gigantically down. . . .

69. FRAGMENT OF AN ODE TO MAIA

MOTHER of Hermes! and still youthful Maia!
      May I sing to thee
As thou wast hymned on the shores of Baiae?
      Or may I woo thee
In earlier Siclian? or thy smiles
Seek as they once were sought, in Grecian isles,
By bards who died content on pleasant sward,
      Leaving great verse unto a little clan?
O, give me their old vigour, and unheard
      Save of the quiet Primrose, and the span
      Of heaven and few ears,
Rounded by thee, my song should die away
      Content as theirs,
Rich in the simple worship of a day.

70. TO THE LORD HIGH TREASURER

My Lord,
Poor wretched States, prest by extremities,

82

Are fain to seek for succours and supplies
Of Princes' aids, or good men's charities.

Disease the Enemy, and his engineers,
Want, with the rest of his conceal'd compeers,
Have cast a trench about me, now five years,

And made those strong approaches by false brays,
Redouts, half-moons, horn-works, and such close
    ways,
The Muse not peeps out, one of hundred days,

But lies block'd up, and straiten's, narrow'd in,
Fix'd to the bed and boards, unlike to win
Health, or scarce breath, as she had never been;

Unless some saving honour of the Crown,
Dare think it, to relieve, no less renown,
A Bed-rid Wit, than a Besieged Town.

71. THE SHOW

We have fallen in the dreams the ever-living
Breathe on the tarnished mirror of the world,
And then smooth out with ivory hands and sigh.
                                    [W. B. YEATS.]

MY soul looked down from a vague height with
    Death,
As unremembering how I rose or why,
And saw a sad land, weak with sweats of dearth,
Gray, cratered like the moon with hollow woe,
And pitted with great pocks and scabs of plagues.

Across its beard, that horror of harsh wire,
There moved thin caterpillars, slowly uncoiled.
It seemed they pushed themselves to be as plugs
Of ditches, where they writhed and shrivelled,
    killed.

By them had slimy paths been trailed and scraped
Round myriad warts that might be little hills.

From gloom's last dregs these long-strung creatures
    crept,
And vanished out of dawn down hidden holes.

(And smell came up from those foul openings
As out of mouths, or deep wounds deepening.)

On dithering feet upgathered, more and more,
Brown strings, towards strings of gray, with bristling
    spines,
All migrants from green fields, intent on mire.

Those that were gray, of more abundant spawns,
Ramped on the rest and ate them and were eaten.

I saw their bitten backs curve, loop, and straighten,
I watched those agonies curl, lift, and flatten.
Whereat, in terror what that sight might mean,
I reeled and shivered earthward like a feather.

And Death fell with me, like a deepening moan.
And He, picking a manner of worm, which half
    had hid
Its bruises in the earth, but crawled no further,
Showed me its feet, the feet of many men,
And the fresh-severed head of it, my head.

72.

NATURE's great masterpiece, an elephant
(The only harmless great thing), the giant
Of beasts, who thought none had to make him
    wise,
But to be just and thankful, loth to offend
(Yet nature hath given him no knees to bend)
Himself he up-props, on himself relies,
And, foe to none, suspects no enemies,
Still sleeping stood; vex'd not his fantasy
Black dreams; like an unbent bow carelessly
His sinewy proboscis did remissly lie.

73.

Now Night descending, the proud scene was o'er,
But liv'd, in Settle's[1] numbers, one day more.
Now Mayors and Shrieves all hush'd and satiate
    lay,
Yet ate, in dreams, the custard of the day;
While pensive Poets painful vigils keep.
Sleepless themselves, to give their readers sleep.

.   .   .   .

Swearing and supperless the Hero sate,
Blasphem'd his Gods, the Dice, and damn'd his
    Fate.
Then gnaw'd his pen, then dash'd it on the ground,
Sinking from thought to thought, a vast profound!
Plung'd for his sense, but found no bottom there,
Yet wrote and flounder'd on, in mere despair.

[1] Poet employed by the City of London to compose
panegyrics on the Lord Mayors, and verses for pageants.

Round him much Embryo, much Abortion lay,
Much future Ode, and abdicated Play;
Nonsense precipitate, like running Lead,
That slipp'd thro' cracks and zig-zags of the head;
All that on Folly Frenzy could beget,
Fruits of dull heat, and Sooterkins of wit.
Next, o'er his Books his eyes began to roll,
In pleasing memory of all he stole;
How here he sipp'd, how there he plunder'd snug,
And suck'd all o'er, like an industrious Bug.
Here lay poor Fletcher's half-eat scenes, and here
The frippery of crucified Molière;
There hapless Shakespear, yet of Tibbald sore,
Wish'd he had blotted for himself before.
The rest on outside merit but presume,
Or serve (like other Fools) to fill a room;
Such with their shelves as due proportion hold,
Or their fond parents dressed in red and gold;
Or where the pictures for the page atone,
And Quarles is sav'd by beauties not his own.
Here swells the shelf with Ogilby the Great;
There, stamp'd with arms, Newcastle shines com-
　　　plete: 　.　　.　　.　　.　　.　　.　　.
A Gothic Library! of Greece and Rome
Well purg'd, and worthy Settle, Banks, and Broome.
　　But, high above, more solid Learning shone,
The Classics of an Age that heard of none;
There Caxton slept, with Wynkyn at his side,
One clasp'd in wood, and one in strong cow-
　　　hide;
There sav'd by spice, like mummies, many a year,
Dry bodies of divinity appear:

De Lyra there a dreadful front extends,
And here the groaning shelves Philemon bends.
  Of these twelve volumes, twelve of amplest size,
Redeem'd from tapers and defrauded pies,
Inspir'd he seizes: these an altar raise:
A hecatomb of pure, unsullied lays
That altar crowns: a folio Common-place
Founds the whole pile, of all his works the base:
Quartos, octavos, shape the less'ning pyre;
A twisted Birth-day Ode completes the spire.
  Then he: Great Tamer of all human art!
First in my care, and ever at my heart;
Dulness! whose good old cause I yet defend,
With whom my Muse began, with whom shall end.

      .   .   .   .

O! ever gracious to perplex'd mankind,
Still spread a healing mist before the mind;
And, lest we err by Wit's wild dancing light,
Secure us kindly in our native night.
Or, if to Wit a coxcomb make pretence,
Guard the sure barrier between that and Sense.

74. IN MEMORY OF MAJOR ROBERT GREGORY

I

Now that we're almost settled in our house
I'll name the friends that cannot sup with us
Beside a fire of turf in th' ancient tower,
And having talked to some late hour
Climb up the narrow winding stair to bed:

Discoverers of forgotten truth
Or mere companions of my youth,
All, all are in my thoughts to-night being dead.

II

Always we'd have the new friend meet the old
And we are hurt if either friend seem cold,
And there is salt to lengthen out the smart
In the affections of our heart,
And quarrels are blown up upon that head;
But not a friend that I would bring
This night can set us quarrelling,
For all that come into my mind are dead.

III

Lionel Johnson comes the first to mind,
That loved his learning better than mankind,
Though courteous to the worst; much falling he
Brooded upon sanctity
Till all his Greek and Latin learning seemed
A long blast upon the horn that brought
A little nearer to his thought
A measureless consummation that he dreamed.

IV

And that enquiring man John Synge comes next,
That dying chose the living world for text
And never could have rested in the tomb
But that, long travelling, he had come
Towards nightfall upon certain set apart
In a most desolate stony place,
Towards nightfall upon a race
Passionate and simple like his heart.

And then I think of old George Pollexfen,
In muscular youth well known to Mayo men
For horsemanship at meets or at racecourses,
That could have shown how pure-bred horses
And solid men, for all their passion, live
But as the outrageous stars incline
By opposition, square and trine;
Having grown sluggish and contemplative.

VI

They were my close companions many a year,
A portion of my mind and life, as it were,
And now their breathless faces seem to look
Out of some old picture-book;
I am accustomed to their lack of breath,
But not that my dear friend's dear son,
Our Sidney and our perfect man,
Could share in that discourtesy of death.

VII

For all things the delighted eye now sees
Were loved by him; the old storm-broken trees
That cast their shadows upon road and bridge;
The tower set on the streams edge;
The ford where drinking cattle make a stir
Nightly, and startled by that sound
The water-hen must change her ground;
He might have been your heartiest welcomer.

When with the Galway foxhounds he would ride
From Castle Taylor to the Roxborough side
Or Esserkelly plain, few kept his pace;
At Mooneen he had leaped a place
So perilous that half the astonished meet
Had shut their eyes; and where was it
He rode a race without a bit?
And yet his mind outran the horses' feet.

IX

We dreamed that a great painter had been born
To cold Clare rock and Galway rock and thorn,
To that stern colour and that delicate line
That are our secret discipline
Wherein the gazing heart doubles her might.
Soldier, scholar, horseman, he,
And yet he had the intensity
To have published all to be a world's delight.

X

What other could so well have counselled us
In all the lovely intricacies of a house
As he that practised or that understood
All work in metal or in wood,
In moulded plaster or in carven stone?
Soldier, scholar, horseman, he,
And all he did done perfectly
As though he had but that one trade alone.

XI

Some burn damp faggots, others may consume
The entire combustible world in one small room
As though dried straw, and if we turn about
The bare chimney is gone black out
Because the work had finished in that flare.
Soldier, scholar, horseman, he,
As 'twere all life's epitome.
What made us dream that he could comb grey
    hair?

XII

I had thought, seeing how bitter is that wind
That shakes the shutter, to have brought to mind
All those that manhood tried, or childhood loved
Or boyish intellect approved,
With some appropriate commentary on each;
Until imagination brought
A fitter welcome; but a thought
Of that late death took all my heart for speech.

75.

OH Happiness! our being's end and aim!
  Good, Pleasure, Ease, Content! whate'er thy
    name:
That something still which prompts th' eternal sigh,
For which we bear to live, or dare to die;
Which still so near us, yet beyond us lies,
O'erlook'd, seen double, by the fool and wise.
Plant of celestial seed! if dropp'd below,
Say, in what mortal soil thou deign'st to grow?

Fair op'ning to some Court's propitious shine,
Or deep with diamonds in the flaming mine?
Twin'd with the wreaths Parnassian laurels yield,
Or reap'd in iron harvests of the field?
Where grow?——where grows it not? If vain our
    toil,
We ought to blame the culture, not the soil.
Fix'd to no spot is Happiness sincere,
Tis nowhere to be found, or every where. . . .

76.

OH! if to dance all night, and dress all day,
Charm'd the small-pox, or chas'd old age away;
Who would not scorn what housewife's cares produce,
Or who would learn one earthly thing of use?

77.

O METAPHYSICAL tobacco,
Fetched as far as from Morocco,
        Thy searching fume
        Exhales the rheum,
O metaphysical tobacco.

78. THE QUEER

O TELL me whence that joy doth spring,
    Whose diet is divine and fair,
Which wears Heaven like a bridal ring,
    And tramples on doubts and despair?

Whose Eastern traffique deals in bright
　And boundless empyrean themes,
Mountains of space, day-stars and light,
　Green trees of life, and living streams?

Tell me, O tell, who did thee bring,
　And here without my knowledge plac'd;
Till thou didst grow and get a wing,
　A wing with eyes, and eyes that taste?

Sure, *Holyness* the magnet is,
　And *love* the lure, that woos thee down:
Which makes the high transcendent bliss
　Of knowing thee, so rarely known!

79.

On thou, that dear and happy isle,
The garden of the world erewhile,
Thou Paradise of the four seas,
Which heaven planted us to please,
But, to exclude the world, did guard
With watery, if not flaming sword,—
What luckless apple did we taste,
To make us mortal, and thee waste?
Unhappy! shall we never more
That sweet militia restore,
When gardens only had their towers
And all the garrisons were flowers;
When roses only arms might bear,
And men did rosy garlands wear?

Tulips, in several colours barred,
Were then the Switzers of our guard;
The gardener had the soldier's place,
And his more gentle forts did trace;
The nursery of all things green
Was then the only magazine;
The winter quarters were the stoves,
Where he the tender plants removes.
But war all this doth overgrow:
We ordnance plant, and powder sow.

80. ADDRESS TO THE DEIL

O THOU! whatever title suit thee,
Auld Hornie, Satan, Nick or Clootie,
Wha in yon cavern grim an' sootie,
   Clos'd under hatches,
Spairges [1] about the brunstane cootie,[2]
   To scaud poor wretches!

Hear me, auld Hangie, for a wee,
An' let poor damnèd bodies be;
I'm sure sma' pleasure it can gie,
   Ev'n to a deil,
To skelp [3] and scaud poor dogs like me,
   An' hear us squeal!

Great is thy pow'r an' great thy fame;
Far kenn'd an' noted is thy name;

[1] splashes. [2] brimstone pail. [3] beat.

An', tho' yon lowin heugh's [1] thy hame,
   Thou travels far;
An' faith! thou's neither lag [2] nor lame,
   Nor blate [3] nor scaur. [4]

Whyles rangin' like a roarin' lion
For prey, a' holes an' corners tryin';
Whyles on the strong-wing'd tempest flyin',
   Tirlin' [5] the kirks;
Whyles, in the human bosom pryin',
   Unseen thou lurks.

I've heard my reverend grannie say,
In lanely glens ye like to stray;
Or, where auld ruin'd castles gray
   Nod to the moon,
Ye fright the nightly wand'rer's way,
   Wi' eldritch croon.

When twilight did my grannie summon
To say her pray'rs, douce, honest woman!
Aft yont the dyke she's heard you bummin',
   Wi' eerie drone;
Or, rustlin', thro' the boortrees comin',
   Wi' heavy groan.

Ae dreary windy winter night
The stars shot down wi' sklentin' light,
Wi' you mysel I gat a fright
   Ayont the lough;
Ye like a rash-buss [6] stood in sight
   Wi' waving sough.

---

[1] flaming pit.   [2] tired.   [3] shy.
[4] frightened.   [5] unroofing.   [6] rush-bush.

The cudgel in my nieve [1] did shake,
Each bristled hair stood like a stake,
When wi' an eldritch stoor 'quaick, quaick,'
    Amang the springs,
Awa ye squatter'd like a drake
      On whistlin' wings.

Let warlocks grim and wither'd hags
Tell how wi' you on ragweed nags
They skim the muirs, an' dizzy crags
    Wi' wicked speed;
And in kirk-yards renew their leagues
      Owre howkit [2] dead.

  .   .   .   .   .   .

Thence mystic knots mak great abuse
On young guidmen, fond, keen, an' crouse; [3]
When the best wark-lume i' the house,
    By cantrip [4] wit,
Is instant made no worth a louse,
      Just at the bit.

When thowes dissolve the snawy hoord,
An' float the jinglin' icy-boord,
Then water-kelpies haunt the foord,
    By your direction,
An' 'nighted trav'llers are allur'd
      To their destruction.

An' aft your moss-traversing spunkies
Decoy the wight that late an' drunk is;

[1] hand.   [2] dug-up.   [3] lively.   [4] magic.

The bleezin', curst, mischievous monkies
　　　　Delude his eyes,
Till in some miry slough he sunk is,
　　　　Ne'er mair to rise.

When masons' mystic word an' grip
In storms an' tempests raise you up,
Some cock or cat your rage maun stop,
　　　　Or, strange to tell!
The youngest brither ye wad whip
　　　　Aff straught to hell.

Lang syne in Eden's bonnie yard,
When youthfu' lovers first were pair'd,
And all the soul of love they shar'd,
　　　　The raptured hour,
Sweet on the fragrant flow'ry swaird,
　　　　In shady bow'r;

Then you, ye auld snick-drawing dog!
Ye cam to Paradise incog.
An' play'd on man a cursèd brogue,[1]
　　　　(Black be your fa'!)
An' gied the infant warld a shog,
　　　　'Maist ruin'd a'.

D'ye mind that day, when in a bizz,
Wi' reekit duds,[2] an' reestit gizz,[3]
Ye did present your smoutie phiz
　　　　'Mang better folk,
An' sklented on the man of Uz
　　　　Your spitefu' joke?

---

[1] trick.　　　[2] smoking clothes.　　　[3] shrivelled wig.

An' how ye gat him i' your thrall,
An' brak him out o' house an' hal',
While scabs an' blotches did him gall
        Wi' bitter claw,
An' lows'd his ill-tongu'd wicked scawl,[1]
        Was warst ava?

But a' your doings to rehearse,
Your wily snares an' fechtin' fierce,
Sin' that day Michael did you pierce,
        Down to this time,
Wad ding a' Lallan tongue, or Erse,
        In prose or rhyme.

An' now, auld Cloots, I ken ye're thinkin'
A certain Bardie's rantin', drinkin',
Some luckless hour will send him linkin',
        To your black pit;
But faith! he'll turn a corner jinkin',
        An' cheat you yet.

But fare you weel, auld Nickie-Ben!
O wad ye tak a thought an' men'!
Ye aiblins[2] might—I dinna ken—
        Still hae a stake:
I'm wae to think upo' yon den,
        Ev'n for your sake!

[1] nagging wife.   [2] perhaps.

81.

O you chorus of indolent reviewers,
Irresponsible, indolent reviewers,
Look, I come to the test, a tiny poem
All composed in a metre of Catullus,
All in quantity, careful of my motion,
Like the skater on ice that hardly bears him,
Lest I fall unawares before the people,
Waking laughter in indolent reviewers.
Should I flounder awhile without a tumble
Thro' this metrification of Catullus,
They should speak to me not without a welcome,
All that chorus of indolent reviewers.
Hard, hard, hard is it, only not to tumble,
So fantastical is the dainty metre.
Wherefore slight me not wholly, nor believe me
Too presumptuous, indolent reviewers.
O blatant Magazines, regard me rather—
Since I blush to belaud myself a moment—
As some rare little rose, a piece of inmost
Horticultural art, or half coquette-like
Maiden, not to be greeted unbenignly.

82.

OF this bad world the loveliest and the best
Has smiled and said 'Good Night,' and gone to
    rest.

83.

OLD YEW, which graspest at the stones
   That name the under-lying dead,
   Thy fibres net the dreamless head,
Thy roots are wrapt about the bones.

The seasons bring the flower again,
   And bring the firstling to the flock;
   And in the dust of thee, the clock,
Beats out the little lives of men.

O not for thee the glow, the bloom,
   Who changest not in any gale,
   Nor branding summer suns avail
To touch thy thousand years of gloom:

And gazing on thee, sullen tree,
   Sick for thy stubborn hardihood,
   I seem to fail from out my blood
And grow incorporate into thee.

84.

              ON a huge hill,
Cragged and steep, Truth stands; and hee that
   will
Reach her, about must and about it goe;
And what the hill's suddennes resists, winne so.

85. THE WRECK OF THE DEUTSCHLAND

   . . . On Saturday sailed from Bremen,
  American-outward-bound,
Take settler and seamen, tell men with women,
    Two hundred souls in the round—
O Father, not under thy feathers nor ever as
    guessing
The goal was a shoal, of a fourth the doom to be
    drowned;
    Yet did the dark side of the bay of thy blessing
Not vault them, the millions of rounds of thy mercy
    not reeve even them in?

    Into the snows she sweeps,
   Hurling the haven behind,
The Deutschland on Sunday; and so the sky keeps,
    For the infinite air is unkind,
And the sea flint-flake, black-backed in the regular
    blow,
Sitting Eastnortheast, in cursed quarter, the wind;
    Wiry and white-fiery and whirlwind-swivellèd
    snow
Spins to the widow-making unchilding unfathering
    deeps.

    She drove in the dark to leeward,
   She struck—not a reef or a rock
But the combs of a smother of sand: night drew her
    Dead to the Kentish Knock;
And she beat the bank down with her bows and
    the ride of her keel:

The breakers rolled on her beam with ruinous
   shock;
      And canvas and compass, the whorl and the
      wheel
Idle for ever to waft her or wind her with, these she
   endured.

      Hope had grown grey hairs,
         Hope had mourning on,
      Trenched with tears, carved with cares,
         Hope was twelve hours gone;
      And frightful a nightfall folded rueful a day
      Nor rescue, only rocket and lightship, shone,
         And lives at last were washing away:
      To the shrouds they took,—they shook in the hurling
         and horrible airs.

      One stirred from the rigging to save
         The wild woman-kind below,
      With a rope's end round the man, handy and
         brave—
         He was pitched to his death at a blow,
      For all his dreadnought breast and braids of
         thew:
      They could tell him for hours, dandled the to and
         fro
         Through the cobbled foam-fleece, what could
         he do
      With the burl of the fountains of air, buck and the
         flood of the wave? . . .

            .   .   .   .

86.

ONCE, as old Lord Gorbals motored
   Round his moors near John o' Groats
He collided with a goatherd
   And a herd of forty goats.
By the time his car got through
They were all defunct but two.

Roughly he addressed the goatherd:
   "Dash my whiskers and my corns!
Can't you teach your goats, you dotard,
   That they ought to sound their horns?
Look, my A.A. badge is bent!
I've a mind to raise your rent!"

87. NOW IT'S HAPPENED

ONE cannot now help thinking
how much better it would have been
if Vronsky and Anna Karenin
had stood up for themselves, and seen
Russia across her crisis,
instead of leaving it to Lenin.

The big, flamboyant Russia
might have been saved, if a pair
of rebels like Anna and Vronsky
had blasted the sickly air
of Dostoevsky and Tchekov,
and spy-government everywhere.

103

But Tolstoi was a traitor
to the Russia that needed him most,
the clumsy, bewildered Russia
so worried by the Holy Ghost.
He shifted his job on to the peasants
and landed them all on toast.

Dostoevsky, the Judas,
with his sham christianity
epileptically ruined
the last bit of sanity
left in the hefty bodies
of the Russian nobility.

So our goody-good men betray us
and our sainty-saints let us down,
and a sickly people will slay us
if we touch the sob-stuff crown
of such martyrs; while Marxian tenets
naturally take hold of the town.

Too much of the humble Willy wet-leg
and the holy can't-help-it touch,
till you've ruined a nation's fibre
and they loathe all feeling as such,
and want to be cold and devilish hard
like machines—and you can't wonder much.—

88.

ONE summer evening (led by her) I found
A little boat tied to a willow tree
Within a rocky cave, its usual home.

Straight I unloosed her chain, and stepping in
Pushed from the shore.   It was an act of stealth
And troubled pleasure, nor without the voice
Of mountain-echoes did my boat move on;
Leaving behind her still, on either side,
Small circles glittering idly in the moon,
Until they melted all into one track
Of sparkling light.   But now, like one who rows,
Proud of his skill, to reach a chosen point
With an unswerving line, I fixed my view
Upon the summit of a craggy ridge,
The horizon's utmost boundary; far above
Was nothing but the stars and the grey sky.
She was an elfin pinnace; lustily
I dipped my oars into the silent lake,
And, as I rose upon the stroke, my boat
Went heaving through the water like a swan;
When, from behind that craggy steep till then
The horizon's bound, a huge peak, black and huge,
As if with voluntary power instinct
Upreared its head.   I struck and struck again,
And growing still in stature the grim shape
Towered up between me and the stars, and still,
For so it seemed, with purpose of its own
And measured motion like a living thing,
Strode after me.   With trembling oars I turned,
And through the silent water stole my way
Back to the covert of the willow tree;
There in her mooring-place I left my bark,—
And through the meadows homeward went, in grave
And serious mood; but after I had seen
That spectacle, for many days, my brain

Worked with a dim and undetermined sense
Of unknown modes of being; o'er my thoughts
There hung a darkness, call it solitude
Or blank desertion. No familiar shapes
Remained, no pleasant images of trees,
Of sea or sky, no colours of green fields;
But huge and mighty forms, that do not live
Like living men, moved slowly through the mind
By day, and were a trouble to my dreams.

89.

OR ever the silver cord be loosed, or the golden
bowl be broken, or the pitcher be broken at the
fountain, or the wheel broken at the cistern.

Then shall the dust return to the earth as it was:
and the spirit shall return unto God who gave it.

90. PROLOGUE TO AURUNG-ZEBE

OUR Author by experience finds it true,
'Tis much more hard to please himself than you;
And out of no feign'd modesty, this day,
Damns his laborious trifle of a Play;
Not that it's worse than what before he writ,
But he has now another taste of wit;
And, to confess a truth (though out of time),
Grows weary of his long-loved Mistris Rhyme.
Passion's too fierce to be in fetters bound,
And Nature flies him like enchanted ground:

What Verse can do he has perform'd in this,
Which he presumes the most correct of his;
But spite of all his pride, a secret shame
Invades his breast at *Shakespear's* sacred name:
Aw'd when he hears his Godlike *Romans* rage,
He in a just despair would quit the stage;
And to an Age less polish'd, more unskill'd,
Does with disdain the foremost honours yield.
As with the greater Dead he dares not strive,
He wou'd not match his verse with those who live:
Let him retire, betwixt two Ages cast,
The first of this, and hindmost of the last.
A losing gamester, let him sneak away;
He bears no ready money from the Play.
The Fate which governs poets, thought it fit,
He shou'd not raise his fortunes by his wit.
The Clergy thrive, and the litigious Bar;
Dull heroes fatten with the spoils of war:
All Southern vices, Heav'n be prais'd, are here;
But wit's a luxury you think too dear.
When you to cultivate the plant are loth,
'Tis a shrewd sign 'twas never of your growth:
And wit in Northern climates will not blow,
Except, like *orange-trees*, 'tis hous'd from snow.
There needs no care to put a play-house down,
'Tis the most desart place of all the Town:
We and our neighbours, to speak proudly, are
Like Monarchs, ruin'd with expensive War;
While, like wise *English*, unconcern'd you sit,
And see us play the Tragedy of Wit.

91. THE HUMAN ABSTRACT

Pity would be no more
If we did not make somebody Poor;
And Mercy no more could be
If all were as happy as we.

And mutual fear brings peace,
Till the selfish loves increase:
Then Cruelty knits a snare,
And spreads his baits with care.

He sits down with holy fears,
And waters the ground with tears;
Then Humility takes its root
Underneath his foot.

Soon spreads the dismal shade
Of Mystery over his head;
And the Caterpillar and Fly
Feed on the Mystery.

And it bears the fruit of Deceit,
Ruddy and sweet to eat;
And the Raven his nest has made
In its thickest shade.

The Gods of the earth and sea
Sought thro' Nature to find this Tree;
But their search was all in vain:
There grows one in the Human Brain.

92. THE POETS AT TEA

I.—MACAULAY, WHO MADE IT

POUR, varlet, pour the water,
  The water steaming hot!
A spoonful for each man of us,
  Another for the pot!
We shall not drink from amber,
  No Capuan slave shall mix
For us the snows of Athos
  With port at thirty-six;
Whiter than snow the crystals
  Grown sweet 'neath tropic fires,
More rich the herb of China's field,
The pasture-lands more fragrance yield;
For ever let Britannia wield
  The teapot of her sires!

II.—TENNYSON, WHO TOOK IT HOT

I think that I am drawing to an end:
For on a sudden came a gasp for breath,
And stretching of the hands, and blinded eyes,
And a great darkness falling on my soul.
O Hallelujah! . . . Kindly pass the milk.

III.—SWINBURNE, WHO LET IT GET COLD

As the sin that was sweet in the sinning
  Is foul in the ending thereof,
As the heat of the summer's beginning
  Is past in the winter of love:
O purity, painful and pleading!
  O coldness, ineffably grey!

O hear us, our handmaid unheeding,
And take it away!

IV.—COWPER, WHO THOROUGHLY ENJOYED IT

The cosy fire is bright and gay,
The merry kettle boils away
    And hums a cheerful song.
I sing the saucer and the cup;
Pray, Mary, fill the teapot up,
    And do not make it strong.

V.—BROWNING, WHO TREATED IT ALLEGORICALLY

Tst! Bah! We take as another case—
  Pass the pills on the window-sill; notice the
    capsule
(A sick man's fancy, no doubt, but I place
  Reliance on trade-marks, Sir)—so perhaps you'll
Excuse the digression—this cup which I hold
  Light-poised—Bah, its spilt in the bed!—well,
    let's on go—
Held Bohea and sugar, Sir; if you were told
  The sugar was salt, would the Bohea be Congo?

VI.—WORDSWORTH, WHO GAVE IT AWAY

"Come, little cottage girl, you seem
    To want my cup of tea;
And will you take a little cream?
    Now tell the truth to me."

She had a rustic, woodland grin,
    Her cheek was soft as silk,
And she replied, "Sir, please put in
    A little drop of milk."

"Why, what put milk into your head?
    'Tis cream my cows supply;"
And five times to the child I said,
    "Why, pig-head, tell me, why?"

"You call me pig-head," she replied;
    "My proper name is Ruth.
I call that milk"—she blushed with pride—
    "You bade me speak the truth."

VII.—POE, WHO GOT EXCITED OVER IT

Here's a mellow cup of tea—golden tea!
What a world of rapturous thought its fragrance
        brings to me!
    Oh, from out the silver cells
    How it wells!
    How it smells!
Keeping tune, tune, tune, tune
To the tintinnabulation of the spoon.
And the kettle on the fire
Boils its spout off with desire,
With a desperate desire
And a crystalline endeavour
Now, now to sit, or never,
On the top of the pale-faced moon,
But he always came home to tea, tea, tea, tea, tea,
            Tea to the n—th.

VIII.—ROSSETTI, WHO TOOK SIX CUPS OF IT

The lilies lie in my lady's bower
    (O weary mother, drive the cows to roost),
They faintly droop for a little hour;
My lady's head droops like a flower.

She took the porcelain in her hand
  (O weary mother, drive the cows to roost):
She poured; I drank at her command;
Drank deep, and now—you understand!
  (O weary mother, drive the cows to roost).

IX.—BURNS, WHO LIKED IT ADULTERATED

Weel, gin ye speir, I'm no inclined,
Whusky or tay—to state my mind
    For ane or ither;
For, gin I tak the first, I'm fou,
And gin the next, I'm dull as you,
    Mix a' thegither.

X.—WALT WHITMAN, WHO DIDN'T STAY MORE THAN A MINUTE

One cup for my self-hood,
Many for you. *Allons, camerados,* we will drink
    together
O hand-in-hand! That tea-spoon, please, when
    you've done with it.
What butter-colour'd hair you've got. I don't want
    to be personal.
All right, then, you needn't — you're a stale —
    cadaver.
Eighteen-pence if the bottles are returned,
Allons, from all bat-eyed formules.

Prepayre you, Parrot, bravely your passage to take,
 Of Mercury under the trynall aspecte,
And sadlye salute ower sullen syre Sydrake,[1]
 And shewe hym that all the world doth conjecte.
 How the matters he mellis in com to small effecte;
For he wantythe of hys wyttes that all wold rule alone;
It is no lytyll burden to bere a grete mylle stone:

To bryng all the see into a cherryston pytte,
 To number all the sterrys in the fyrmament,
To rule ix realmes by one mannes wytte
 To such thynges impossybyll reason cannot
  consent:
 Much money, men say, there madly he hath spent:
Parrot, ye may prate thys under protestation
Was never such a senatour synce Crystes incarnation.

94. DON'S HOLIDAY

Professor Robinson each summer beats
The fishing record of the world—such feats
As one would hardly credit from a lesser
Person than a history professor.

95.

Ring out ye Crystal spheres,
Once bless our human ears,
(If ye have power to touch our senses so)

    [1] Cardinal Wolsey.

And let your silver chime
Move in melodious time;
And let the Bass of Heaven's deep Organ blow,
And with your ninefold harmony
Make up full consort to th' Angelick symphony.

For if such holy Song
Enwrap our fancy long,
Time will run back, and fetch the age of gold,
And speckl'd vanity
Will sicken soon and die,
And leprous sin will melt from earthly mould,
And Hell itself will pass away,
And leave her dolorous mansions to the peering
day. . . .

96. ROOKHOPE RYDE

ROOKHOPE stands in a pleasant place,
　　If the false thieves wad let it be,
But away they steal our goods apace,
　　And ever an ill death may they dee!

And so is the man of Thirlwall and Willie-haver,
　　And all their companies thereabout,
That is minded to do mischief,
　　And at their stealing stands not out.

But yet we will not slander them all,
　　For there is of them good enough;
It is a sore consumed tree
　　That on it bears not one fresh bough.

Lord god! is not this a pitiful case,
  That men dare not drive their goods to the fell,
But limmer [1] thieves drives them away,
  That fears neither heaven nor hell?

Lord, send us peace into the realm,
  That every man may live on his own!
I trust to God, if it be his will,
  That Weardale men may never be overthrown.

For great troubles they've had in hand,
  With borderers pricking hither and thither,
But the greatest fray that e'er they had,
  Was with the men of Thirlwall and Willie-haver.

They gather'd together so royally,
  The stoutest men and the best in gear;
And he that rade not on a horse,
  I wat he rade on a weil-fed mear.

So in the morning, before they came out,
  So weel I wot they broke their fast;
In the forenoon they came unto a bye fell,
  Where some of them did eat their last.

When they had eaten aye and done,
  They say'd, some captains here needs must be:
Then they choosed forth Harry Corbyl,
  And 'Symon Fell,' and Martin Ridley.

Then o'er the moss, where as they came,
  With many a brank and whew,
One of them could to another say,
  "I think this day we are men enew."

[1] base.

For Weardale-men have a journey ta'en,
   They are so far out o'er yon fell,
That some of them's with the two earls,
   And others fast in Bernard castell.

There we shall get gear enough,
   For there is nane but women at hame;
The sorrowful fend that they can make,
   Is loudly cries as they were slain.

Then in at Rookhope-head they came,
   And there they thought tul a'had their prey,
But they were spy'd coming over the Dry-rig,
   Soon upon Saint Nicholas' day.

Then in at Rookhope-head they came,
   They ran the forest but a mile;
They gather'd together in four hours
   Six hundred sheep within a while.

And horses I trow they gat,
   But either ane or twa,
And they gat them all but ane
   That belanged to great Rowley.

That Rowley was the first man that did them spy,
   With that he raised a mighty cry;
The cry it came down Rookhope-burn,
   And spread through Weardale hasteyly.

Then word came to the bailif's house
   At the East-gate, where he did dwell;
He was walk'd out to the Smale-burns,
   Which stands above the Hanging-well.

His wife was wae when she heard tell,
    So well she wist her husband wanted gear;
She gar'd saddle him his horse in haste,
    And neither forget sword, jack, nor spear.

The bailif got wit before his gear came,
    That such news was in the land,
He was sore troubled in his heart,
    That on no earth that he could stand.

His brother was hurt three days before,
    With limmer thieves that did him prick;
Nineteen bloody wounds lay him upon,
    What ferly[1] was't that he lay sick?

But yet the bailif shrinked nought,
    But fast after them he did hye,
And so did all his neighbours near,
    That went to bear him company.

But when the bailif was gathered,
    And all his company,
They were number'd to never a man
    But forty under fifty.

The thieves was numbered a hundred men,
    I wat they were not of the worst:
That could be choosed out of Thirlwall and
        Willie-haver
    I trow they were the very first.

[1] wonder.

But all that was in Rookhope-head,
    And all that was i' Nuketon-cleugh,
Where Weardale-men o'ertook the thieves,
    And there they gave them fighting eneugh.

So sore they made them fain to flee,
    As many was a' out of hand,
And, for tul have been at home again,
    They would have been in iron bands.

And for the space of long seven years
    As sore they mighten a'had their lives,
But there was never one of them
    That ever thought to have seen their wives.

About the time the fray began,
    I trow it lasted but an hour,
Till many a man lay weaponless,
    And was sore wounded in that stour.

Also before that hour was done,
    Four of the thieves were slain,
Besides all those that wounded were,
    And eleven prisoners there was ta'en.

George Carrick, and his brother Edie,
    Them two, I wot, they were both slain;
Harry Corbyl, and Lennie Carrick,
    Bore them company in their pain.

One of our Weardale-men was slain,
    Rowland Emerson his name hight;
I trust to God his soul is well,
    Because he fought unto the right.

But thus they say'd, We'll not depart
   While we have one:—Speed back again!
And when they came amongst the dead men,
   There they found George Carrick slain.

And when they found George Carrick slain,
   I wot it went well near their heart;
Lord, let them never make a better end
   That comes to play them sicken a part.

I trust to God, no more they shall,
   Except it be one for a great chance;
For God will punish all those
   With a great heavy pestilence.

Thir limmer thieves, they have good hearts,
   They never think to be o'erthrown;
Three banners against Weardale-men they bare,
   As if the world had been all their own.

Thir Weardale-men, they have good hearts,
   They are as stiff as any tree;
For, if they'd every one been slain,
   Never a foot back man would flee.

And such a storm amongst them fell,
   As I think you never heard the like;
For he that bears his head so high,
   He oft-times falls into the dyke.

And now I do entreat you all,
   As many as are present here,
To pray for the singer of this song,
   For he sings to make blithe your cheer.

97. DEATH OF GEORGE III

SAINT PETER sat by the celestial gate:
　His keys were rusty, and the lock was dull,
So little trouble had been given of late;
　Not that the place by any means was full,
But since the Gallic era "eighty-eight"
　The Devils had ta'en a longer, stronger pull,
And "a pull altogether," as they say
At sea—which drew most souls another way.

The Angels all were singing out of tune,
　And hoarse with having little else to do,
Excepting to wind up the sun and moon,
　Or curb a runaway young star or two,
Or wild colt of a comet, which too soon
　Broke out of bounds o'er the ethereal blue,
Splitting some planet with its playful tail,
As boats are sometimes by a wanton whale.

The guardian Seraphs had retired on high,
　Finding their charges past all care below;
Terrestrial business filled nought in the sky
　Save the Recording Angel's black bureau;
Who found, indeed, the facts to multiply
　With such rapidity of vice and woe,
That he had stripped off both his wings in quills,
And yet was in arrear of human ills.

His business so augmented of late years,
　That he was forced, against his will, no doubt,
(Just like those cherubs, earthly ministers,)
　For some resource to turn himself about,

And claim the help of his celestial peers,
  To aid him ere he should be quite worn out
By the increased demand for his remarks:
Six Angels and twelve Saints were named his clerks.

This was a handsome board—at least for Heaven;
  And yet they had even then enough to do,
So many Conquerors' cars were daily driven,
  So many kingdoms fitted up anew;
Each day, too, slew its thousands six or seven,
  Till at the crowning carnage, Waterloo,
They threw their pens down in divine disgust—
The page was so besmeared with blood and dust.

This by the way; 'tis not mine to record
  What Angels shrink from: even the very Devil
On this occasion his own work abhorred,
  So surfeited with the infernal revel:
Though he himself had sharpened every sword,
  It almost quenched his innate thirst of evil.
(Here Satan's sole good work deserves insertion—
'Tis, that he has both Generals in reversion.)

Let's skip a few short years of hollow peace,
  Which peopled earth no better, Hell as wont,
And Heaven none—they form the tyrant's lease,
  With nothing but new names subscribed upon't;
'Twill one day finish: meantime they increase,
  "With seven heads and ten horns," and all in
    front,
Like Saint John's foretold beast; but ours are born
Less formidable in the head than horn.

In the first year of Freedom's second dawn
    Died George the Third; although no tyrant, one
Who shielded tyrants, till each sense withdrawn
    Left him nor mental nor external sun:
A better farmer ne'er brushed dew from lawn,
    A worse king never left a realm undone!
He died—but left his subjects still behind,
One half as mad—and t'other no less blind.

He died! his death made no great stir on earth:
    His burial made some pomp; there was profusion
Of velvet—gilding—brass—and no great dearth
    Of aught but tears—save those shed by collusion:
For these things may be bought at their true worth;
    Of elegy there was the due infusion—
Bought also; and the torches, cloaks and banners,
Heralds, and relics of old Gothic manners,

Formed a sepulchral melodrame.   Of all
    The fools who flocked to swell or see the show,
Who cared about the corpse?   The funeral
    Made the attraction, and the black the woe.
There throbbed not there a thought which pierced
        the pall;
    And when the gorgeous coffin was laid low,
It seemed the mockery of hell to fold
The rottenness of eighty years in gold.

So mix his body with the dust!   It might
    Return to what it *must* far sooner, were
The natural compound left alone to fight
    Its way back into earth, and fire, and air;

But the unnatural balsams merely blight
   What Nature made him at his birth, as bare
As the mere million's base unmummied clay—
   Yet all his spices but prolong decay.

He's dead—and upper earth with him has done;
   He's buried; save the undertaker's bill,
Or lapidary scrawl, the world is gone
   For him, unless he left a German will:
But where's the proctor who will ask his son?
   In whom his qualities are reigning still,
Except that household virtue, most uncommon,
Of constancy to a bad, ugly woman.

"God save the king!" It is a large economy
   In God to save the like; but if he will
Be saving, all the better; for not one am I
   Of those who think damnation better still:
I hardly know too if not quite alone am I
   In this small hope of bettering future ill
By circumscribing, with some slight restriction,
The eternity of Hell's hot jurisdiction.

I know this is unpopular; I know
   'Tis blasphemous; I know one may be damned
For hoping no one else may e'er be so;
   I know my catechism; I know we're crammed
With the best doctrines till we quite o'erflow;
   I know that all save England's Church have shammed,
And that the other twice two hundred churches
And synagogues have made a *damned* bad purchase.

God help us all! God help me too! I am,
  God knows, as helpless as the Devil can wish,
And not a whit more difficult to damn,
  Than is to bring to land a late-hooked fish,
Or to the butcher to purvey the lamb;
  Not that I'm fit for such a noble dish,
As one day will be that immortal fry
Of almost every body born to die.

Saint Peter sat by the celestial gate,
  And nodded o'er his keys: when, lo! there came
A wondrous noise he had not heard of late—
  A rushing sound of wind, and stream, and flame;
In short, a roar of things extremely great,
  Which would have made aught save a Saint
    exclaim;
But he, with first a start and then a wink,
Said, "There's another star gone out, I think!"

But ere he could return to his repose,
  A Cherub flapped his right wing o'er his eyes—
At which Saint Peter yawned, and rubbed his nose:
  "Saint porter," said the angel, "prithee rise!"
Waving a goodly wing, which glowed, as glows
  An earthly peacock's tail, with heavenly dyes:
To which the saint replied, "Well, what's the matter?
Is Lucifer come back with all this clatter?"

"No," quoth the Cherub: "George the Third is
    dead."
  "And who *is* George the Third?" replied the
    apostle:

"*What George? what Third?*" "The King of
  England," said
The angel. "Well! he won't find kings to jostle
Him on his way; but does he wear his head?
  Because the last we saw here had a tustle,
And ne'er would have got into Heaven's good graces,
Had he not flung his head in all our faces.

"He was—if I remember—King of France;
  That head of his, which could not keep a crown
On earth, yet ventured in my face to advance
  A claim to those of martyrs—like my own:
If I had had my sword, as I had once
  When I cut ears off, I had cut him down;
But having but my *keys*, and not my brand,
I only knocked his head from out his hand.

"And then he set up such a headless howl,
  That all the Saints came out and took him in;
And there he sits by Saint Paul, cheek by jowl;
  That fellow Paul—the parvenu! The skin
Of Saint Bartholomew, which makes his cowl
  In heaven, and upon earth redeemed his sin,
So as to make a martyr, never sped
Better than did this weak and wooden head.

"But had it come up here upon its shoulders,
  There would have been a different tale to tell:
The fellow-feeling in the Saint's beholders
  Seems to have acted on them like a spell;

And so this very foolish head Heaven solders
   Back on its trunk: it may be very well,
And seems the custom here to overthrow
Whatever has been wisely done below."

The Angel answered, "Peter! do not pout:
   The King who comes has head and all entire,
And never knew much what it was about—
   He did as doth the puppet—by its wire,
And will be judged like all the rest, no doubt:
   My business and your own is not to inquire
Into such matters, but to mind our cue—
Which is to act as we are bid to do."

.   .   .   .

98.

SHUT, shut the door, good John! fatigued I said;
Tie up the knocker, say I'm sick, I'm dead.
The Dog-star rages! nay, 'tis past a doubt,
All Bedlam, or Parnassus, is let out:
Fire in each eye, and papers in each hand,
They rave, recite, and madden round the land.
   What walls can guard me, or what shades can hide?
They pierce my thickets, through my grot they glide,
By land, by water, they renew the charge,
They stop the chariot, and they board the barge.
No place is sacred, not the church is free,
Ev'n Sunday shines no Sabbath-day to me:
Then from the Mint walks forth the man of rhyme,
Happy! to catch me, just at dinner-time.

Is there a parson, much bemused in beer,
A maudlin poetess, a rhyming peer,
A clerk, foredoom'd his father's soul to cross,
Who pens a stanza, when he should engross?
Is there, who, lock'd from ink and paper, scrawls
With desperate charcoal round his darkened walls?
All fly to Twit'nam, and in humble strain
Apply to me, to keep them mad or vain.
Arthur, whose giddy son neglects the laws,
Imputes to me and my damn'd works the cause:
Poor Cornus sees his frantic wife elope,
And curses wit, and poetry, and Pope. . . .

99.

SIMKIN said that Sis was fair
   And that he meant to love her;
He set her on his ambling mare;
   All this he did to prove her.
When they came home Sis floted cream,
   And poured it through a strainer;
But sware that Simkin should have none
   Because he did disdain her.

100.

SINCE Bonny-boots was dead, that so divinely
Could toot and foot it, (O he did it finely!)
   We ne'er went more a-Maying
   Nor had that sweet fa-laing.

101. JOHANNES MILTON, SENEX

SINCE I believe in God the Father Almighty,
Man's Maker and Judge, Overruler of Fortune,
'Twere strange should I praise anything and refuse
   Him praise,
Should love the creature forgetting the Creator,
Nor unto Him in suff'ring and sorrow turn me:
Nay how cou'd I withdraw me from His embracing?

But since that I have seen not, and cannot know Him,
Nor in my earthly temple apprehend rightly
His wisdom and the heav'nly purpose eternal;
Therefore will I be bound to no studied system
Nor argument, nor with delusion enslave me,
Nor seek to please Him in any foolish invention,
Which my spirit within me, that loveth beauty
And hateth evil, hath reprov'd as unworthy:

But I cherish my freedom in loving service,
Gratefully adoring for delight beyond asking
Or thinking, and in hours of anguish and darkness
Confiding always on His excellent greatness.

102.

SING we the two lieutenants, Parer and M'Intosh,
After the War wishing to hie them home to Australia,
Planned they would take a high way, a hazardous
   crazy air-way:

Death their foregone conclusion, a flight headlong to
  failure,
We said.   For no silver posh
Plane was their pigeon, no dandy dancer quick-
  stepping through heaven,
But a craft of obsolete design, a condemned D. H.
  nine;
Sold for a song it was, patched up though to write an
  heroic
Line across the world as it reeled on its obstinate stoic
Course to that southern haven.

On January 8, 1920, their curveting wheels kissed
England goodbye. Over Hounslow huddled in
  morning mist
They rose and circled like buzzards while we rubbed
  our sleepy eyes:
Like a bird scarce-fledged they flew, whose flying
  hours are few—
Still dear is the nest but deeper its desire unto the
  skies—
And they left us to our sleeping.
They felt earth's warning tug on their wings: vain
  to advance
Asking a thoroughfare through the angers of the air
On so flimsy a frame: but they pulled up her nose
  and the earth went sloping
Away, and they aimed for France.

Fog first, a wet blanket, a kill-joy, the primrose-of-
  morning's blight,
Blotting out the dimpled sea, the ample welcome of
  land,

The gay glance from the bright
Cliff-face behind, snaring the sky with treachery,
    sneering
At hope's loss of height.   But they charged it, flying
    blind;
They took a compass-bearing against that dealer of
    doubt,
As a saint when the field of vision is fogged gloriously
    steels
His spirit against the tainter of air, the elusive
    taunter:
They climbed to win a way out,
Then downward dared till the moody waves snarled
    at their wheels.

Landing at last near Conteville, who had skimmed
    the crest of oblivion,
They could not rest, but rose and flew on to Paris,
    and there
Trivially were delayed—a defective petrol feed—
Three days: a time hung heavy on
Hand and heart, till they leapt again to the upper
    air,
Their element, their lover, their angel antagonist.
Would have taken a fall without fame, but the sinewy
    framework the wrist
Of steel the panting engine wrestled well: and they
    went
South while the going was good, as a swallow that
    guide nor goad
Needs on his sunny scent.

At Lyons the petrol pump failed again, and forty-
    eight hours
They chafed to be off, the haughty champions whose
    breathing-space
Was an horizon span and the four winds their fan.
Over Italy's shores
A reverse, the oil ran out and cursing they turned
    about
Losing a hundred miles to find a landing-place.
Not a coast for a castaway this, no even chance of
    alighting
On sward or wind-smooth sand:
A hundred miles without pressure they flew, the
    engine fighting
For breath, and its heart nearly burst before they
    dropped to land.

And now the earth they had spurned rose up against
    them in anger,
Tier upon tier it towered, the terrible Apennines:
No sanctuary there for wings, not flares nor landing-
    lines,
No hope of floor and hangar.
Yet those ice-tipped spears that disputed the passage
    set spurs
To their two hundred and forty horse power;
    grimly they gained
Altitude, though the hand of heaven was heavy upon
    them,
The downdraught from the mountains: though
    desperate eddies spun them

Like a coin, yet unkindly tossed their luck came
    uppermost
And mastery remained.

Air was all ambushes round them, was avalanche
    earthquake
Quicksand, a funnel deep as doom, till climbing
    steep
They crawled like a fly up the face of perpendicular
    night
And levelled, finding a break
At fourteen thousand feet. Here earth is shorn from
    sight:
Deadweight a darkness hangs on their eyelids, and
    they bruise
Their eyes against a void: vindictive the cold airs
    close
Down like a trap of steel and numb them from head
    to heel;
Yet they kept an even keel,
For their spirit reached forward and took the con-
    trols while their fingers froze.

They had not heard the last of death. When the
    mountains were passed,
He raised another crest, the long crescendo of pain
Kindled to climax, the plane
Took fire. Alone in the sky with the breath of their
    enemy
Hot in their face they fought: from three thousand
    feet they tilted
Over, side-slipped away—a trick for an ace, a race

And running duel with death: flame streamed out
    behind,
A crimson scarf of, as life-blood out of a wound, but
    the wind
Of their downfall staunched it; death wilted,
Lagged and died out in smoke—he could not stay
    their pace.

A lull for a while. The powers of hell rallied their
    legions.
On Parer now fell the stress of the flight; for the
    plane had been bumped,
Buffeted, thrashed by the air almost beyond repair:
But he tinkered and coaxed, and they limped
Over the Adriatic on into warmer regions.
Erratic their course to Athens, to Crete: coolly they
    rode her
Like a tired horse at the water-jumps, they jockeyed
    her over seas,
Till they came at last to a land whose dynasties of
    sand
Had seen Alexander, Napoleon, many a straddling
    invader,
But never none like these. . . .

103.

Sir Joshua praised Rubens with a Smile,
By calling his the ornamental Style;
And yet his praise of Flaxman was the smartest
When he call'd him the Ornamental Artist.
But sure such ornaments we well may spare,
As Crooked limbs and louzy heads of hair.

104. À TERRE

(Being the Philosophy of Many Soldiers)

Sit on the bed. I'm blind, and three parts shell.
Be careful; can't shake hands now; never shall.
Both arms have mutinied against me,—brutes.
My fingers fidget like ten idle brats.

I tried to peg out soldierly,—no use!
One dies of war like any old disease.
This bandage feels like pennies on my eyes.
I have my medals?—Discs to make eyes close.
My glorious ribbons?—Ripped from my own back
In scarlet shreds. (That's for your poetry book.)

A short life and a merry one, my buck!
We used to say we'd hate to live dead-old,—
Yet now . . . I'd willingly be puffy, bald,
And patriotic. Buffers catch from boys
At least the jokes hurled at them. I suppose
Little I'd ever teach a son, but hitting,
Shooting, war, hunting, all the arts of hurting.
Well, that's what I learnt,—that, and making money.
Your fifty years ahead seem none too many?
Tell me how long I've got? God! For one year
To help myself to nothing more than air!
One Spring! Is one too good to spare, too long?
Spring wind would work its own way to my lung,
And grow me legs as quick as lilac-shoots.

My servant's lamed, but listen how he shouts!
When I'm lugged out, he'll still be good for that.
Here in this mummy-case, you know, I've thought
How well I might have swept his floors for ever.

I'd ask no nights off when the bustle's over,
Enjoying so the dirt.   Who's prejudiced
Against a grimed hand when his own's quite dust,
Less live than specks that in the sun-shaft turn,
Less warm than dust that mixes with arms' tan?
I'd love to be a sweep, now, black as Town,
Yes; or a muckman.   Must I be his load?

O Life, Life, let me breathe,—a dug-out rat!
Not worse than ours the existences rats lead—
Nosing along at night down some safe rut,
They find a shell-proof home before they rot.
Dead men may envy living mites in cheese,
Or good germs even.   Microbes have their joys,
And subdivide, and never come to death.
Certainly flowers have the easiest time on earth.
"I shall be one with nature, herb, and stone,"
Shelley would tell me.   Shelley would be stunned:
The dullest Tommy hugs that fancy now.
"Pushing up daisies" is their creed, you know.
To grain, then, go my fat, to buds my sap,
For all the usefulness there is in soap.
D'you think the Boche will ever stew man-soup?
Some day, no doubt, if . . .

                     Friend, be very sure
I shall be better off with plants that share
More peaceably the meadow and the shower.
Soft rains will touch me,—as they could touch once,
And nothing but the sun shall make me ware.
Your guns may crash around me.   I'll not hear;
Or, if I wince, I shall not know I wince.

Don't take my soul's poor comfort for your jest.
Soldiers may grow a soul when turned to fronds,
But here the thing's best left at home with friends.
My soul's a little grief, grappling your chest,
To climb your throat on sobs; easily chased
On other sighs and wiped by fresher winds.

Carry my crying spirit till it's weaned
To do without what blood remained these wounds.

105. THE FRAY OF SUPORT

SLEEP'RY SIM of the Lamb-hill,
And snoring Jock of Suport-mill,
Ye are baith right het and fou';—
But my wae wakens na you.
Last night I saw a sorry sight—
Nought left me, o' four-and-twenty gude ousen and kye,
My weel-ridden gelding, and a white quey,[1]
But a toom[2] byre and a wide,
And the twelve nogs[3] on ilka side.
     Fy, lads! shout a' a' a' a' a',
     My gear's a' gane.

Weel may ye ken,
Last night I was right scarce o' men:
But Toppet Hob o' the Mains had guesten'd in my
    house by chance;
I set him to wear the fore-door wi' the speir, while I
    kept the back-door wi' the lance;

    [1] pony.   [2] empty.   [3] stakes.

But they hae run him thro' the thick o' the thie, and
    broke his knee-pan,
And the mergh [1] o' his shin-bane has run down on his
    spur-leather whang [2]:
He's lame while he lives, and where'er he may gang.
      Fy, lads! shout a' a' a' a' a',
      My gear's a' gane.

But Peenye, my gude son, is out at the Hagbut-head,
His een glittering for anger like a fiery gleed;
Crying—"Mak sure the nooks
Of Maky's-muir crooks;
For the wily Scot takes by nooks, hooks, and crooks.
Gin we meet a' together in a head the morn,
We'll be merry men."
      Fy, lads! shout a' a' a' a' a',
      My gear's a' gane.

There's doughty Cuddy in the Heughhead,
Thou was aye gude at a need:
With thy brock-skin bag at thy belt,
Aye ready to mak a puir man help.
Thou maun awa' out to the Cauf-craigs,
(Where anes ye lost your ain twa naigs),
And there toom thy brock-skin bag.
      Fy, lads! shout a' a' a' a' a',
      My gear's a' ta'en.

Doughty Dan o' the Houlet Hirst,
Thou was aye gude at a birst:
Gude wi' a bow, and better wi' a speir,
The bauldest March-man that e'er followed gear;

      [1] marrow.   [2] thong.

Come thou here.
>   Fy, lads! shout a' a' a' a' a'.
>   My gear's a' gane.

Rise, ye carle coopers, frae making o' kirns and tubs,
In the Nicol forest woods.
Your craft hasna left the value of an oak rod,
But if you had had only fear o' God,
Last night ye hadna slept sae sound,
And let my gear be a' ta'en.
>   Fy, lads! shout a' a' a' a' a',
>   My gear's a' ta'en.

Ah! lads, we'll fang them a' in a net,
For I hae a' the fords o' Liddel set;
The Dunkin, and the Door-loup,
The Willie-ford and the Water-Slack,
The Black-rack and the Trout-dub of Liddel;
There stands John Forster wi' five men at his back,
Wi' buft coat and cap of steil:
Boo! ca' at them e'en, Jock;
That ford's sicker, I wat weil.
>   Fy, lads! shout a' a' a' a' a',
>   My gear's a' ta'en.

.   .   .   .

106.

So now, this poet, who forsakes the stage
Intends to gratify the present age.
One warrant shall be signed for every man;
All shall be wits that will and beaux that can . . .

138

He dies, at least to us and to the stage,
And what he has, he leaves this noble age.
He leaves you first all plays of his inditing,
The whole estate which he has got by writing.
The beaux may think this nothing but vain praise;
They'll find it something the testator says;
For half their love is made from scraps of plays.
To his worst foes he leaves his honesty,
That they may thrive upon't as much as he.
He leaves his manners to the roaring boys,
Who come in drunk, and fill the house with noise.
He leaves to the dire critics of his wit
His silence and contempt of all they writ.
To Shakespeare's critic, he bequeaths the curse,
To find his faults, and yet himself make worse. . . .
Last for the fair, he wishes you may be
From your dull critics, the lampooners, free.
Tho' he pretends no legacy to leave you,
An old man may at least good wishes give you. . . .

107.

So, on the bloody sand, Sohrab lay dead.
And the great Rustum drew his horseman's cloak
Down o'er his face, and sate by his dead son.
As those black granite pillars, once high-rear'd
By Jemshid in Persepolis, to bear
His house, now, mid their broken flights of steps,
Lie prone, enormous, down the mountain side—
So in the sand lay Rustum by his son.

And night came down over the solemn waste,
And the two gazing hosts, and that sole pair,
And darkened all; and a cold fog, with night,
Crept from the Oxus. Soon a hum arose,
As of a great assembly loosed, and fires
Began to twinkle through the fog; for now
Both armies moved to camp, and took their meal:
The Persians took it on the open sands
Southward; the Tartars by the river marge:
And Rustum and his son were left alone.

But the majestic River floated on,
Out of the mist and hum of that low land,
Into the frosty starlight, and there moved,
Rejoicing, through the hush'd Chorasmian waste,
Under the solitary moon:—he flow'd
Right for the Polar Star, past Orgunjè,
Brimming, and bright, and large: then sands begin
To hem his watery march, and dam his streams,
And split his currents; that for many a league
The shorn and parcell'd Oxus strains along
Through beds of sand and matted rushy isles—
Oxus, forgetting the bright speed he had
In his high mountain cradle in Pamere,
A foil'd circuitous wanderer—till at last
The long'd for dash of waves is heard, and wide
His luminous home of waters opens, bright
And tranquil, from whose floor the new-bathed stars
Emerge, and shine upon the Aral Sea.

108

Sol through white curtains shot a tim'rous ray,
And ope'd those eyes that must eclipse the day:
Now lapdogs give themselves the rousing shake,
And sleepless lovers, just at twelve, awake:
Thrice rung the bell, the slipper knock'd the ground,
And the press'd watch return'd a silver sound.

109.

Stay, Corydon, thou swain,
Talk not so soon of dying.
What though thy heart be slain?
What though thy love be flying?
She threatens thee but dares not strike.
Thy nymph is light and shadow-like;
For if thou follow her, she'll fly from thee,
But if thou fly from her, she'll follow thee.

110.

The beauty of Israel is slain upon thy high places;
how are the mighty fallen!

.   .   .   .

From the blood of the slain, from the fat of the
mighty, the bow of Jonathan turned not back, and
the sword of Saul returned not empty.

Saul and Jonathan were lovely and pleasant in
their lives, and in their death they were not divided:

they were swifter than eagles, they were stronger than lions.

. . . .

How are the mighty fallen in the midst of battle!
O Jonathan, thou wast slain in thine high places.

I am distressed for thee, my brother Jonathan:
very pleasant hast thou been unto me: thy love to me was wonderful, passing the love of women.

How are the mighty fallen, and the weapons of war perished!

III.

THE Eagle soars in the summit of Heaven,
The Hunter with his dogs pursues his circuit.
O perpetual revolution of configured stars,
O perpetual recurrence of determined seasons,
O world of spring and autumn, birth and dying!
The endless cycle of idea and action,
Endless invention, endless experiment,
Brings knowledge of motion, but not of stillness;
Knowledge of speech, but not of silence;
Knowledge of words, and ignorance of the Word.
All our knowledge brings us nearer to our ignorance,
All our ignorance brings us nearer to death,
But nearness to death no nearer to God.
Where is the Life we have lost in living?
Where is the wisdom we have lost in knowledge?
Where is the knowledge we have lost in information?
The cycles of Heaven in twenty centuries
Bring us farther from God and nearer to the Dust.

I journeyed to London, to the timekept City,
Where the River flows, with foreign flotations.
There I was told: we have too many churches,
And too few chop-houses.   There I was told
Let the vicars retire.   Men do not need the Church
In the place where they work, but where they spend
    their Sundays.
In the City, we need no bells:
Let them waken the suburbs.
I journeyed to the suburbs, and there I was told:
We toil for six days, on the seventh we must motor
To Hindhead, or Maidenhead.
If the weather is foul we stay at home and read the
    papers.
In industrial districts, there I was told
Of economic laws.
In the pleasant countryside, there it seemed
That the country now is only fit for picnics.
And the Church does not seem to be wanted
In country or in suburb; and in the town
Only for important weddings.

112. THE SACK OF TROY

ÆNEAS: The Grecian soldiers, tired with ten years'
    war,
Began to cry, "Let us unto our ships,
Troy is invincible, why stay we here?"
With whose outcries Atrides being appalled,
Summoned the Captains to his princely tent;

Who, looking on the scars we Trojans gave,
Seeing the number of their men decreased,
And the remainder weak and out of heart,
Gave up their voices to dislodge the camp,
And so in troops all marched to Tenedos:
Where when they came, Ulysses on the sand
Assayed with honey words to turn them back;
And as he spoke to further his intent,
The winds did drive huge billows to the shore,
And heaven was darkened with tempestuous clouds:
Then he alleged the Gods would have them stay,
And prophesied Troy should be overcome:
And therewithal he called false Sinon forth,
A man compact of craft and perjurie,
Whose ticing tongue was made of Hermes' pipe,
To force an hundred watchful eyes to sleep;
And him, Epeus having made the horse,
With sacrificing wreaths upon his head,
Ulysses sent to our unhappy town:
Who, grovelling in the mire of Xanthus' banks,
His hands bound at his back, and both his eyes
Turned up to heaven, as one resolved to die,
Our Phrygian shepherds hailed within the gates,
And brought unto the Court of Priamus:
To whom he used action so pitiful,
Looks so remorseful, vows so forcible,
As therewithal the old man, overcome,
Kissed him, embraced him, and unloosed his bands:
And then—O Dido, pardon me.
Dido: Nay, leave not here; resolve me of the rest.
Æneas: O th' enchanting words of that base slave
Made him to think Epeus' pine-tree Horse

A sacrifice t' appease Minerva's wrath:
The rather, for that one Laocoon
Breaking a spear upon his hollow breast,
Was with two winged Serpents stung to death.
Whereat aghast, we were commanded straight
With reverence to draw it into Troy.
In which unhappy worke was I employed.
These hands did help to hail it to the gates,
Through which it could not enter, 'twas so huge.
O had it never entered, Troy had stood.
But Priamus impatient of delay,
Enforced a wide breach in that rampiered wall,
Which thousand battering rams could never pierce,
And so came in this fatal instrument:
At whose accursed feet as overjoyed,
We banquetted till, overcome with wine,
Some surfcited, and others soundly slept.
Which Sinon viewing, caused the Greekish spies
To haste to Tenedos and tell the Camp.
Then he unlocked the Horse, and suddenly
From out his entrails, Neoptolemus
Setting his spear upon the ground, lept forth,
And after him a thousand Grecians more,
In whose stern faces shined the quenchless fire
That after burnt the pride of Asia.
By this, the Camp was come unto the walls,
And through the breach did march into the streets,
Where, meeting with the rest, "Kill, kill!" they
    cried.
Frighted with this confused noise, I rose,
And, looking from a turret, might behold
Young infants swimming in their parents' blood,

Headless carcasses piled up in heaps,
Virgins half-dead, dragged by their golden hair,
And with main force flung on a ring of pikes,
Old men with swords thrust through their aged
    sides,
Kneeling for mercy to a Greekish lad,
Who with steel pole-axes dashed out their brains.
Then buckled I mine armour, drew my sword
And thinking to go down, came Hector's ghost,
With ashy visage, blueish sulphur eyes,
His arms torn from his shoulders, and his breast
Furrow'd with wounds, and, that which made me
    weep,
Thongs at his heels, by which Achilles' horse
Drew him in triumph through the Greekish camp,
Burst from the earth, crying "Æneas, fly!
Troy is a-fire, the Grecians have the town!"

113.

THE groves of Blarney they look so charming,
Down by the purling of sweet, silent streams,
Being banked with posies that spontaneous grow there,
Planted in order by the sweet rock close.
'Tis there's the daisy and the sweet carnation,
The blooming pink and the rose so fair,
The daffodowndilly, likewise the lily,
All flowers that scent the sweet, fragrant air.

'Tis Lady Jeffers that owns this station;
Like Alexander, or Queen Helen fair,
There's no commander in all the nation,

For emulation, can with her compare.
Such walls surround her, that no nine-pounder
Could dare to plunder her place of strength;
But Oliver Cromwell her he did pommell,
And made a breach in her battlement.

There's gravel walks there for speculation
And conversation in sweet solitude.
'Tis there the lover may hear the dove, or
The gentle plover in the afternoon;
And if a lady would be so engaging
As to walk alone in those shady bowers,
'Tis there the courtier he may transport her
Into some fort, or all under ground.

For 'tis there's a cave where no daylight enters,
But cats and badgers are for ever bred;
Being mossed by nature, that makes it sweeter
Than a coach-and-six or a feather bed.
'Tis there the lake is, well stored with perches,
And comely eels in the verdant mud;
Besides the leeches, and groves of beeches,
Standing in order for to guard the flood.

There's statues gracing this noble place in—
All heathen gods and nymphs so fair;
Bold Neptune, Plutarch, and Nicodemus,
All standing naked in the open air!
So now to finish this brave narration,
Which my poor genii could not entwine;
But were I Homer, or Nebuchadnezzar,
'Tis in every feature I would make it shine.

114

THE heavens themselves, the planets, and this
    centre,
Observe degree, priority, and place,
Insisture, course, proportion, season, form,
Office, and custom, in all line of order:
And therefore is the glorious planet Sol
In noble eminence enthroned and sphered
Amidst the ether; whose med'cinable eye
Corrects the ill aspects of planets evil,
And posts, like the commandment of a king,
Sans check, to good and bad: but when the planets,
In evil mixture, to disorder wander,
What plagues, and what portents, what mutiny,
What raging of the sea, shaking of earth,
Commotion in the winds, frights, changes, horrors,
Divert and crack, rend and deracinate
The unity and married calm of states
Quite from their fixure! O, when degree is shaked,
Which is the ladder to all high designs,
The enterprise is sick! How could communities,
Degrees in schools and brotherhoods in cities,
Peaceful commerce from dividable shores,
The primogenitive and due of birth,
Prerogative of age, crowns, sceptres, laurels,
But by degree, stand in authentic place?
Take but degree away, untune that string,
And, hark, what discord follows! each thing meets
In mere oppugnancy: the bounded waters
Should lift their bosoms higher than the shores,
And make a sop of all this solid globe:

Strength should be lord of imbecility,
And the rude son should strike his father dead:
Force should be right; or rather, right and wrong
(Between whose endless jar justice resides),
Should lose their names, and so should justice too.
Then every thing includes itself in power,
Power into will, will into appetite;
And appetite, an universal wolf,
So doubly seconded with will and power,
Must make perforce an universal prey,
And last eat up himself.

115. INCIDENT IN HYDE PARK, 1803

THE impulses of April, the rain-gems, the rose-
cloud,
The frilling of flowers in the westering love-wind!
And here through the Park come gentlemen riding,
And there through the Park come gentlemen riding,
And behind the glossy horses Newfoundland dogs
follow.
Says one dog to the other, 'This park, sir, is mine,
sir.'
The reply is not wanting: hoarse clashing and
mouthing
Arouses the masters.
Then Colonel Montgomery, of the Life-Guards,
dismounts.
'Whose dog is this?' The reply is not wanting,
From Captain Macnamara, Royal Navy: 'My
dog.'

'Then call your dog off, or by God he'll go
  sprawling.'
'If my dog goes sprawling, you must knock me
  down after.'
'Your name?' 'Macnamara, and yours is——'
  'Montgomery.'
'And why, sir, not call your dog off?' 'Sir, I chose
Not to do so, no man has dictated to me yet,
And you, I propose, will not change that.' 'This
  place,
For adjusting disputes, is not proper'—and the
  Colonel,
Back to the saddle, continues, 'If your dog
Fights my dog, I warn you, I knock your dog
  down.
For the rest, you are welcome to know where to
  find me,
Colonel Montgomery; and you will of course
Respond with the due information.' 'Be sure of
  it.'

Now comes the evening, green-twinkling, clear-
  echoing,
And out to Chalk-farm the Colonel, the Captain,
Each with his group of believers, have driven.
    Primrose Hill on an April evening
    Even now in a fevered London
    Sings a vesper sweet; but these
    Will try another music. Hark!
These are the pistols; let us test them; quite
  perfect.
Montgomery, Macnamara six paces, two faces;

Montgomery, Macnamara—both speaking together
In nitre and lead, the style is incisive,
Montgomery fallen, Macnamara half-falling,
The surgeon exploring the work of the evening—
And the Newfoundland dogs stretched at home in
     the firelight.

The coroner's inquest; the view of one body;
And then, pale, supported, appears at Old Bailey
James Macnamara, to whom this arraignment:
  You stand charged
  That you
  With force and arms
  Did assault Robert Montgomery,
  With a certain pistol
  Of the value of ten shillings,
  Loaded with powder and a leaden bullet,
  Which the gunpowder, feloniously exploded,
  Drove into the body of Robert Montgomery,
  And gave
  One mortal wound;
  Thus you did kill and slay
  The said Robert Montgomery.

O heavy imputation! O dead that yet speaks!
  O evening transparency, burst to red thunder!

Speak, Macnamara. He, tremulous as a wind-
     flower,
Exactly imparts what had slaughtered the Colonel.
'Insignificant the origin of the fact now before you;
Defending our dogs, we grew warm; that was
     nature;

That heat of itself had not led to disaster.
From defence to defiance was the leap that destroyed.
At once he would have at my deity, Honour—
"If you are offended you know where to find
    me."
On one side, I saw the wide mouths of Contempt,
Mouth to mouth working, a thousand vile gun-
    mouths;
On the other my Honour; Gentlemen of the Jury,
I am a Captain in the British Navy.'

Then said Lord Hood: 'For Captain Macnamara,
He is a gentleman and so says the Navy.'
Then said Lord Nelson: 'I have known Macnamara
Nine years, a gentleman, beloved in the Navy,
Not to be affronted by any man, true,
Yet as I stand here before God and my country,
Macnamara has never offended, and would not,
Man, woman, child.' Then a spring tide of
    admirals,
Almost Neptune in person, proclaim Macnamara
Mild, amiable, cautious, as any in the Navy
And Mr. Garrow rises, to state that if need be,
To assert the even temper and peace of his client,
He would call half the Captains in the British
    Navy.

Now we are shut from the duel that Honour
Must fight with the Law; no eye can perceive
The fields wherein hundreds of shadowy combats
Must decide between a ghost and a living idolon—
A ghost with his army of the terrors of bloodshed,

A half-ghost with the grand fleet of names that like
    sunrise
Have dazzled the race with their march on the
    ocean.
Twenty minutes. How say you?
  Not guilty.

Then from his chair with his surgeon the Captain
Walks home to his dog, his friends' acclamations
Supplying some colour to the pale looks he had,
Less pale than Montgomery's; and Honour rides on.

116. NOVEMBER

THE lonely season in lonely lands, when fled
Are half the birds, and mists lie low, and the sun
Is rarely seen, nor strayeth far from his bed;
The short days pass unwelcomed one by one.

  Out by the ricks the mantled engine stands
Crestfallen, deserted,—for now all hands
Are told to the plough,—and ere it is dawn appear
The teams following and crossing far and near,
As hour by hour they broaden the brown bands
Of the striped fields; and behind them firk and
    prance
The heavy rooks, and daws grey-pated dance:
As awhile, surmounting a crest, in sharp outline
(A miniature of toil, a gem's design,)
They are pictured, horses and men, or now near by
Above the lane they shout lifting the share,
By the trim hedgerow bloom'd with purple air;

Where, under the thorns, dead leaves in huddle lie
Packed by the gales of Autumn, and in and out
The small wrens glide
With a happy note of cheer,
And yellow amorets flutter above and about,
Gay, familiar in fear.

And now, if the night shall be cold, across the sky
Linnets and twites, in small flocks helter-skelter,
All the afternoon to the gardens fly,
From thistle-pastures hurrying to gain the shelter
Of American rhododendron or cherry-laurel:
And here and there, near chilly setting of sun,
In an isolated tree a congregation
Of starlings chatter and chide,
Thickset as summer leaves, in garrulous quarrel:
Suddenly they hush as one,—
The tree top springs,—
And off, with a whirr of wings,
They fly by the score
To the holly-thicket, and there with myriads more
Dispute for the roosts; and from the unseen nation
A babel of tongues, like running water unceasing,
Makes live the wood, the flocking cries increasing,
Wrangling discordantly, incessantly,
While falls the night on them self-occupied;
The long dark night, that lengthens slow,
Deepening with Winter to starve grass and tree,
And soon to bury in snow
The Earth, that, sleeping 'neath her frozen stole,
Shall dream a dream crept from the sunless pole
Of how her end shall be.

117. THE PYLONS

THE secret of these hills was stone, and cottages
Of that stone made,
And crumbling roads
That turned on sudden hidden villages.

Now over these small hills they have built the
    concrete
That trails black wire:
Pylons, those pillars
Bare like nude, giant girls that have no secret.

The valley with its gilt and evening look
And the green chestnut
Of customary root
Are mocked dry like the parched bed of a brook.

But far above and far as sight endures
Like whips of anger
With lightning's danger
There runs the quick perspective of the future.

This dwarfs our emerald country by its trek
So tall with prophecy:
Dreaming of cities
Where often clouds shall lean their swan-white
    neck.

118.

THE sely wydow, and hir doughtres tuo,
Herden these hennys crie and maken wo,
And out at dores starte thay anoon,

And sawen the fox toward the grove goon,
And bar upon his bak the cok away;
They criden, 'Out! harrow and wayleway!
Ha, ha, the fox!' and after him thay ranne,
And eek with staves many another manne;
Ran Colle our dogge, and Talbot, and Garlond,
And Malkyn, with a distaf in hir hond;
Ran cow and calf, and eek the verray hogges
Sore fered were for berkyng of dogges,
And schowtyng of the men and wymmen eke,
Thay ronne that thay thought her herte breke.
Thay yelleden as feendes doon in helle;
The dokes criden as men wold hem quelle;
The gees for fere flowen over the trees;
Out of the hyves cam the swarm of bees;
So hidous was the noyse, a *benedicite*!
Certes he Jakke Straw, and his meyné,
Ne maden schoutes never half so schrille,
Whan that thay wolden eny Flemyng kille,
As thilke day was maad upon the fox.
Of bras thay broughten hornes and of box,
Of horn and boon, in which thay blew and powpede,
And therwithal thay schryked and thay howpede;
It semed tho as that heven schulde falle.

119.

THE silver swan, who living had no note
When death approached unlocked her silent throat;
Leaning her breast against the reedy shore,
Thus sung her first and last, and sung no more:
Farewell, all joys; O death, come close mine eyes;
More geese than swans now live, more fools than wise.

120. DEATH OF CHARLES II

THE Sons of Art all med'cines try'd,
And every noble remedy applied,
With emulation each essay'd
His utmost skill, nay more they pray'd:
Never was losing game with better conduct plaid.
Death never won a stake with greater toyl,
Nor e're was Fate so near a foil:
But, like a fortress on a Rock
Th' impregnable Disease their vain attempts did
    mock;
They min'd it near, they batter'd from afar
With all the cannon of the Med'cinal War;
No gentle means could be essay'd,
'Twas beyond parly when the siege was laid:
The extreamest ways they first ordain,
Prescribing such intolerable pain
As none but Cæsar could sustain;
Undaunted Cæsar underwent
The malice of their Art, nor bent
Beneath what e're their pious rigour cou'd invent.
In five such days he suffer'd more
Than any suffer'd in his reign before;
More, infinitely more than he
Against the worst of rebels cou'd decree,
A Traytor, or twice pardon'd Enemy.
Now Art was tir'd without success,
No Racks could make the stubborn malady confess.
    The vain *Insurancers* of life,
And He who most perform'd and promis'd less,
    Even Short himself forsook the unequal strife.

Death and despair were in their looks,
No longer they consult their memories or books;
Like helpless friends, who view from shoar
The labouring Ship and hear the tempest roar,
  So stood they with their arms across;
Not to assist; but to deplore
    Th' inevitable loss.

121. MAD SONG

THE wild winds weep,
  And the night is a-cold;
Come hither, Sleep,
  And my griefs enfold!
But lo! the morning peeps
Over the eastern steeps,
And the rustling birds of dawn
The earth do scorn.

Lo! to the vault
  Of pavèd heaven,
With sorrow fraught
  My notes are driven:
They strike the ear of Night,
  Make weep the eyes of Day;
They make mad the roaring winds,
  And with tempests play.

Like a fiend in a cloud,
  With howling woe
After night I do crowd,
  And with night will go;

I turn my back to the east
From whence comforts have increased;
For light doth seize my brain
With frantic pain.

122.

THEN Flattery fetched forth florins unnumbered,
Bidding Guile to go giving much gold all about,
Notably to notaries, none should be missed,
And to fee False-witness with florins at will;
"He'll be master of Meed, and will make her
assent!"

When given was the gold, full great was the
thanking
Of False and of Flattery, for their fair gifts;
Soon came they to comfort from care Sir False,
And said, "Sir, for certain, now cease will we never,
Till Meed be thy wife, through the wits of us all.
We have mastered Meed with our merry speech;
She has granted to go, with a right good will,
To London, to know if the law will allow
The judges to join you in joy everlasting."
Then fain was Sir False, and Flattery blithe;
And summoned all sage men from shires around,
And bade them be bound, both beggars and others,
To wend soon to Westminster, to witness this deed.
They hunted for horses, to hasten the journey,
And Flattery fetched forth some foals of the best.

Meed sat on a sheriff, new shod for the nonce,
False rode an assize-man, that softly trotted,
And Flattery a flatterer, finely attired.

Then had notaries none, annoyed were they all
That Civil-law and Simony should follow on foot;
But Simony swore, and Civil-law also,
That sumners should be saddled, to serve them at need,
And provisors apparelled as palfreys also;
Sir Simony himself was to sit on their backs.

"Ye deans and ye subdeans, now draw you
    together,
Archdeacons, officials, and registrars all,
Be saddled with silver, our sins to allow,
Adultery, divorces, and doubling of debts,
And payments for bishops that visit abroad.
The Paulines' people, for plaints in consistory,
Shall serve here myself, who am Civil-law named.
Cart-saddle the commissary, our cart shall he draw,
And lewd men shall fee us for lewdnesses winked at.
Give Liar a long cart, to lead all the others,
Such as friars and false men, that run all afoot."

Thus False and Sir Flattery fared on their way,
With Meed in the midst, and all these men after.
Time fails me to tell of the tail that did follow,
All manner of men that on earth's mould live;
But Guile was foregoer, and guided them all.
Soothness perceived them, and said but a little,
But pricked well his palfrey, and passed all the rout,
And came to the king's court, and told it to
    Conscience,
And Conscience to the king recounted it after.

160

"Now by Christ," quoth the king, "if I could but catch
False or Sir Flattery, or any of their fellows,
I'd wreak me on those wretches, that wrought have so ill,
And hang in a halter each hound that abets them!
Not a bairn or a brother should bail out the least,
But the sentence of law should be served upon all!"

He commanded a constable, that came at his call,
"Go, attach me those tyrants, I tell thee for sooth,
And fast fetter False, never free him for bribes;
Let Guile be beheaded, nor go a foot further.
If you light upon Liar, ne'er let him escape,
But put him in the pillory, in spite of his prayers;
And bring Meed to me, in spite of them all."

Dread stood at the door, and this doom heard,
How the king had commanded constables and sergeants
To fetter Sir False, and to bind all his fellows.
Then went Dread away, and gave warning to False,
Bade him flee for fear, and his fellows go with him.

Then False in his fear fled fast to the friars;
And Guile too was going, aghast for his life,
But met with some merchants, who made him abide,
Shut him in their shops, to show forth their ware,
And apparelled him as a 'prentice, the people to serve.

Then lightly did Liar go leaping away,
Lurking through lanes, and belaboured by many;

He was nowhere welcome for his wily tales,
But everywhere hooted, and hustled to flee,
Till pardoners had pity, and pulled him indoors,
Washed him and wiped him, and wound him in
    raiment,
And sent him with seals on Sundays to churches,
Giving pardons for pence, by pounds at a time.
Then leeches had envy, and letters they sent him
To dress as a doctor, and dwell with them ever.

The grocers besought him to sell men their spices,
And tout for their trade; their terms well he knew.
But minstrels and messengers met with him once,
And withheld him a half-year, and eleven days.
Friars with fair speech fetched him at last,
And coped him as a friar, lest comers should know
    him;
He has leave to go loose, as oft as he liketh,
And hie when he will to their house as his home.

All fled they for fear, and had flown into holes;
Save Meed the maid, not a man durst abide.

123.

THEN sang Deborah and Barak the son of Abinoam
on that day, saying,

Praise ye the Lord for the avenging of Israel, when
the people willingly offered themselves.

Hear, O ye kings; give ear, O ye princes; I, even
I, will sing unto the Lord; I will sing praise to the
Lord God of Israel.

Lord, when thou wentest out of Seir, when thou marchedst out of the field of Edom, the earth trembled, and the heavens dropped, the clouds also dropped water.

The mountains melted from before the Lord, even that Sinai from before the Lord God of Israel.

In the days of Shamgar the son of Anath, in the days of Jael, the highways were unoccupied, and the travellers walked through byways.

The inhabitants of the villages ceased, they ceased in Israel, until that I Deborah arose, that I arose a mother in Israel.

They chose new gods; then was war in the gates: was there a shield or spear seen among forty thousand in Israel?

My heart is toward the governors of Israel, that offered themselves willingly among the people. Bless ye the Lord.

Speak, ye that ride on white asses, ye that sit in judgment, and walk by the way.

They that are delivered from the noise of archers in the places of drawing water, there shall they rehearse the righteous acts of the Lord, even the righteous acts toward the inhabitants of his villages in Israel: then shall the people of the Lord go down to the gates.

Awake, awake, Deborah: awake, awake, utter a song: arise, Barak, and lead thy captivity captive, thou son of Abinoam.

Then he made him that remaineth have dominion

over the nobles among the people: the Lord made me have dominion over the mighty.

Out of Ephraim was there a root of them against Amalek; after thee, Benjamin, among thy people; out of Machir came down governors, and out of Zebulun they that handle the pen of the writer.

And the princes of Issachar were with Deborah; even Issachar, and also Barak: he was sent on foot into the valley. For the divisions of Reuben there were great thoughts of heart.

Why abodest thou among the sheepfolds, to hear the bleatings of the flocks? For the divisions of Reuben there were great searchings of heart.

Gilead abode beyond Jordan: and why did Dan remain in ships? Asher continued on the sea shore, and abode in his breaches.

Zebulun and Napthali were a people that jeoparded their lives unto the death in the high places of the field.

The kings came and fought, then fought the kings of Canaan in Taanach by the waters of Megiddo; they took no gain of money.

They fought from heaven; the stars in their courses fought against Sisera.

The river of Kishon swept them away, that ancient river, the river Kishon. O my soul, thou hast trodden down strength.

Then were the horsehoofs broken by the means of the pransings, the pransings of their mighty ones.

Curse ye Meroz, said the angel of the Lord, curse

ye bitterly the inhabitants thereof; because they came not to the help of the Lord, to the help of the Lord against the mighty.

Blessed above women shall Jael the wife of Heber the Kenite be, blessed shall she be above women in the tent.

He asked water, and she gave him milk; she brought forth butter in a lordly dish.

She put her hand to the nail, and her right hand to the workman's hammer; and with the hammer she smote Sisera, she smote off his head, when she had pierced and stricken through his temples.

At her feet he bowed, he fell, he lay down: at her feet he bowed, he fell: where he bowed, there he fell down dead.

The mother of Sisera looked out at a window, and cried through the lattice, Why is his chariot so long in coming? why tarry the wheels of his chariots?

Her wise ladies answered her, yea, she returned answer to herself,

Have they not sped? have they not divided the prey; to every man a damsel or two; to Sisera a prey of divers colours, a prey of divers colours of needlework, of divers colours of needlework on both sides, meet for the necks of them that take the spoil?

So let all thine enemies perish, O Lord: but let them that love him be as the sun when he goeth forth in his might.

THERE lived a wife at Usher's Well,
 And a wealthy wife was she;
She had three stout and stalwart sons,
 And sent them o'er the sea.

They hadna been a week from her,
 A week but barely ane,
When word came to the carline [1] wife,
 That her three sons were gane.

They hadna been a week from her,
 A week but barely three,
When word came to the carline wife,
 That her sons she'd never see.

"I wish the wind may never cease,
 Nor fishes in the flood,
Till my three sons come hame to me,
 In earthly flesh and blood!"

It fell about the Martinmas,
 When nights are lang and mirk,
The carline wife's three sons came hame,
 And their hats were o' the birk.

It neither grew in syke [2] nor ditch,
 Nor yet in ony sheugh [3];
But at the gates o' Paradise,
 That birk grew fair eneugh.

  . . . . . .

[1] old.   [2] stream.   [3] trench.

"Blow up the fire, my maidens!
  Bring water from the well!
For a' my house shall feast this night,
  Since my three sons are well."

And she has made to them a bed,
  She's made it large and wide;
And she's ta'en her mantle her about,
  Sat down at the bedside.

      .   .   .   .   .   .

Up then crew the red red cock,
  And up and crew the gray;
The eldest to the youngest said,
  "'Tis time we were away."

The cock he hadna craw'd but once,
  And clapp'd his wings at a',
When the youngest to the eldest said,
  "Brother, we must awa.

"The cock doth craw, the day doth daw,
  The channerin' worm doth chide;
Gin we be mist out o' our place,
  A sair pain we maun bide.

"Fare ye weel, my mother dear!
  Fareweel to barn and byre!
And fare ye weel, the bonny lass,
  That kindles my mother's fire."

      .   .   .   .   .   .

THERE's a certain slant of light,
On winter afternoons,
That oppresses, like the weight
Of cathedral tunes.

Heavenly hurt it gives us;
We can find no scar,
But internal difference
Where the meanings are.

None may teach it anything,
'T is the seal, despair,—
An imperial affliction
Sent us of the air.

When it comes, the landscape listens,
Shadows hold their breath;
When it goes, 't is like the distance
On the look of death.

·126. ON MONSIEUR COUÉ

THIS very remarkable man
Commends a most practical plan;
You can do what you want
    If you don't think you can't,
So don't think you can't think you can.

THOU who, when fears attack,
Bidst them avaunt, and Black
Care, at the horseman's back
   Perching, unseatest;
Sweet, when the morn is gray;
Sweet, when they've cleared away
Lunch; and at close of day
   Possibly sweetest:

I have a liking old
For thee, though manifold
Stories, I know, are told,
   Not to thy credit;
How one (or two at most)
Drops make a cat a ghost—
Useless, except to roast—
   Doctors have said it:

How they who use fusees
All grow by slow degrees
Brainless as chimpanzees,
   Meagre as lizards:
Go mad, and beat their wives;
Plunge (after shocking lives)
Razors and carving knives
   Into their gizzards.

Confound such knavish tricks!
Yet know I five or six
Smokers who freely mix
   Still with their neighbours;

Jones—(who, I'm glad to say,
Asked leave of Mrs. J.)—
Daily absorbs a clay
    After his labours.

Cats may have had their goose
Cooked by tobacco-juice;
Still why deny its use
    Thoughtfully taken?
We're not as tabbies are:
Smith, take a fresh cigar!
Jones, the tobacco-jar!
    Here's to thee, Bacon!

128.

TIRED with all these, for restful death I cry,—
As, to behold desert a beggar born,
And needy nothing trimm'd in jollity,
And purest faith unhappily forsworn,
And gilded honour shamefully misplaced,
And maiden virtue rudely strumpeted,
And right perfection wrongfully disgraced,
And strength by limping sway disabled,
And art made tongue-tied by authority,
And folly, doctor-like, controlling skill,
And simple truth miscall'd simplicity,
And captive good attending captain ill:
    Tired with all these, from these would I be gone,
    Save that, to die, I leave my love alone.

129. THE DIVINE IMAGE

To Mercy, Pity, Peace, and Love,
　All pray in their distress,
And to these virtues of delight
　Return their thankfulness.

For Mercy, Pity, Peace, and Love,
　Is God, our Father dear;
And Mercy, Pity, Peace, and Love,
　Is man, His child and care.

For Mercy has a human heart;
　Pity, a human face;
And Love, the human form divine:
　And Peace, the human dress.

Then every man, of every clime,
　That prays in his distress,
Prays to the human form divine:
　Love, Mercy, Pity, Peace.

And all must love the human form,
　In heathen, Turk, or Jew.
Where Mercy, Love, and Pity dwell,
　There God is dwelling too.

130.

To-night the winds begin to rise
　And roar from yonder dropping day:
　The last red leaf is whirl'd away,
The rooks are blown about the skies;

The forest crack'd, the waters curl'd,
  The cattle huddled on the lea;
  And wildly dash'd on tower and tree
The sunbeam strikes along the world:

And but for fancies, which aver
  That all thy motions gently pass
  Athwart a plane of molten glass,
I scarce could brook the strain and stir

That makes the barren branches loud;
  And but for fear it is not so,
  The wild unrest that lives in woe
Would dote and pore on yonder cloud

That rises upward always higher,
  And onward drags a labouring breast,
  And topples round the dreary west,
A looming bastion fringed with fire.

131.

TOWARDS me did runne
A thing more strange, than on Niles slime, the Sunne
E'r bred; or all which into Noahs Arke came;
A thing, which would have pos'd Adam to name;
Stranger then seaven Antiquaries studies;
Than Africks monsters, Guianaes rarities.
Stranger than strangers; One, who for a Dane,
In the Danes Massacre had sure beene slaine,
If he had liv'd then: And without helpe dies,
When next the Prentises 'gainst Strangers rise.

One, whom the watch at noone lets scarce goe by,
One, to whom, the examining Justice sure would cry,
Sir, by your priesthood tell me what you are.
His cloths were strange, though coarse; and black,
    though bare;
Sleeveless his jerkin was, and it had beene
Velvet, but 'twas now (so much ground was seene)
Become Tufftaffatie; and our children shall
See it plaine Rashe awhile, then nought at all.
This thing hath travail'd, and saith, speakes all
    tongues
And only knoweth what to all states belongs.
Made of th' Accents, and best phrase of all these
He speakes one language.   If strange meats displease,
Art can deceive, or hunger force my tast,
But Pedants moteley tongue, souldiers bumbast,
Mountebankes drug-tongue, nor the termes of law
Are strong enough preparatives, to draw
Me to beare this: yet I must be content
With his tongue, in his tongue, call'd complement.

132. ASLEEP

Under his helmet, up against his pack,
After the many days of work and waking,
Sleep took him by the brow and laid him back.
And in the happy no-time of his sleeping,
Death took him by the heart.   There was a quaking
Of the aborted life within him leaping ......
Then chest and sleepy arms once more fell slack.

And soon the slow, stray blood came creeping
From the intrusive lead, like ants on track.

* * * * * * * *

Whether his deeper sleep lie shaded by the shaking
Of great wings, and the thoughts that hung the
    stars,
High-pillowed on calm pillows of God's making
Above these clouds, these rains, these sleets of lead,
And these winds' scimitars;
—Or whether yet his thin and sodden head
Confuses more and more with the low mould,
His hair being one with the grey grass
Of finished fields and wire-scrags rusty old ......
Who knows? Who hopes? Who troubles? Let it
    pass!
He sleeps. He sleeps less tremulous, less cold,
Than we who wake, and waking, say Alas!

133

WAKE all the dead! what ho! what ho!
  How soundly they sleep whose pillows lie low?
They mind not poor lovers who walk above
On the decks of the world in storms of love.
  No whisper now nor glance shall pass
    Through thickets or through panes of glass;
For our windows and doors are shut and barred.
Lie close in the church, and in the churchyard.
  In every grave, make room, make room!
  The world's at an end, and we come, we come.

WE know him, out of Shakspeare's art,
   And those fine curses which he spoke;
The old Timon, with his noble heart,
   That, strongly loathing, greatly broke.

So died the Old: here comes the New.
   Regard him: a familiar face:
I *thought* we knew him: What, it's you,
   The padded man—that wears the stays—

Who kill'd the girls and thrill'd the boys,
   With dandy pathos when you wrote,
A Lion, you, that made a noise,
   And shook a mane en papillotes.

And once you tried the Muses too;
   You fail'd, Sir: therefore now you turn,
You fall on those who are to you,
   As Captain is to Subaltern.

But men of long-enduring hopes,
   And careless what this hour may bring,
Can pardon little would-be Popes
   And Brummels, when they try to sting.

An artist, Sir, should rest in Art,
   And waive a little of his claim;
To have the deep Poetic heart
   Is more than all poetic fame.

But you, Sir, you are hard to please;
    You never look but half content:
Nor like a gentleman at ease,
    With moral breadth of temperament.

And what with spites and what with fears,
    You cannot let a body be:
It's always ringing in your ears,
    'They call this man as good as *me*.'

What profits now to understand
    The merits of a spotless shirt—
A dapper boot—a little hand—
    If half the little soul is dirt?

You talk of tinsel! why we see
    The old mark of rouge upon your cheeks.
You prate of Nature! you are he
    That spilt his life about the cliques.

A Timon you! Nay, nay, for shame:
    It looks too arrogant a jest—
The fierce old man—to take *his* name,
    You bandbox. Off, and let him rest.

135.

Weep, O mine eyes, and cease not;
Your spring-tides, out alas, methinks increase not.
    O when, O when begin you
To swell so high that I may drown me in you?

136.

WELAND, the resolute warrior, had knowledge of exile; he suffered hardships; sorrow and longing he had for companions, wintry cold exile. Often he found woes after *Nithad* put compulsion upon him, supple bonds of sinew upon a more excellent man.

That passed away, so may this.

137. CONFERENCE IN HELL

"WELL have ye judged, well ended long debate,
Synod of gods, and like to what ye are,
Great things resolved; which from the lowest deep
Will once more lift us up, in spite of Fate,
Nearer our ancient Seat; perhaps in view
Of those bright confines, whence with neighbouring
        arms
And opportune excursion, we may chance
Re-enter Heaven; or else in some mild zone
Dwell not unvisited of Heaven's fair light,
Secure, and at the brightening Orient beam
Purge off this gloom; the soft delicious air,
To heal the scar of these corrosive fires,
Shall breathe her balm. But first whom shall we
        send
In search of this new world, whom shall we find
Sufficient? who shall tempt with wandering feet
The dark unbottomed infinite abyss,
And through the palpable obscure find out
His uncouth way, or spread his aery flight

Upborne with indefatigable wings
Over the vast abrupt, ere he arrive
The happy isle; what strength, what art can then
Suffice, or what evasion bear him safe
Through the strict senteries and stations thick
Of angels watching round?   Here he had need
All circumspection, and we now no less
Choice in our suffrage; for on whom we send,
The weight of all and our last hope relies."

　　This said, he sat; and expectation held
His look suspense, awaiting who appeared
To second, or oppose, or undertake
The perilous attempt; but all sat mute,
Pondering the danger with deep thoughts;   and
　　each
In others countenance read his own dismay
Astonished: none among the choice and prime
Of those Heaven-warring champions could be
　　found
So hardy as to proffer or accept,
Alone the dreadful voyage; till, at last
Satan, whom now transcendent glory raised
Above his fellows, with monarchal pride,
Conscious of highest worth, unmoved thus spake.

　　"O Progeny of Heaven, Empyreal Thrones,
With reason hath deep silence and demur
Seized us, though undismayed: long is the way
And hard, that out of Hell leads up to Light;
Our prison strong, this huge convex of fire,
Outrageous to devour, immures us round
Ninefold, and gates of burning adamant
Barred over us prohibit all egress.

These passed, if any pass, the void profound
Of unessential Night receives him next
Wide gaping, and with utter loss of being
Threatens him, plunged in that abortive gulf.
If thence he 'scape into whatever world,
Or unknown region, what remains him less
Than unknown dangers and as hard escape.
But I should ill become this throne, O Peers,
And this imperial sovereignty, adorned
With splendour, armed with power, if aught
    proposed
And judged of public moment, in the shape
Of difficulty or danger could deter
Me from attempting.   Wherefore do I assume
These royalties, and not refuse to reign,
Refusing to accept as great a share
Of hazard as of honour, due alike
To him who reigns, and so much to him due
Of hazard more, as he above the rest
High honoured sits?   Go therefore mighty Powers,
Terror of Heaven, though fallen; intend at home,
While here shall be our home, what best may
    ease
The present misery, and render Hell
More tolerable; if there be cure or charm
To respite or deceive, or slack the pain
Of this ill mansion: intermit no watch
Against a wakeful Foe, while I abroad
Through all the coasts of dark destruction seek
Deliverance for us all: this enterprise
None shall partake with me." Thus saying rose
The monarch, and prevented all reply,

Prudent lest from his resolution raised
Others among the chief might offer now
(Certain to be refused) what erst they feared;
And so refused might in opinion stand
His rivals, winning cheap the high repute
Which he through hazard huge must earn.   But
    they
Dreaded not more the adventure than his voice
Forbidding; and at once with him they rose;
Their rising all at once was as the sound
Of thunder heard remote.   Towards him they bend
With awful reverence prone; and as a God
Extol him equal to the highest in Heaven:
Nor failed they to express how much they praised,
That for the general safety he despised
His own; for neither do the Spirits damned
Lose all their virtue; lest bad men should boast
Their specious deeds on earth, which glory excites,
Or close ambition varnished o'er with zeal.
Thus they their doubtful consultations dark
Ended rejoicing in their matchless Chief.

138. THE MOTOR BUS

WHAT is this that roareth thus?
Can it be a Motor Bus?
Yes, the smell and hideous hum
Indicat Motorem Bum!
Implet in the Corn and High
Terror me Motoris Bi:
Bo Motori clamitabo
Ne Motore caedar a Bo—

Dative be or Ablative
So thou only let us live:
Whither shall thy victims flee?
Spare us, spare us, Motor Be!
Thus I sang; and still anigh
Came in hordes Motores Bi,
Et complebat omne forum
Copia Motorum Borum.
How shall wretches live like us
Cincti Bis Motoribus?
Domine, defende nos
Contra hos Motores Bos!

139.

WHAT slender Youth bedew'd with liquid odours
Courts thee on Roses in some pleasant Cave,
   Pyrrha for whom bind'st thou
   In wreaths thy golden Hair,
Plain in thy neatness? O how oft shall he
On Faith and changed Gods complain: and Seas
   Rough with black winds and storms
   Unwonted shall admire:
Who now enjoys thee credulous, all Gold,
Who always vacant, always amiable
   Hopes thee, of flattering gales
   Unmindful. Hapless they
To whom thou untried seem'st fair. Me in my
     vow'd
Picture the sacred wall declares t' have hung
   My dank and dropping weeds
   To the stern God of Sea.

140

I

1

WHAT's become of Waring
Since he gave us all the slip,
Chose land-travel or seafaring,
Boots and chest or staff and scrip,
Rather than pace up and down
Any longer London town?

2

Who'd have guessed it from his lip
Or his brow's accustomed bearing,
On the night he thus took ship
Or started landward?—little caring
For us, it seems, who supped together
(Friends of his too, I remember)
And walked home thro' the merry weather,
The snowiest in all December.
I left his arm that night myself
For what's-his-name's, the new prose-poet
Who wrote the book there, on the shelf—
How, forsooth, was I to know it
If Waring meant to glide away
Like a ghost at break of day?
Never looked he half so gay!

. . . .

6

Ichabod, Ichabod,
The glory is departed!
Travels Waring East away?

Who, of knowledge, by hearsay,
Reports a man upstarted
Somewhere as a god,
Hordes grown European-hearted,
Millions of the wild made tame
On a sudden at his fame?
In Vishnu-land what Avatar?
Or who in Moscow, toward the Czar,
With the demurest of footfalls
Over the Kremlin's pavement bright
With serpentine and syenite,
Steps, with five other Generals
That simultaneously take snuff,
For each to have pretext enough
And kerchiefwise unfold his sash
Which, softness' self, is yet the stuff
To hold fast where a steel chain snaps,
And leave the grand white neck no gash?
Waring in Moscow, to those rough
Cold northern natures born perhaps,
Like the lambwhite maiden dear
From the circle of mute kings
Unable to repress the tear,
Each as his sceptre down he flings,
To Dian's fane at Taurica,
Where now a captive priestess, she alway
Mingles her tender grave Hellenic speech
With theirs, tuned to the hailstone-beaten beach
As pours some pigeon, from the myrrhy lands
Rapt by the whirlblast to fierce Scythian strands
Where breed the swallows, her melodious cry
Amid their barbarous twitter!

In Russia? Never! Spain were fitter!
Ay, most likely 'tis in Spain
That we and Waring meet again
Now, while he turns down that cool narrow lane
Into the blackness, out of grave Madrid
All fire and shine, abrupt as when there's slid
Its stiff gold blazing pall
From some black coffin-lid.
Or, best of all,
I love to think
The leaving us was just a feint;
Back here to London did he slink,
And now works on without a wink
Of sleep, and we are on the brink
Of something great in fresco-paint:
Some garret's ceiling, walls and floor,
Up and down and o'er and o'er
He splashes, as none splashed before
Since great Caldara Polidore.
Or Music means this land of ours
Some favour yet, to pity won
By Purcell from his Rosy Bowers,—
"Give me my so-long promised son,
"Let Waring end what I begun!"
Then down he creeps and out he steals
Only when the night conceals
His face; in Kent 'tis cherry-time,
Or hops are picking: or at prime
Of March he wanders as, too happy,
Years ago when he was young.

. . . . . .

II

I

"When I last saw Waring . . . "
(How all turned to him who spoke!
You saw Waring?   Truth or joke?
In land-travel or sea-faring?)

2

"We were sailing by Triest
"Where a day or two we harboured:
"A sunset was in the West,
"When, looking over the vessel's side,
"One of our company espied
"A sudden speck to larboard.
"And as a sea-duck flies and swims
"At once, so came the light craft up,
"With its sole lateen sail that trims
"And turns (the water round its rims
"Dancing, as round a sinking cup)
"And by us like a fish it curled,
"And drew itself up close beside,
"Its great sail on the instant furled,
"And o'er its thwarts a shrill voice cried,
"(A neck as bronzed as a Lascar's)
"'Buy wine of us, you English Brig?
"'Or fruit, tobacco and cigars?
"'A pilot for you to Triest?
"'Without one, look you ne'er so big,
"'They'll never let you up the bay!
"'We natives should know best.'
"I turned, and 'just those fellows' way,'

"Our captain said, 'The 'long-shore thieves
"'Are laughing at us in their sleeves.'

3

"In truth, the boy leaned laughing back;
"And one, half-hidden by his side
"Under the furled sail, soon I spied,
"With great grass hat and kerchief black,
"Who looked up with his kingly throat,
"Said somewhat, while the other shook
"His hair back from his eyes to look
"Their longest at us; then the boat,
"I know not how, turned sharply round,
"Laying her whole side on the sea
"As a leaping fish does; from the lee
"Into the weather, cut somehow
"Her sparkling path beneath our bow
"And so went off, as with a bound,
"Into the rosy and golden half
"O' the sky, to overtake the sun
"And reach the shore, like the sea-calf
"Its singing cave; yet I caught one
"Glance ere away the boat quite passed,
"And neither time nor toil could mar
"Those features: so I saw the last
"Of Waring!"—You?   Oh, never star
Was lost here but it rose afar!
Look East, where whole new thousands are!
In Vishnu-land what Avatar?

141. L'ENFANT GLACÉ

WHEN Baby's cries grew hard to bear
I popped him in the Frigidaire.
I never would have done so if
I'd known that he'd be frozen stiff.
My wife said: "George, I'm so unhappé!
Our darling's now completely *frappé*!"

142. ON BUNGALOID GROWTH

WHEN England's multitudes observed with frowns
   That those who came before had spoiled the towns,
'This can no longer be endured!' they cried,
   And set to work to spoil the countryside.

143. FANCY'S KNELL

WHEN lads were home from labour
   At Abdon under Clee,
A man would call his neighbour
   And both would send for me.
And where the light in lances
   Across the mead was laid,
There to the dances
   I fetched my flute and played.

Ours were idle pleasures,
   Yet oh, content we were,
The young to wind the measures,
   The old to heed the air;

And I to lift with playing
   From tree and tower and steep
The light delaying,
   And flute the sun to sleep.

The youth toward his fancy
   Would turn his brow of tan,
And Tom would pair with Nancy
   And Dick step off with Fan;
The girl would lift her glances
   To his, and both be mute:
Well went the dances
   At evening to the flute.

Wenlock Edge was umbered,
   And bright was Abdon Burf,
And warm between them slumbered
   The smooth green miles of turf;
Until from grass and clover
   The upshot beam would fade,
And England over
   Advanced the lofty shade.

The lofty shade advances,
   I fetch my flute and play:
Come, lads, and learn the dances
   And praise the tune to-day.
To-morrow, more's the pity,
   Away we both must hie,
To air the ditty,
   And to earth I.

144. OPPORTUNITY

WHEN Mrs. Gorm (Aunt Eloïse)
Was stung to death by savage bees,
Her husband (Prebendary Gorm)
Put on his veil, and took the swarm.
He's publishing a book, next May,
On "How to Make Bee-keeping Pay."

145.

WHEN the eye of day is shut,
　And the stars deny their beams,
And about the forest hut
　Blows the roaring wood of dreams,

From deep clay, from desert rock,
　From the sunk sands of the main,
Come not at my door to knock,
　Hearts that loved me not again.

Sleep, be still, turn to your rest
　In the lands where you are laid;
In far lodgings east and west
　Lie down on the beds you made.

In gross marl, in blowing dust,
　In the drowned ooze of the sea,
Where you would not, lie you must,
　Lie you must, and not with me.

146. THE DAY OF JUDGMENT

WHEN the fierce North-wind with his airy forces
Rears up the Baltic to a foaming fury;
And the red lightning with a storm of hail comes
                  Rushing amain down;

How the poor sailors stand amazed and tremble,
While the hoarse thunder, like a bloody trumpet,
Roars a loud onset to the gaping waters
                  Quick to devour them.

Such shall the noise be, and the wild disorder
(If things eternal may be like these earthly),
Such the dire terror when the great Archangel
                  Shakes the creation;

Tears the strong pillars of the vault of Heaven,
Breaks up old marble, the repose of princes,
Sees the graves open, and the bones arising,
                  Flames all around them.

    .   .   .   .   .   .

147. AFTERWARDS

WHEN the Present has latched its postern behind
    my tremulous stay,
And the May month flaps its glad green leaves
    like wings,
Delicate-filmed as new-spun silk, will the neighbours
    say,
    "He was a man who used to notice such things"?

If it be in the dusk when, like an eyelid's soundless
    blink,
  The dewfall-hawk comes crossing the shades to
    alight
Upon the wind-warped upland thorn, a gazer may
    think,
  "To him this must have been a familiar sight."

If I pass during some nocturnal blackness, mothy
    and warm,
  When the hedgehog travels furtively over the
    lawn,
One may say, "He strove that such innocent
    creatures should come to no harm,
  But he could do little for them; and now he is
    gone."

If, when hearing that I have been stilled at last,
    they stand at the door,
  Watching the full-starred heavens that winter
    sees,
Will this thought rise on those who will meet my
    face no more,
  "He was one who had an eye for such mysteries"?

And will any say when my bell of quittance is heard
    in the gloom,
  And a crossing breeze cuts a pause in its out-
    rollings,
Till they rise again, as they were a new bell's boom,
  "He hears it not now, but used to notice such
    things?"

148. NIGHTMARE

WHEN you're lying awake with a dismal headache,
    and repose is taboo'd by anxiety,
I conceive you may use any language you choose to
    indulge in, without impropriety;
For your brain is on fire—the bedclothes conspire of
    usual slumber to plunder you:
First your counterpane goes, and uncovers your toes,
    and your sheet slips demurely from under you;
Then the blanketing tickles—you feel like mixed
    pickles—so terribly sharp is the pricking,
And you're hot, and you're cross, and you tumble
    and toss till there's nothing 'twixt you and the
    ticking.
Then the bedclothes all creep to the ground in a heap,
    and you pick 'em all up in a tangle;
Next your pillow resigns and politely declines to
    remain at its usual angle!
Well, you get some repose in the form of a doze, with
    hot eye-balls and head ever aching,
But your slumbering teems with such horrible dreams
    that you'd very much better be waking;
For you dream you are crossing the Channel, and
    tossing about in a steamer from Harwich—
Which is something between a large bathing machine
    and a very small second-class carriage—
And you're giving a treat (penny ice and cold meat)
    to a party of friends and relations—
They're a ravenous horde—and they all come on
    board at Sloane Square and South Kensington
    Stations.

And bound on that journey you find your attorney
    (who started that morning from Devon);
He's a bit undersized, and you don't feel surprised
    when he tells you he's only eleven.
Well, you're driving like mad with this singular lad
    (by-the-bye the ship's now a four-wheeler),
And you're playing round games, and he calls you
    bad names when you tell him that "ties pay the
    dealer";
But this you can't stand, as you throw up your hand,
    and you find you're as cold as an icicle,
In your shirt and your socks (the black silk with gold
    clocks), crossing Salisbury Plain on a bicycle:
And he and the crew are on bicycles too—which
    they've somehow or other invested in—
And he's telling the tars, all the particu*lars* of a com-
    pany he's interested in—
It's a scheme of devices, to get at low prices all goods
    from cough mixtures to cables
(Which tickled the sailors) by treating retailers, as
    though they were all vege*ta*bles—
You get a good spadesman to plant a small trades-
    man (first take off his boots with a boot-
    tree),
And his legs will take root, and his fingers will shoot,
    and they'll blossom and bud like a fruit-tree—
From the greengrocer tree you get grapes and green-
    pea, cauliflower, pineapple, and cranberries,
While the pastrycook plant, cherry brandy will grant,
    apple puffs, and three-corners, and Banburys—
The shares are a penny, and ever so many are taken
    by Rothschild and Baring,

And just as a few are allotted to you, you awake with
　　a shudder despairing—
You're a regular wreck, with a crick in your neck,
　　and no wonder you snore, for your head's on
　　the floor, and you've needles and pins from
　　your soles to your shins, and your flesh is a-creep,
　　for your left leg's asleep, and you've cramp in
　　your toes, and a fly on your nose, and some fluff
　　in your lung, and a feverish tongue, and a thirst
　　that's intense, and a general sense that you
　　haven't been sleeping in clover;
But the darkness has passed, and it's daylight at
　　last, and the night has been long—ditto ditto
　　my song—and thank goodness they're both of
　　them over!

149. THE DUCHESS OF ORMOND VISITS IRELAND

WHEN westward, like the Sun, you took your way,
And from benighted Britain bore the Day,
Blue Triton gave the signal from the Shore,
The ready nereids heard, and swam before
To smooth the seas; a soft Etesian Gale
But just inspir'd, and gently swell'd the sail;
Portunus took his turn, whose ample hand
Heav'd up the lighten'd keel, and sunk the sand,
And steer'd the sacred Vessel safe to land.
The land, if not restrain'd, had met your way,
Projected out a neck, and jutted to the sea.
Hibernia, prostrate at your feet, ador'd
In You the Pledge of her expected Lord;

Due to her Isle; a venerable name;
His father and his grandsire known to Fame;
Aw'd by that House, accustom'd to command,
The sturdy Kerns in due subjection stand,
Nor hear the reins in any foreign hand.

At your approach, they crowded to the port;
And scarcely landed, You create a court:
As Ormond's harbinger, to You they run,
For Venus is the promise of the Sun.

The waste of civil wars, their towns destroy'd,
Pales unhonour'd, Ceres unemploy'd,
Were all forgot; and one triumphant Day
Wip'd all the tears of three campaigns away.

150. AN ANCIENT TO ANCIENTS

WHERE once we danced, where once we sang,
        Gentlemen,
The floors are sunken, cobwebs hang,
And cracks creep; worms have fed upon
The doors.   Yea, sprightlier times were then
Than now, with harps and tabrets gone,
        Gentlemen!

Where once we rowed, where once we sailed,
        Gentlemen,
And damsels took the tiller, veiled
Against too strong a stare (God wot
Their fancy, then or anywhen!)
Upon that shore we are clean forgot,
        Gentlemen!

We have lost somewhat, afar and near,
          Gentlemen,
The thinning of our ranks each year
Affords a hint we are nigh undone,
That we shall not be ever again
The marked of many, loved of one,
          Gentlemen.

In dance the polka hit our wish,
          Gentlemen,
The paced quadrille, the spry schottische,
"Sir Roger."—And in opera spheres
The "Girl" (the famed "Bohemian"),
And "Trovatore," held the ears,
          Gentlemen.

This season's paintings do not please,
          Gentlemen,
Like Etty, Mulready, Maclise;
Throbbing romance has waned and wanned;
No wizard wields the witching pen
Of Bulwer, Scott, Dumas, and Sand,
          Gentlemen.

The bower we shrined to Tennyson,
          Gentlemen,
Is roof-wrecked; damps there drip upon
Sagged seats, the creeper-nails are rust,
The spider is sole denizen;
Even she who voiced those rhymes is dust,
          Gentlemen!

We who met sunrise sanguine-souled,
  Gentlemen,
Are wearing weary. We are old;
These younger press; we feel our rout
Is imminent to Aïdes' den,—
That evening shades are stretching out,
  Gentlemen!

And yet, though ours be failing frames,
  Gentlemen,
So were some others' history names,
Who trode their track light-limbed and fast
As these youth, and not alien
From enterprise, to their long last,
  Gentlemen.

Sophocles, Plato, Socrates,
  Gentlemen,
Pythagoras, Thucydides,
Herodotus, and Homer,—yea,
Clement, Augustin, Origen,
Burnt brightlier towards their setting-day,
  Gentlemen.

And ye, red-lipped and smooth-browed; list,
  Gentlemen;
Much is there waits you we have missed;
Much lore we leave you worth the knowing,
Much, much has lain outside our ken:
Nay, rush not: time serves: we are going,
  Gentlemen.

WHILE going the road to sweet Athy,
    Hurroo! Hurroo!
While going the road to sweet Athy,
    Hurroo! Hurroo!
While going the road to sweet Athy,
A stick in my hand and a drop in my eye,
A doleful damsel I heard cry:—
    "Och, Johnny, I hardly knew ye!
With drums and guns, and guns and drums
    The enemy nearly slew ye,
    My darling dear, you look so queer,
    Och, Johnny, I hardly knew ye!

"Where are your eyes that looked so mild?
    Hurroo! Hurroo!
Where are your eyes that looked so mild?
    Hurroo! Hurroo!
Where are your eyes that looked so mild
When my poor heart you first beguiled?
Why did you run from me and the child?
    Och, Johnny, I hardly knew ye!
With drums, etc.

"Where are the legs with which you run?
    Hurroo! Hurroo!
Where are the legs with which you run?
    Hurroo! Hurroo!
Where are the legs with which you run
When you went to carry a gun?—
Indeed your dancing days are done!
    Och, Johnny, I hardly knew ye!
With drums, etc.

"It grieved my heart to see you sail,
    Hurroo! Hurroo!
It grieved my heart to see you sail,
    Hurroo! Hurroo!
It grieved my heart to see you sail
Though from my heart you took leg bail,—
Like a cod you're doubled up head and tail.
    Och, Johnny, I hardly knew ye!
With drums, etc.

"You haven't an arm and you haven't a leg,
    Hurroo! Hurroo!
You haven't an arm and you haven't a leg,
    Hurroo! Hurroo!
You haven't an arm and you haven't a leg,
You're an eyeless, noseless, chickenless egg;
You'll have to be put in a bowl to beg;
    Och, Johnny, I hardly knew ye!
With drums, etc.

"I'm happy for to see you home,
    Hurroo! Hurroo!
I'm happy for to see you home,
    Hurroo! Hurroo!
I'm happy for to see you home,
All from the island of Sulloon,
So low in flesh, so high in bone,
    Och, Johnny, I hardly knew ye!
With drums, etc.

"But sad as it is to see you so,
    Hurroo! Hurroo!
But sad as it is to see you so,
    Hurroo! Hurroo!

But sad as it is to see you so,
And to think of you now as an object of woe,
Your Peggy'll still keep ye on as her beau;
　　Och, Johnny, I hardly knew ye!
With drums and guns, and guns and drums
　　The enemy nearly slew ye,
　　　My darling dear, you look so queer,
　　　Och, Johnny, I hardly knew ye!"

152.　EVE

"WHILE I sit at the door,
Sick to gaze within,
Mine eye weepeth sore
For sorrow and sin:
As a tree my sin stands
To darken all lands;
Death is the fruit it bore.

"How have Eden bowers grown
Without Adam to bend them!
How have Eden flowers blown,
Squandering their sweet breath,
Without me to tend them!
The Tree of Life was ours,
Tree twelvefold-fruited,
Most lofty tree that flowers,
Most deeply rooted:
I chose the Tree of Death.

"Hadst thou but said me nay,
Adam, my brother,
I might have pined away;
I, but none other:
God might have let thee stay
Safe in our garden
By putting me away
Beyond all pardon.

"I, Eve, sad mother
Of all who must live,
I, not another,
Plucked bitterest fruit to give
My friend, husband, lover.
O wanton eyes run over;
Who but I should grieve?—
Cain hath slain his brother:
Of all who must die mother,
Miserable Eve!"

Thus she sat weeping,
Thus Eve our mother,
Where one lay sleeping
Slain by his brother.
Greatest and least
Each piteous beast
To hear her voice
Forgot his joys
And set aside his feast.

The mouse paused in his walk
And dropped his wheaten stalk;

Grave cattle wagged their heads
In rumination;
The eagle gave a cry
From his cloud station:
Larks on thyme beds
Forbore to mount or sing;
Bees drooped upon the wing;
The raven perched on high
Forgot his ration;
The conies in their rock,
A feeble nation,
Quaked sympathetical;
The mocking-bird left off to mock;
Huge camels knelt as if
In deprecation;
The kind hart's tears were falling;
Chattered the wistful stork;
Dove-voices with a dying fall
Cooed desolation
Answering grief by grief.
Only the serpent in the dust,
Wriggling and crawling,
Grinned an evil grin and thrust
His tongue out with its fork.

153.

"WHO's in the next room?—who?
I seemed to see
Somebody in the dawning passing through,
Unknown to me."
"Nay: you saw nought. He passed invisibly."

"Who's in the next room?—who?
      I seem to hear
Somebody muttering firm in a language new
      That chills the ear."
"No: you catch not his tongue who has entered
    there."

      "Who's in the next room?—who?
      I seem to feel
His breath like a clammy draught, as if it drew
      From the Polar Wheel."
"No: none who breathes at all does the door
    conceal."

      "Who's in the next room?—who?
      A figure wan
With a message to one in there of something due?
      Shall I know him anon?"
"Yea he; and he brought such; and you'll know
    him anon."

154. THE POET TO THE PAINTER

WHY, though I seem of a prodigious waist,
I am not so voluminous and vast,
But there are lines wherewith I might be embrac'd.

'Tis true, as my womb swells so my back stoops,
And the whole lump grows round, deform'd, and
      droops;
But yet the Tun at Heidelberg had hoops.

You were not tied by any painter's law
To square my circle, I confess, but draw
My superficies: that was all you saw.

Which if in compass of no art it came
To be described by a monogram
With one great blot you had form'd me as I am.

But whilst you curious were to have it be
An archetype, for all the world to see,
You made it a brave piece, but not like me.

O had I now your manner, mastery, might,
Your power of handling shadow, air, and spright,
How I would draw, and take hold and delight!

But you are he can paint, I can but write:
A Poet hath no more but black and white,
Nor knows he flattering colours, or false light.

Yet when of Friendship I would draw the face,
A letter'd mind, and a large heart would place
To all posterity; I will write *Burlase*.

155. THE BELLS OF SHANDON

WITH deep affection,
And recollection,
I often think of
  Those Shandon bells,
Whose sounds so wild would,
In the days of childhood,
Fling around my cradle
  Their magic spells.

204

On this I ponder
Where'er I wander,
And thus grow fonder,
　　Sweet Cork, of thee;
With thy bells of Shandon,
That sound so grand on
The pleasant waters
　　Of the River Lee.

I've heard bells chiming
Full many a clime in,
Tolling sublime in
　　Cathedral shrine,
While at a glib rate
Brass tongues would vibrate—
But all their music
　　Spoke naught like thine;
For memory, dwelling
On each proud swelling
Of the belfry knelling
　　Its bold notes free,
Made the bells of Shandon
Sound far more grand on
The pleasant waters
　　Of the River Lee.

I've heard bells tolling
Old Adrian's Mole in,
There thunder rolling
　　From the Vatican,
And cymbals glorious
Swinging uproarious

In the gorgeous turrets
    Of Notre Dame;
But thy sounds were sweeter
Than the dome of Peter
Flings o'er the Tiber,
    Pealing solemnly—
O, the bells of Shandon
Sound far more grand on
The pleasant waters
    Of the River Lee.

There's a bell in Moscow,
While on tower and kiosk O!
In Saint Sophia
    The Turkman gets,
And loud in air
Calls men to prayer
From the tapering summits
    Of tall minarets.
Such empty phantom
I freely grant them;
But there's an anthem
    More dear to me,—
'Tis the bells of Shandon,
That sound so grand on
The pleasant waters
    Of the River Lee.

156. STREPHON AND KLAIUS

STREPHON

Ye Gote-heard Gods, that love the grassie
    mountaines,
Ye Nymphs that haunt the springs in pleasant vallies,
Ye Satyrs joy'd with free and quiet forrests,
Vouchsafe your silent eares to plaining musike,
Which to my woes give still an earlie morning,
And drawes the dolor on till wearie evening.

KLAIUS

O Mercurie, foregoer to the evening,
O heavenly huntresse of the savage mountaines,
O lovely starre, entitled of the morning,
While that my voice doth fill the wofull vallies,
Vouchsafe your silent eares to plaining musike,
Which oft hath Echo tyr'd in secret forrests.

STREPHON

I that was once free burgesse of the forrests,
Where shade from Sunne, and sports I sought at
    evening,
I that was once esteem'd for pleasant musike,
Am banisht now among the monstrous mountaines
Of huge despaire, and foule afflictions vallies,
Am growne a shrich-owle to my selfe each morning.

KLAIUS

I that was once delighted everie morning,
Hunting the wild inhabiters of forrests:
I that was once the musike of these vallies,
So darkened am, that all my day is evening,

Hart broken so, that molehilles seeme high
  mountaines,
And fill the vales with cries in steed of musike.

STREPHON

Long since alas, my deadlie swannish musike,
Hath made it selfe a crier of the morning,
And hath with wailing strength clim'd highest
  mountaines:
Long since my thoughts more desert be then
  forrests:
Long since I see my joyes come to their evening,
And state throwne downe to overtroden vallies.

KLAIUS

Long since the happie dwellers of these vallies,
Have pray'd me leave my straunge exclaming
  musike,
Which troubles their dayes worke, and joyes of
  evening:
Long since I hate the night, more hate the morning:
Long since my thoughts chase me like beasts in
  forrests,
And make me wish my selfe laid under mountaines.

STREPHON

Me seemes I see the high and statelie mountaines,
Transforme themselves to low dejected vallies:
Me seemes I heare in these ill chaunged forrests,
The Nightingales do learne of Owles their musike:
Me seems I feele the comfort of the morning,
Turn'd to the mortall serene of an evening.

KLAIUS

Me seemes I see a filthy cloudy evening,
As soone as Sunne begins to clime the mountaines:
Me seemes I feele a noysome sent, the morning
When I doo smell the flowers of these vallies:
Me seemes I heare, when I doo heare sweete musike,
The dreadfull cries of murdred men in forrests.

STREPHON .

I wish to fire the trees of all those forrests,
I give the Sunne a last farewell each evening,
I curse the fidling finders out of musike:
With envie I doo hate the loftie mountaines;
And with dispite despise the humble vallies;
I doo detest night, evening, day, and morning.

KLAIUS

Curse to my selfe my praier is, the morning;
My fire is more then can be made with forrests;
My state more base, then are the basest vallies
I wish no evenings more to see, each evening;
Shamed I hate my selfe in sight of mountaines,
And stoppe mine eares, lest I grow mad with
  musike.

STREPHON

For she whose parts maintainde a perfect musike,
Whose beautie shin'de more then the blushing
  morning,
Who much did passe in state the stately mountaines,
In streightnesse past the Cedars of the forrests,
Hath cast me wretch into eternall evening,
By taking her two Sunnes from these darke vallies.

KLAIUS

For she, to whome compar'd, the Alps are vallies,
She, whose least word brings from the sphears their
    musike,
At whose approch the Sunne rose in the evening,
Who where she went bare in her forhead morning,
Is gone, is gone, from these our spoyled forrests,
Turning to desarts our best pastur'de mountaines.

STREPHON

These mountaines witnesse shall, so shal these
    vallies,
These forrests eke, made wretched by our musike,

KLAIUS

Our morning hymne is this, and song at evening.

APPENDIX

KING LEAR

[Scene : Before a Hovel on a Heath.
Characters : Lear, Kent, and the Fool.]

Kent.   Here is the place, my lord; good my lord,
   enter:
The tyranny of the open night 's too rough
For nature to endure.   *[Storm still.*

   Lear.   Let me alone.

Kent.   Good my lord, enter here.

Lear.   Wilt break my heart?

Kent.   I'd rather break mine own.   Good my
   lord, enter.

Lear.   Thou think'st 'tis much that this con-
   tentious storm
Invades us to the skin: so 'tis to thee;
But where the greater malady is fix'd,
The lesser is scarce felt.   Thou 'dst shun a bear;
But if thy flight lay toward the roaring sea,
Thou 'dst meet the bear i' the mouth.   When the
   mind's free
The body's delicate: the tempest in my mind
Doth from my senses take all feeling else
Save what beats there.—Filial ingratitude!
Is it not as this mouth should tear this hand
For lifting food to 't?—But I will punish home:—
No, I will weep no more.—In such a night
To shut me out!—Pour on; I will endure:—
In such a night as this!   O Regan, Goneril!
Your old kind father, whose frank heart gave all,—

O, that way madness lies; let me shun that;
No more of that.

   Kent.   Good my lord, enter here.

   Lear.   Prithee, go in thyself; seek thine own ease:
This tempest will not give me leave to ponder
On things would hurt me more.—But I'll go in.
[*To the* Fool.] In, boy; go first. You houseless
    poverty,—
Nay, get thee in. I'll pray, and then I'll sleep.—

                        [Fool *goes in.*

Poor naked wretches, wheresoe'er you are,
That bide the pelting of this pitiless storm,
How shall your houseless heads and unfed sides,
Your loop'd and window'd raggedness, defend you
From seasons such as these? O, I have ta'en
Too little care of this! Take physic, pomp;
Expose thyself to feel what wretches feel,
That thou mayst shake the superflux to them,
And show the heavens more just.

   Edgar. [*Within.*] Fathom and half, fathom and
    half! Poor Tom!

               [*The* Fool *runs out from the hovel.*

   Fool. Come not in here, nuncle, here 's a spirit.
Help me, help me!

   Kent. Give me thy hand.—Who 's there?

   Fool. A spirit, a spirit: he says his name 's poor
    Tom.

   Kent. What art thou that dost grumble there i'
    the straw?
Come forth.

     Enter EDGAR *disguised as a madman.*

   Edgar. Away! the foul fiend follows me:—

Through the sharp hawthorn blows the cold
   wind.—
   Hum! go to thy cold bed, and warm thee.
Lear. Didst thou give all to thy two daughters?
And art thou come to this?
Edgar. Who gives any thing to poor Tom? whom
the foul fiend hath led through fire and through
flame, through ford and whirlpool, o'er bog and
quagmire; that hath laid knives under his pillow,
and halters in his pew; set ratsbane by his porridge;
made him proud of heart, to ride on a bay trotting-
horse over four-inched bridges, to course his own
shadow for a traitor.—Bless thy five wits!—Tom
's a-cold.—O, do de, do de, do de.—Bless thee
from whirlwinds, star-blasting, and taking! Do
poor Tom some charity, whom the foul fiend vexes:
There could I have him now,—and there,—and there
again, and there.   [*Storm continues.*
Lear. What! have his daughters brought him to
this pass?—
   Couldst thou save nothing? Didst thou give them
all?
Fool. Nay, he reserved a blanket, else we had
been all shamed.
Lear. Now, all the plagues that in the pendulous air
Hang fated o'er men's faults light on thy daughters!
Kent. He hath no daughters, sir.
Lear. Death, traitor! nothing could have sub-
   du'd nature
To such a lowness but his unkind daughters.—
Is it the fashion, that discarded fathers
Should have thus little mercy on their flesh?

Judicious punishment! 'twas this flesh begot
Those pelican daughters.

Edgar. Pillicock sat on Pillicock-hill:
Halloo, halloo, loo, loo!

Fool. This cold night will turn us all to fools and
madmen.

Edgar. Take heed o' the foul fiend; obey thy
parents; keep thy word justly; swear not; set not
thy sweet heart on proud array. Tom 's a-cold.

Lear. What hast thou been?

Edgar. A serving-man, proud in heart and mind;
that curl'd my hair; wore gloves in my cap; swore
as many oaths as I spake words, and broke them in
the sweet face of heaven: wine loved I deeply, dice
dearly: false of heart, light of ear, bloody of hand;
hog in sloth, fox in stealth, wolf in greediness, dog
in madness, lion in prey. Let not the creaking of
shoes nor the rustling of silks betray thy poor heart
to woman: keep thy pen from lenders' books, and
defy the foul fiend.—Still through the hawthorn
blows the cold wind; says suum, mun, ha, no,
nonny. Dolphin my boy, my boy, sessa! let him
trot by.   [*Storm still continues.*

Lear. Why, thou wert better in thy grave than to
answer with thy uncover'd body this extremity of the
skies.—Is man no more than this? Consider him well.
Thou owest the worm no silk, the beast no hide, the
sheep no wool, the cat no perfume.—Ha! here's three
on's are sophisticated!—Thou art the thing itself:
—unaccommodated man is no more but such a poor,
bare, forked animal as thou art.—Off, off, you lend-
ings:—Come; unbutton here. [*Tearing off his clothes.*

214

Fool. Prithee, nuncle, be contented; 'tis a naughty night to swim in.—Now a little fire in a wild field were like an old sinner's heart; a small spark, all the rest on's body cold.—Look, here comes a walking fire.

Enter GLOUCESTER *with a torch.*

Edgar. This is the foul fiend Flibbertigibbet: he begins at curfew, and walks till the first cock; he gives the web and the pin, squints the eye, and makes the hare-lip; mildews the white wheat, and hurts the poor creature of earth.

> Saint Withold footed thrice the wold;
> He met the night-mare and her nine-fold;
> > Bid her alight,
> > And her troth plight,
> And, aroint thee, witch, aroint thee!

Kent. How fares your Grace?

Lear. What's he?

Kent. Who's there? What is't you seek?

Gloucester. What are you there? Your names?

Edgar. Poor Tom; that eats the swimming frog, the toad, the tadpole, the wall-newt, and the water; that in the fury of his heart, when the foul fiend rages, eats cow-dung for sallets; swallows the old rat and the ditch-dog; drinks the green mantle of the standing pool; who is whipp'd from tithing to tithing, and stock-punished, and imprison'd; who hath had three suits to his back, six shirts to his body, horse to ride, and weapon to wear,—

> But mice and rats, and such small deer,
> Have been Tom's food for seven long year.

Beware my follower. Peace, Smulkin; peace, thou
fiend!

Gloucester. What, hath your Grace no better
company?

Edgar. The prince of darkness is a gentleman:
Modo he's call'd, and Mahu.

Gloucester. Our flesh and blood, my lord, is
grown so vile,
That it doth hate what gets it.

Edgar. Poor Tom 's a-cold.

Gloucester. Go in with me; my duty cannot
suffer
To obey in all your daughters' hard commands:
Though their injunction be to bar my doors,
And let this tyrannous night take hold upon you,
Yet have I ventur'd to come seek you out,
And bring you where both fire and food is ready.

Lear. First let me talk with this philosopher.—
What is the cause of thunder?

Kent. Good my lord, take his offer; go into the
house.

Lear. I'll talk a word with this same learned
Theban.
What is your study?

Edgar. How to prevent the fiend and to kill
vermin.

Lear. Let me ask you one word in private.

Kent. Importune him once more to go, my lord;
His wits begin t' unsettle.

Gloucester. Canst thou blame him?
His daughters seek his death:—ah, that good Kent!
He said it would be thus,—poor banish'd man!—

Thou say'st the king grows mad; I'll tell thee,
   friend,
I am almost mad myself: I had a son,
Now outlaw'd from my blood; he sought my life,
But lately, very late: I lov'd him, friend,
No father his son dearer: true to tell thee,
                              [*Storm continues.*
The grief hath craz'd my wits.   What a night's this!
I do beseech your Grace,—

Lear.   O, cry you mercy, sir.
Noble philosopher, your company.

Edgar.   Tom 's a-cold.

Gloucester.   In, fellow, there, into the hovel: keep
   thee warm.

Lear.   Come, let's in all.

Kent.   This way, my lord.

Lear.   With him;
I will keep still with my philosopher.

Kent.   Good my lord, soothe him; let him take
   the fellow.

Gloucester.   Take him you on.

Kent.   Sirrah, come on; go along with us.

Lear.   Come, good Athenian.

Gloucester.   No words, no words: hush.

Edgar.   *Child Rowland to the dark tower came;*
         His word was still,—'Fie, foh, and fum,
         I smell the blood of a British man.'

                              [*Exeunt.*

THE DUCHESS OF MALFI

[*Scene: A Room in the Duchess of Malfi's Lodging.*
Characters: The Duchess of Malfi; Daniel de Bosola (one of her household) and Cariola (her woman).]

Bos. I am come to make thy tomb.

Duch. Ha! my tomb!
    Thou speak'st as if I lay upon my deathbed,
    Gasping for breath: dost thou perceive me sick?

Bos. Yes, and the more dangerously, since thy sickness is insensible.

Duch. Thou art not mad, sure: dost know me?

Bos. Yes.

Duch. Who am I?

Bos. Thou art a box of worm-seed, at best but a salvatory of green mummy. What's this flesh? a little crudded milk, fantastical puff-paste. Our bodies are weaker than those paper-prisms boys use to keep flies in; more contemptible, since ours is to preserve earth-worms. Didst thou ever see a lark in a cage? Such is the soul in the body: this world is like her little turf of grass, and the Heaven o'er our heads, like her looking-glass, only gives us a miserable knowledge of the small compass of our prison.

Duch. Am not I thy duchess?

Bos. Thou art some great woman, sure, for riot begins to sit on thy forehead (clad in grey hairs) twenty years sooner than on a merry milkmaid's. Thou sleepest worse than if a mouse should be forced to take up her lodging in a cat's ear: a little infant that breeds its teeth, should it lie with thee, would cry out, as if thou wert the more unquiet bedfellow.

Duch. I am Duchess of Malfi still.

Bos. That makes thy sleep so broken :
    Glories, like glow-worms, afar off shine bright,
    But looked to near, have neither heat nor
       light.

Duch. Thou art very plain.

Bos. My trade is to flatter the dead, not the living ;
I am a tomb maker.

Duch. And thou comest to make my tomb?

Bos. Yes.

Duch. Let me be a little merry :—of what stuff wilt
thou make it?

Bos. Nay, resolve me first, of what fashion?

Duch. Why do we grow fantastical in our death-bed?
do we affect fashion in the grave?

Bos. Most ambitiously. Princes' images on their
tombs do not lie, as they were wont, seeming to
pray up to Heaven ; but with their hands under
their cheeks, as if they died of the toothache : they
are not carved with their eyes fixed upon the stars ;
but as their minds were wholly bent upon the world,
the self-same way they seem to turn their faces.

Duch. Let me know fully therefore the effect
    Of this thy dismal preparation,
    This talk fit for a charnel.

Bos. Now I shall :—

ENTER EXECUTIONERS, WITH A COFFIN,
CORDS, AND A BELL.

Here is a present from your princely brothers ;
And may it arrive welcome, for it brings
Last benefit, last sorrow.

Duch. Let me see it:
　　　　I have so much obedience in my blood,
　　　　I wish it in their veins to do them good.
Bos.　This is your last presence-chamber.
Cari.　O my sweet lady!
Duch. Peace; it affrights not me.
Bos.　I am the common bellman,
　　　　That usually is sent to condemned persons
　　　　The night before they suffer.
Duch. Even now thou said'st
　　　　Thou wast a tomb-maker.
Bos.　'Twas to bring you
　　　　By degrees to mortification.　Listen.
　　　　　Hark, now every thing is still
　　　　　The screech-owl and the whistler shrill
　　　　　Call upon our dame aloud,
　　　　　And bid her quickly don her shroud!
　　　　　Much you had of land and rent;
　　　　　Your length in clay's now competent:
　　　　　A long war disturbed your mind;
　　　　　Here your perfect peace is signed.
　　　　　Of what is't fools make such vain keeping?
　　　　　Sin their conception, their birth weeping,
　　　　　Their life a general mist of error,
　　　　　Their death a hideous storm of terror.
　　　　　Strew your hair with powders sweet,
　　　　　Don clean linen, bathe your feet,
　　　　　And (the foul fiend more to check)
　　　　　A crucifix let bless your neck:
　　　　　'Tis now full tide 'tween night and day;
　　　　　End your groan, and come away.
Cari.　Hence, villains, tyrants, murderers! alas!

What will you do with my lady?—Call for help.

Duch. To whom? to our next neighbours? they are
mad-folks.

Bos. Remove that noise.

Duch. Farewell, Cariola.
In my last will I have not much to give:
A many hungry guests have fed upon me;
Thine will be a poor reversion.

Cari. I will die with her.

Duch. I pray thee, look thou giv'st my little boy
Some syrup for his cold, and let the girl
Say her prayers ere she sleep.

> [CARIOLA IS FORCED OUT BY THE
> EXECUTIONERS.]

Now what you please:
What death?

Bos. Strangling; here are your executioners.

Duch. I forgive them:
The apoplexy, catarrh, or cough o' the lungs,
Would do as much as they do.

Bos. Doth not death fright you?

Duch. Who would be afraid on't,
Knowing to meet such excellent company
In the other world?

Bos. Yet, methinks,
The manner of your death should much
afflict you:
This cord should terrify you.

Duch. Not a whit:
What would it pleasure me to have my throat
cut

With diamonds? or to be smotherèd
With cassia? or to be shot to death with
    pearls?
I know death hath ten thousand several doors
For men to take their exits; and 'tis found
They go on such strange geometrical hinges,
You may open them both ways; any way, for
    Heaven sake,
So I were out of your whispering. Tell my
    brothers
That I perceive death, now I am well awake,
Best gift is they can give or I can take.
I would fain put off my last woman's fault,
I'd not be tedious to you.

1st Execut. We are ready.

Duch. Dispose my breath how please you; but my
    body
Bestow upon my women, will you?

1st Execut. Yes.

Duch. Pull, and pull strongly, for your able strength
Must pull down Heaven upon me:—
    Yet stay; Heaven-gates are not so highly
    arched
As princes' palaces; they that enter there
Must go upon their knees [KNEELS].—Come,
    violent death,
Serve for mandragora to make me sleep!
Go tell my brothers, when I am laid out,
They then may feed in quiet.

    [THE EXECUTIONERS STRANGLE THE
                DUCHESS.]

BOOK SUGGESTIONS

MAUD BODKIN: *Archetypal Patterns in Poetry* (Oxford University Press).

T. S. ELIOT: *Selected Essays* (Faber).

WILLIAM EMPSON: *Seven Types of Ambiguity* (Chatto).

A. H. GARDINER: *The Theory of Speech and Language* (Oxford University Press).

ROBERT GRAVES: *Poetic Unreason and other Studies* (Cecil Palmer).

GEORGE GRODDECK: *The World of Man* (Daniel).
Exploring the Unconscious (Daniel).

W. P. KER: *Collected Essays* (Macmillan).
Epic and Romance (Macmillan).
Form and Style in Poetry (Macmillan).
English Literature: Medieval (Home University Library, Thornton Butterworth).

C. DAY LEWIS: *A Hope for Poetry* (Blackwell).

WYNDHAM LEWIS: *The Lion and the Fox: Rôle of the Hero in the Plays of Shakespeare* (Richards Press).

HERBERT READ: *Form in Modern Poetry* (Sheed & Ward).

I. A. RICHARDS: *Principles of Literary Criticism* (Routledge).
Practical Criticism (Routledge).
Science and Poetry (Routledge).

STEPHEN SPENDER: *The Destructive Element* (Cape).

EDMUND WILSON: *Axel's Castle* (Scribner).